MW00651675

Ancient Middle East

A Captivating Guide to Civilizations and Empires of the Ancient Near East and Ancient Anatolia

Free Bonus from Captivating History (Available for a Limited time)

Hi History Lovers!

Now you have a chance to join our exclusive history list so you can get your first history ebook for free as well as discounts and a potential to get more history books for free! Simply visit the link below to join.

Captivatinghistory.com/ebook

Also, make sure to follow us on Facebook, Twitter and Youtube by searching for Captivating History.

Table of Contents

Part 1: Ancient Near East

A Captivating Guide to Ancient Civilizations of the Middle East, Including Regions Such as Mesopotamia, Ancient Iran, Egypt, Anatolia, and the Levant

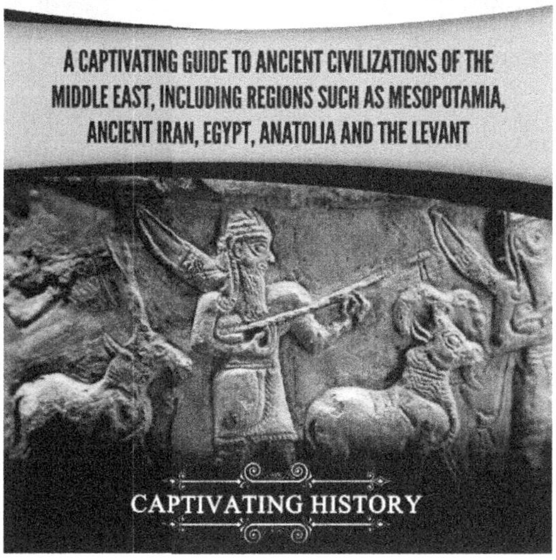

Introduction

Where did the first signs of civilization appear in the ancient world? When did people start to transition from the nomadic life of hunters and gatherers to living in the first urbanized settlements? Who was the first emperor in history? Which empire was the strongest and mightiest, and for how long? Where did the title "King of the Universe" come from, and who was the "True King?" All these answers are hidden in the ancient history of the Fertile Crescent, and now, they are unveiled to you in our comprehensive and captivating guide to the ancient civilizations of the Near East.

Take a journey back in time and meet the first emperor and the mysterious legend that surrounds his origins. Find out who was the first pharaoh to unite the kingdom of Egypt, and discover the time when a woman ruled ancient Mesopotamia. You will also find out about the first people to inhabit the Levant and Anatolia, as well as how Persia lost their hegemony in the Levant. Join us as we discover the power of agriculture, trading, writing, and commerce, to the rise and fall of the first major empires in the world.

Between myths and facts, one can discover an ancient world that set the first stone to the foundation of civilization. The beautiful Near East, the cradle of different ethnicities, nationalities, legends, and religions, has slowly been unveiling its ancient secrets, and in these pages, you can travel the hallways of time to uncover a distant past that gave life to society as we know it.

Chapter 1 – Mesopotamia: The Birth of the First Civilization

We are going back to the late 4th millennium BCE to get to know the oldest literate civilization: the Sumerians in Mesopotamia. Sumer encompassed the southernmost part of the great civilization of Mesopotamia, where southern Iraq now lies. Mesopotamia itself covered a vast region, and it included the modern-day territories of Iraq, Kuwait, Syria, and Turkey. Interestingly, the name of Sumer means "the land of civilized kings." Based by the river system of the Tigris and Euphrates, this powerful civilization rose to become the home of some of the most powerful empires over the centuries to come. One such empire was ruled by the Akkadian dynasty.

Washukanni, Nineveh, Hatra, Assur, Nuzi, Palmyra, Mari, Sippar, Babylon, Kish, Nippu, Isin, Lagash, Uruk, Charax Spasinu, and Ur, from north to south.

Goran tek-en, CC BY-SA 4.0 <https://creativecommons.org/licenses/by-sa/4.0>, via Wikimedia Commons https://commons.wikimedia.org/wiki/File:N-Mesopotamia_and_Syria_english.svg

Numerous positive factors affected the rise of the first civilization in Mesopotamia. For one, the area was practically booming in life when it came to agriculture. Where one can find fertile soil and a favorable climate, there is food, and where there is food, there is always most certainly life. And this time, it was not just any form of life—it was civilized life. To grow a true civilization, the Sumerians had to do more than farm and irrigate successfully. They invested in magnificent architecture, promoted literacy, and had a sophisticated military system.

Sargon: The Emperor among Kings

According to the scriptures and legends dating from the late 4th millennium BCE and even centuries later, Sargon wasn't the first ruler of Mesopotamia and the Fertile Crescent. However, Sargon of Akkad became the first ideal model of a ruler, and he created the first empire known in the history of civilized men. The dynasty of

Akkad is known to have commenced with Sargon of Akkad, who was once a cupbearer for Ur-Zababa, the second king of the Fourth Dynasty of Kish, who ruled around 2334 BCE.

Before Sargon rose up to transform the Fertile Crescent into an empire, a feat that had been unseen in the ancient world, dynasties oversaw Mesopotamia, which the people considered to be sacred. And it all began with one man: Alulim. According to the ancient scriptures found in the area and the mythological portion of the Sumerian King List, Alulim was the first king of Mesopotamia, and he ruled over Eridu, a city in southern Mesopotamia, sometime before 2900 BCE. Sumerians believed the gods themselves appointed the rulers, as the kingship is said to have descended from the heavens. Ancient scriptures created by the Sumerians thousands of years ago even list a king that supposedly lived and ruled in Mesopotamia for over 48,000 years. And supposedly, women ruled Kish as well. According to the Sumerian King List, a woman named Kubaba ruled from around 2500 to 2330 BCE. It is very unlikely she ruled for this long, but it is believed that she was the grandmother to none other than Ur-Zababa.

Ur-Zababa, like other rulers before him, resided in the city of Kish, which was located in today's territory of Tell al-Uhaymir. Ur-Zababa and the Kish dynasty was defeated by the king of Uruk in around 2375 BCE. Uruk was another ancient city of Sumer; it was located east of the present-day Euphrates River. Lugal-zage-si, who was originally the king of Umma, another ancient Sumerian city, was the leader behind this attack. He was perhaps the first king to come near the title of emperor before Sargon of Akkad appeared on the scene. Besides Kish and Uruk, Lugal-zage-si is said to have conquered other Sumerian cities, such as Lagash, with his main goal being to form a unified kingdom of Mesopotamia. According to the Sumerian List of Kings, Lugal-zage-si, who ruled Kish for twenty-five years, was overthrown by Sargon of Akkad.

It is hard to differentiate between fact and the whimsical legends that surround the life and deeds of Sargon of Akkad. Even Sargon's origins are veiled in myth, but the Sumerian King List states that he was the son of a farmer and the king's cupbearer.

But why would a king choose a modest farmer's son to serve him as a cupbearer? To answer the question, historians can only turn to the ancient scripture known as *The Legend of Sargon*. The legend is actually Sargon's autobiography, which is why it must be analyzed with reserved accuracy. Sargon weaved an interesting story to justify his right to the throne. He particularly wanted to present his rule in an appealing light to the commoners, who were suffering from famine at the time due to unflattering political conditions.

Sargon appeared to be very much aware of the demographics he ruled over as emperor and the times he lived in. He belonged to both worlds after his conquest—the world of commoners and the world of kings—but yet, he was neither. He was an emperor. Sargon made sure to emphasize his modest origins instead of hiding the fact that he was the son of a farmer. However, Sargon added fantastic details to his origin story that made him into a half-god—a man in the favor of the goddess Inanna. His autobiography states that he was born to a changeling priestess serving in the temple of Inanna, which gives him a connection to the divine, something that all kings searched for to prove their legitimacy to rule. Although historians can't claim with complete certainty what the word "changeling" means in *The Legend of Sargon*, it is thought that "changeling" refers to the temple priestesses who worshipped Inanna, as they were androgynous. Since Sargon was illegitimately brought into this world by a priestess who couldn't keep him, Sargon says he was placed in a basket and set upon the currents of the Euphrates River. According to the legend Sargon wrote himself, he was found by a modest farmer, who took care of him as if Sargon was his own flesh and blood. The man who found Sargon in a tar-sealed basket was named Akki, and he was a farmer or a gardener in the service of

King Ur-Zababa, who ruled the Sumerian city of Kish. If Akki was a gardener, he most likely would have taken care of the royal gardens, as this would explain how Sargon came in contact with King Ur-Zababa and became his cupbearer.

The scripture considered to be Sargon's "autobiography" was written long after the first emperor was gone; however, historians believe the written version represents Sargon's own story of his modest upbringing and birth under strange circumstances. Sargon wanted the people to see a poor boy, a castaway who had made it against the kings and the elite to do what no one else before him could—build an empire and unite all of Mesopotamia under a single ruler. In reality, historians can confirm that there are not many clear pieces of evidence that reveal the true origin of Sargon. The very fact that Sargon wasn't his real name helps to show this. Sargon was a cleverly minted name that means "True King."

Regardless of his true origins, Sargon successfully formed the first multi-national empire and also formed a new line of monarchs known as the Akkadian dynasty. To this day, no opposing version of Sargon's origins has emerged, which is why Sargon is still presented as an orphaned son of a priestess. Sargon is the first known ruler to have conquered all of Mesopotamia, although this feat would take him some time. The first emperor was to be remembered as Sargon the Great, the first of his name, "king of Akkad, overseer of Inanna, king of Kish, anointed of Anu, king of the land, governor of Enlil."

The Rise of an Empire and the Battling Cities of Sumer

Even though it may not appear so, Lugal-zage-si cleared the path for Sargon to become the first emperor of Mesopotamia. Before Lugal-zage-si's conquest, Sumerian cities were frequently at war, battling over territory and the water supply. Lugal-zage-si managed to unify the cities of Sumer; however, his kingdom was still an incohesive union. Lugal-zage-si made his own glory by becoming the first king of Sumer to succeed in conquering the majority of Sumerian city-states; he is also remembered as the last king before the rise of the Akkadian Empire. After conquering Uruk, he decided to try his luck with Kish. Upon hearing Lugal-zage-si's plans, Ur-Zababa decided to offer a treaty. According to *The Legend of Sargon*, Ur-Zababa had a dream where he was told that Sargon would be his end. So, the king decided to send Sargon to take the treaty to Lugal-zage-si, asking the conqueror to kill Sargon after he read the message. For some unknown reason, Lugal-zage-si decided not to kill Sargon but instead offered him an alliance. Sargon joined Lugal-zage-si, and together, they defeated and subdued Kish. In the chaos, Ur-Zababa escaped and went into hiding. There are numerous legends revolving around Sargon, so it is not clear what happened afterward. What is known is that Sargon and Lugal-zage-si soon came to be enemies. Some sources indicate that Sargon was banished by King Lugal-zage-si for having an affair with the queen. Sargon decided to take Uruk by marching into the city, after which Lugal-zage-si challenged him in the city of Kish, a challenge he lost. After capturing Lugal-zage-si, Sargon made him march in chains to acknowledge his own demise. Sargon then proclaimed himself the king of Kish and continued to conquer the rest of Sumer.

In addition to warfare and conquests, Sargon also had to face internal conflicts. The reason Sargon most likely decided to place emphasis on his modest origins was the steaming political situation between the elite and poor laborers. Of course, the poor laborers outnumbered the rich and powerful. Sargon's politics and the image he created of himself, in combination with his unquestionable talent in military skills, appealed to the oppressed Sumerian society. It is crucial to note that very few people at the time lived in abundance and prosperity. The wealthy, who controlled the cities of Mesopotamia, were only becoming wealthier, while the poor were suffering, with no chances to acquire a more prosperous life. Long days of work with little to show for it created discontent among the poor. When Sargon took over the leadership, this discontent seemed to settle somewhat. By conquering the entire region and subduing all the Mesopotamian city-states, Sargon could equally dispense the collected riches across his new empire, which could help resolve the discontent caused by famine to some extent. Sargon also created a centralized authority in Mesopotamia with effective administration that employed people he trusted across different regions and cities.

The path toward building the first empire wasn't easy, but the image Sargon presented to the poor and rich alike granted the emperor the hegemony he needed in the southern parts of Mesopotamia. However, Sargon's political ideals and claim to the throne didn't appeal to everyone. Sargon described numerous revolts he needed to deal with before he was able to create a cohesive empire.

After defeating Lugal-zage-si and conquering Kish, Sargon established a new capital—Akkad, also known as Agade—by the banks of the Euphrates River. He wasn't satisfied with ruling a small territory, and with the Sumerian elite challenging his right to the throne, Sargon decided to continue with war campaigns. He had support from the military, as Sargon himself was described as an exceptional military leader. He decided to cross the Tigris River and take the Elamite lands, in which he succeeded. He didn't stop there, for he decided to take his campaigns north and conquer Mari. Sargon went pushed even deeper to demonstrate his power in the land of the Amorites, west of the Caspian Sea. Ashur and Nineveh were next in line, which were farther to the north, and Sargon campaigned in Asia Minor as well. Every march and every campaign only helped Sargon grow his empire. It is entirely possible that he even conquered Cyprus and enabled trade with India, which would make his growing empire even richer.

Sargon conquered one city after another, and any ruler who didn't recognize him as the new king was soon forced to accept him as the ultimate ruler. One of the reasons Sargon's military campaigns were so successful is that he created the first institutionalized military practices, which made his army more adaptable and mobile.

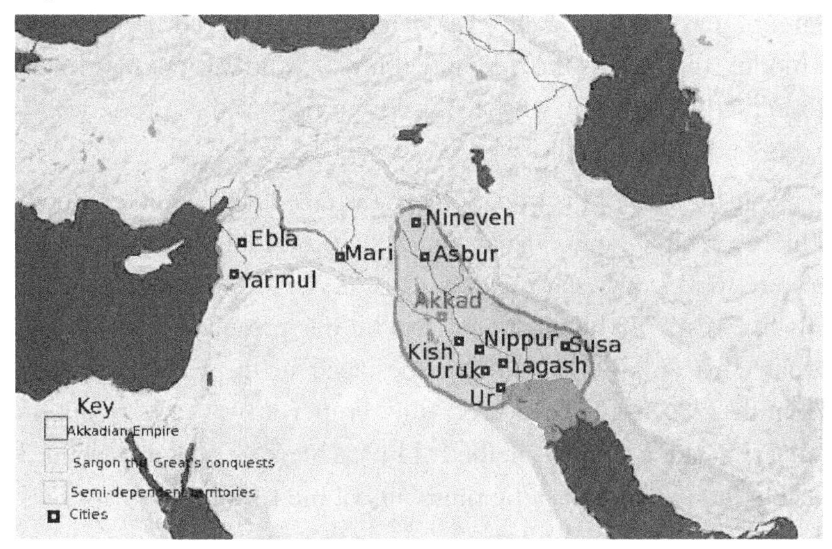

Sargon the Great's conquests: Ebla, Yarmul, Mari, Nineveh, Asbur, Akkad, Nippur, Susa, Lagash, Kish, Uruk, and Ur

Interchange88, CC BY 3.0 <https://creativecommons.org/licenses/by/3.0>, via Wikimedia Commons https://commons.wikimedia.org/wiki/File:Akkadian_Empire_Map.gif

Sargon was equally capable of leading an empire. He ended up ruling over sixty-five cities. Sargon wanted to make sure that the administration would reaffirm his rulership, so he employed sixty-five governors to lead these cities on his behalf.

The Children of Sargon the Great and the Fall of the Akkadian Empire

Sargon the Great conquered sixty-five cities of the Fertile Crescent in thirty-four battles. Those who wouldn't kneel before him were soon forced to, as Sargon managed to unite all the cities of Mesopotamia, including the people of Sumer and Akkad, under his rule. It is hard to know when Sargon accomplished the following feats, as the chronology of his rule only covers the first five years; after this point, it is just descriptions of his conquests. Sargon attacked the land of Subartu and conquered the tribes of Kazallu, decimating the land so badly that there was nothing left. All of the regions that bordered the Akkadian Empire became vassals to Sargon. Two millennia after his death, Sargon would be held up as a model ruler across the Semitic empires, as he was the first ruler of a multi-ethnic empire, who acquired the right to the throne with his might and military skill.

Near the end of his rule, Sargon was faced with famine and wars. The revolts that Sargon successfully silenced in the early days of his empire were slowly starting to rise again. Sargon was already around fifty-five years old by this point, and he was presumably too weak to protect his empire. Sargon was besieged in the capital of Akkad around 2286 BCE; however, the emperor was an exceptional military leader, which helped him achieve a victory when he decided to battle against the members of the revolt.

Sargon had three children: a daughter, who became a priestess serving the goddess Inanna, and two sons. The throne was inherited by his first son, Rimush, in around 2279 BCE. It is perhaps needless to say that he and all his successors were more or less in the shadow of Sargon, who had even created the title "King of Everything," also interpreted as "King of the Universe." The title was used by Mesopotamian kings who reigned long after Sargon's death.

Rimush was immediately faced with revolts by the cities his father had previously conquered. Rimush was forced to reclaim the cities of Umma, Der, Lagash, Kazallu, Ur, and Adab from the rebels. The cause of Rimush's death remains unknown, as he didn't die in any of the battles he conducted against the rebelling cities, nor did he fall during his victorious campaigns against Barakhshe and Elam. It is presumed that Sargon's first successor died by the hands of his own courtiers. Regardless, Rimush only ruled for nine years before his brother took over.

Manishtushu, Rimush's brother, inherited the throne around 2270 BCE. His rule would last for fifteen years. There were few to no rebellions during the rule of Manishtushu, so the king focused on campaigns in the Persian Gulf, south of the Akkadian Empire, and the cities along the Tigris River. His son would take over the rule after Manishtushu died in c. 2255 BCE.

Manishtushu's son, Naram-Sin, would bring the empire to the peak of its glory. Naram-Sin justified the name of his grandfather's dynasty and created the title "King of Four Quarters"; he also carried the title forged by his grandfather, "King of Everything." Naram-Sin translates to "Beloved by the Moon God," and he was the first ruler of Mesopotamia to consider himself a divinity. Naram-Sin also gave himself the title of "God of Akkad." Naram-Sin conquered the regions by the Mediterranean Sea, as well as Armenia. He faced a rebellion from the city of Kish but was able to silence it with his military power. He took control over Elam and also conquered Armanum and Ebla, facilitating another golden age for the Akkadians. Naram-Sin's rule was the longest after the approximate fifty-five-year rule of his grandfather, Sargon.

The fall of the empire would become obvious during the rule of Shar-Kali-Sharri, the son of Naram-Sin. Shar-Kali-Sharri was the last king to rule the Akkadian Empire as a whole, and he came to power in circa 2217 BCE. He united all the cities of Sumer and the regions his father had conquered during his thirty-six-year rule. The Akkadian Empire started to fall apart around the time of his death in around 2193 BCE, as a severe drought occurred, which brought famine to the people. After the king's death, four potential successors—Igigi, Imi, Nanum, and Ilulu—took turns on the throne, with all four ruling for short periods of time due to the chaotic nature of the empire. Dudu took the throne in around 2189 BCE. He ruled for a longer period of time, about twenty-one years, but he was the penultimate ruler of the Akkadian dynasty. Shu-turul, his son, would inherit the throne around 2168 BCE. Little did he know that the Gutian invasion would put an end to his reign in circa 2154 BCE. The famine made it easier for the Gutian people to conquer the Akkadian Empire when they descended from the Zagros Mountains at the end of the 3rd millennium BCE. The Guti, who were nomadic people before their conquest of the Akkadian Empire, formed their own dynasty after overrunning southern Mesopotamia. Most of the cities in the southern area of Mesopotamia were deserted due to the severe drought at the time. However, one empire's demise meant another empire would rise. And one of the most notable empires of Mesopotamia did so: the Assyrian Empire. This empire will be covered in more depth later on. In the meantime, another civilization in the ancient Near East was developing and achieving glory on the banks of another powerful but more predictable river, that of the Nile. This civilization was none other than Egypt.

Culture, Government, and Military of the Akkadian Empire

Before the Akkadians, the city-states of Sumer didn't have a standing army. There were professional soldiers employed to protect the city, but there were no legions of soldiers with the capacity to carry on conquests like those led by Sargon. This army counted perhaps several hundred soldiers or even a thousand. It is not known whether the soldiers were paid or simply volunteered to protect the territory of Sargon's conquests. As time went by, Sargon's army became larger. After all was said and done, Sargon had an army of around 5,500 men. Sargon came up with an idea to recruit soldiers from defeated city-states after conquests, which set new standards and military traditions for empires that came later. Sargon appeared to have had a great talent in warfare, which can be testified through the invention and use of the composite bow. This bow had three times greater impact power when compared to the commonly used wooden bow. For the most, the army was composed of infantry units, but it is possible that some units included horses and chariots later on. It is not difficult to imagine how the threatened city-states viewed the first standing army ever to be seen in the history of the ancient world. Watching an army march toward the city gates with Sargon the Great at its head would bring fear to anyone's heart. It was an effective military strategy as well, as people would often surrender without a fight.

Sargon must have been a talented statesman as well, or else his newly conquered empire would have crumbled. However, he understood the need and importance of administration, as it would keep his war-won empire intact. While his empire was growing larger, he created an organized administration, where he employed people he trusted to oversee the city-states he had conquered. These people were known as *ensi.* Some of the city-states were overseen and administered by local *ensi,* while some cities were governed by Sargon's most trusted officials. This decentralized administration worked in unison with the emperor. For the first time in history, an empire with colorful cultural, political, ethnic, and religious backgrounds was founded, and these differences had to be somehow tamed and neutralized so as not to cause the demise of the Akkadian Empire.

Sargon wanted to establish a strong, unified, powerful, and rich kingdom—an ambitious endeavor that he succeeded in. Sargon realized during the process of unification that the peripheral city-states would be difficult to control under the autonomy of the Akkadian Empire. Some of these cities were located far from the center of the empire, and they varied in demographics and agricultural production. Their use was quite limited, so instead of subduing these states, Sargon used treaties. Through these treaties, the emperor was able to create a strong commercial network while also keeping the city-states under his control. His grandson and successor, Naram-Sin, built strongholds to gain better control over this trading network. One such stronghold was in Tell Brak, an ancient city-state in Syria whose original name is not known to history. It is presumed there were more strongholds built across the commercial system that Sargon created.

Civilized and organized societies in the ancient world are noted by their development of a collective identity through language and an alphabet. In the case of the Akkadians, they used the now-extinct East Semitic language known as the Akkadian language. The language used a cuneiform script, which is one of the earliest forms of writing that uses wedged marks on clay tablets. Thanks to the political and imperialistic influence of the Akkadian Empire, the Akkadian language became the common language of Mesopotamia and a great part of the ancient Near East before the end of the Bronze Age around 1200 BCE.

Chapter 2 –Egypt: The Unification of Upper and Lower Egypt and the Birth of the Pharaohs

Before the Early Bronze Age brought the Akkadian Empire to the top of the ancient world and then into oblivion, Predynastic Egypt had yet to dream of its future glory. Predynastic Egypt, also known as prehistoric Egypt, is presumed to have begun with some of the earliest human settlements in the ancient Near East. This period ended with the Early Dynastic Period, which occurred around 3100 BCE when the first pharaoh ruled over the fertile soil of the Nile. The Predynastic period is marked by numerous different civilizations and settlements that found their home around the Nile River. They would help shape the future glory of ancient Egypt. In the Neolithic period, Upper Egypt was settled by the Tasian, Badarian, and Amratian cultures. The Tasian culture flourished around 4500 BCE on the eastern bank of the Nile. It is the oldest-known culture that existed in Upper Egypt in the Predynastic period. To archaeologists, this culture is best known for its brown and red pottery, which they coated in black paint outside and inside.

Archaeologists were able to keep track of the general development of the Tasian culture based on the pottery handles. Over time, the pottery handles would gradually transition from practical to ornamental. This pottery also indicates that the Badarian and Tasian cultures overlapped at one point between 4500 BCE and 4400 BCE, as the pottery found in both cultures don't have any significant differences.

The Badarian culture flourished between 4400 BCE and 4000 BCE. The Badarian sites have revealed some of the first agricultural settlements. These people were located in El-Badari, Egypt, which is about 200 kilometers (124 miles) northwest from modern-day Luxor. Their settlements revealed signs of an early civilized society based on the excavation of graves. It was discovered that the Badarian people used to bury the more prominent members of their community in separate tombs. The Badarian culture made tools such as axes, arrowheads, and hooks. Besides agriculture, they also relied on fishing and the domestication of animals for wool, milk, and meat. Their art was rather simple, usually depicting animals, such as hippopotami, and they were buried with objects such as female mortuary figures and ore amulets.

The Amratian culture, also known as the Naqada I culture, developed between 4000 BCE and 3500 BCE. The archaeological site of el-Amra, after which the Amratian culture was named, is around 120 kilometers south of Badari, Egypt. The black-topped ware found in the Tasian and Badarian cultures was still produced; however, a unique type of white-lined pottery appeared with the Amratian culture. The Amratian was also noted as the first culture in Upper Egypt to own slaves, and they used papyrus-based rowboats to sail the Nile. They started to trade goods with Lower Egypt, sending them items like vases, beads, and other similar artifacts. The Amratian people imported smaller amounts of gold and obsidian from Nubia. Other items they traded for include emery, cedar, and marble. Their deceased were occasionally buried with dogs, and each village in the settlement had its own statue protector of an animal deity.

During the period of the Gerzeh culture, also known as the Naqada II culture, which lasted from around 3500 BCE to 3200 BCE, the first brick of the foundation of dynastic Egypt was laid. The Gerzeh period in Upper Egypt coincides with the Uruk period in Mesopotamia (during the 4th millennium), which was the first time the two cultures ever met.

At this point, the Akkadian Empire had yet to rise. Before this happened, the Nile River was about to give birth to one of the strongest and most glorious civilizations of the ancient world: ancient Egypt. During the Gerzeh period, Egyptians started to farm along the Nile due to the radical decline in rainfall, although hunting was not a forgotten skill. With more advanced agriculture, food supplies started to rise, and the number of people living in the cities of Upper Egypt was increasing as well. Mud bricks, which were first found in the Amratian period, were mass-produced in Upper Egypt to meet the demand for more homes.

During the Gerzeh period, Egyptian culture was significantly influenced by Mesopotamia in the domain of art and through the exchange of letters. The two civilizations also traded goods, such as pottery, art, grain, linen, papyrus, iron, copper, timber, lapis lazuli, ebony, myrrh, and incense. The Sumerian script that originated in Mesopotamia probably influenced the development of Egyptian hieroglyphs. Although the Gerzeh culture is considered to be the most predominant in prehistoric Egypt by many Egyptologists, Naqada III, also known as the Protodynastic period, is considered to be the true introduction to the future glory of ancient Egypt. Naqada III brought about Egyptian hieroglyphs, advanced irrigation systems, and a glimpse into the first royal burial places that somewhat resembled the majestic pyramids that appeared in the Old Kingdom of Egypt.

The Protodynastic period is also known as Dynasty 0, as it was when the first concept of rulers appeared in ancient Egypt. The people of ancient Egypt now had advanced irrigation systems, copper tools for multiple purposes, weapons, and trade relations with other civilizations in the ancient Near East. This led to an ever-increasing population in the cities and the development of city-states along the banks of the Nile. The series of conquests led by the different cities in the area created three bigger city-states in Upper Egypt: Thinis, Nekhen, and Naqada. The time was ripe for someone to rule.

The first king of Egypt is veiled in mystery, as his existence can't be proven. His name was Iry-Hor. While some historians argue that Iry-Hor wasn't a king since his name was not written in a serekh—a heraldic crest that contained royal names—he is still considered to be the first Predynastic pharaoh. It is presumed that Ka succeeded Iry-Hor, although it is not known for certain who Iry-Hor's immediate successor was. Ka ruled the city of Thinis around the 32nd century BCE, and many historians believe he conquered all of Upper Egypt, thus placing this region under the ruling hand of the Thinite royal family.

Succeeding Ka, which is read as "King's Arms" or *Sekhen* ("to embrace"), was another king from the Thinite line: Narmer. Narmer is sometimes known as Menes, but historians are divided on the issue. Menes is the name given to the first king of Egypt in ancient sources. However, the coronation of pharaohs included an Egyptian tradition that bestowed a name in honor of Horus. This practice has its roots in Iry-Hor's name, which means the "Companion of Horus." If that is the case, Menes would be the name Narmer received after he was coronated with his two crowns—a red crown to signify his rule over Upper Egypt and a white one to mark his hegemony in Lower Egypt. This was the first time in the history of Egypt that this unification happened. Once Narmer took the throne, Upper Egypt invaded Lower Egypt, forming a united

Egyptian kingdom. The act of unification marked the start of the First Dynasty and the beginning of a new era for Egypt.

Narmer: The Founder of the First Dynasty and the Pharaoh of a United Egypt

When Narmer took the throne, Egypt was already partially unified. Although the unification of Egypt is attributed to him, it began long before, although it was perhaps not seen as official.

After the unification, Horus became the main deity of the kingdom, which both Upper and Lower Egypt agreed upon. Lower and Upper Egypt also shared an alphabet and culture, taking on the form of a true kingdom. According to Manetho, an Egyptian priest and historian who lived in the early 3rd century BCE, Narmer ruled for sixty-two years. According to Manetho, Narmer was killed by a hippopotamus sometime in the 31st century BCE. The First Dynasty continued with Hor-Aha, who is believed to be Narmer's son, although some claim he was the real Menes.

Hor-Aha, abbreviated from Horus Aha, translates to "Horus the Fighter." By the time Hor-Aha came to the throne, his father had already improved the quality of life in the Egyptian kingdom. Narmer had introduced improvements to the everyday life of ancient Egyptians, including irrigation systems, a system of mathematics, practical and effective healthcare, roads, obelisks, and increased agricultural production. People started to use cloths to cover their tables and couches, introducing a more elegant way of life on an everyday basis. Narmer also promoted the idea of human sacrifices, which were supposed to assure company and protection for the pharaoh in the afterlife. An average Egyptian wouldn't be affected by this practice, as this tradition didn't include the mass killing of commoners. Instead, the pharaohs would take a couple of servants to accompany them in the afterlife. Hor-Aha continued that tradition. In fact, all of the pharaohs of the First Dynasty engaged in this practice; once the First Dynasty ended, so, too, did the tradition of human sacrifices. Before his death, Narmer transferred the capital of the kingdom from Thinis, where his line had begun their rule as Dynasty 0, to Memphis. As such, Memphis would be the capital of Hor-Aha.

Memphis was chosen as a capital for strategic reasons, as the only threat to Egypt would have come from across the Mediterranean. Memphis was located near modern-day Cairo to the south. That way, Egypt could see any threat arriving, which would give them time to prepare defenses. Even though Memphis was made the capital of unified Egypt, pharaohs would be buried in Abydos. Abydos plays a major role in Egyptian religion. According to Egyptian myth, Abydos was sacred to Osiris, as it was the place where Isis buried Osiris after assembling his cut-off body parts. It was also the city where Osiris was resurrected. Symbolically, pharaohs of the First Dynasty were buried in Abydos in hopes of resurrection.

To continue his father's legacy over the unified kingdom of Egypt, Hor-Aha performed many religious duties and focused on the luxuries Egypt had at the time, such as marvelous craftsmanship and abundant food.

The Rise and Fall of the First Dynasty in Egypt

Hor-Aha didn't have the ambition to continue the trading relations Narmer had developed with other civilizations in the Fertile Crescent. However, Egyptians still enjoyed a life of luxury, at least by ancient standards. Even though Hor-Aha reduced commerce between Egypt and other regions of the Crescent, such as the southern Levant, the pharaoh engaged in war campaigns. For instance, he attacked the Nubians while leading an expedition.

After the death of his father, Hor-Aha's mother possibly married one of her son's most trusted grand viziers. The king's mother, Neithhotep, is believed to have outlived her son, and she took over the throne as queen regent before her grandson, Djer, was old enough to inherit the throne as the rightful pharaoh. It is thought that Djer ruled around forty years in the mid-31st century BCE. Djer is said to have had five wives, who were all buried in tombs next to his own. Djer fathered a daughter, Merneith, and a son, Djet. After Djer died around 2980 BCE, Djet assumed the throne. At some point, Djet and Merneith married. Egyptologists believe that Djet had more than one wife, just like his father, continuing the tradition of polygamous marriage. Moreover, when Djet married his sister, the Egyptian pharaohs began another tradition, that of marrying their closest relatives to protect the bloodline. They were practicing incest for the sake of the dynasty. Before this tradition, earlier kings were known to have married their daughters and sons to other wealthy families to establish diplomatic relations with powerful families. With Egypt unified under a single pharaoh, it appears the goal was to keep the land in unison by limiting the power to one family—the royals of the First Dynasty.

Historians are not certain about the exact time of Djet's rule, although some inscriptions indicate that his reign lasted ten years. After his death, Djet's throne is presumed to have been inherited by his sister-wife, Merneith, who ruled before their son. Their son, known as Hor-Den or simply as Den, was the fourth pharaoh of the First Dynasty. He began his reign around 2970 BCE and ruled for forty-two years. During his long reign, Pharaoh Den is said to have brought prosperity to the kingdom, as well as innovation to court life. Even though his rule commenced decades after the unification of Egypt, Den was the first pharaoh of Egypt to adopt the title of "King of Lower and Upper Egypt," and he was the first to be depicted wearing the double crown colored in white and red to signify the unification of Lower and Upper Egypt, although it is believed Menes invented it.

Den is the first well-attested king of the First Dynasty, as many sources mention him. Moreover, it is thought that he was the most praised pharaoh that Egypt had seen so far. Den had many sons and daughters, but it is not known for sure if his successor, Adjib, was actually his child. The First Dynasty is more or less veiled in mystery, and there are no reliable sources that credit Adjib as being one of Den's sons. However, what is certain is that Adjib took the throne after Den.

Adjib, also known as Anedjib, Hor-Adjib, Hor-Adjib, and Enezib, ruled around 2930 BCE. The ancient Egyptian historian Manetho credits Adjib with ruling for twenty-six years, while other sources state that the king ruled for seventy-six years. However, modern Egyptologists suggest that Adjib couldn't have ruled for more than ten years, as Manetho often exaggerated the length of pharaohs' reigns. Adjib wanted to legitimize his rule over all of Egypt, so he introduced a new title to the reign of pharaohs, known as the Nebuy-title. This title was written with the representations of two falcons, and it means "the two lords," which refers to Seth and Horus. The title also symbolically indicates that the pharaoh's rule was established in Upper and Lower Egypt. What makes Adjib stand out as an ambitious king is the extraordinarily high number of cult statues he created for himself and the building of a new royal fortress. This was done to create an appealing image of the ruler for the people of Egypt. Judging by the inscriptions found in Adjib's tomb, his rule may have ended violently. Unfortunately, the cause of his death remains unknown. Historians suggest that Adjib had many children, but none of their names are known to history, except for possibly one: Semerkhet.

The name of Semerkhet's mother in the Palermo Stone—a fragment of an ancient stele, also known as the Royal Annals—is Batirset, although the name is not attested by other sources. However, since Egyptologists believe the throne was inherited within the bloodline of the First Dynasty, Semerkhet is thought to be one of the many sons Adjib had during his life. Although there are speculations that Semerkhet might have been a usurper, this theory can't be confirmed. Based on Manetho's records on Semerkhet's reign, the rule of Semerkhet started with some sort of calamity, which, judging by the records, marked his short rule as the king of Egypt. Manetho believes that the occurrence of natural disasters during his reign indicates that he was a usurper who was being punished for assuming a throne that was not rightfully his. Semerkhet was buried close to the tomb where Den was buried, suggesting that he was closer to Den than Adjib, his predecessor. Since Semerkhet is known to have removed the name of Adjib, his predecessor, from many contemporary scriptures, along with the fact that he was buried close to Den, it is presumed that Den was Semerkhet's father. That would make Adjib his brother.

Semerkhet began his rule around 2920 BCE, and he ruled for eight and a half years. His name is translated as "thoughtful friend" and "companion of the divine community," which is why some Egyptologists suggest that Semerkhet might have been a priest. He didn't use the title Adjib used–the Nebuy-title–but took the title Nebty, signifying "Two Ladies." The two ladies are most likely the goddesses Nekhbet and Wadjet. Semerkhet's full prenomen (throne name) was "he of the two ladies, the king of Upper and Lower Egypt." One of the most interesting facts about Semerkhet is that his name features a rare hieroglyph. The hieroglyph shows a man in a cloak carrying a stick, and there are many theories on what the hieroglyph could mean. The symbol could be translated as "divine guardian," "guardian of the Two Ladies," or simply "guardian." This hieroglyph depicted a ceremony that was performed by priests.

The throne was next inherited by Qa'a, also known as Ka'a. Qa'a is thought to be the last king of the First Dynasty, as a war between the First and the Second Dynasties occurred. Qa'a could have been Semerkhet's son, but according to modern-day historians, he might have been the son of Adjib. According to the scriptures and the fact that Qa'a celebrated two Sed festivals, the last pharaoh of the First

Dynasty probably ruled for at least thirty-three years. The Sed festival was used to celebrate the thirty-year mark of a pharaoh, and it repeated every three to four years after the first celebration. Qa'a appears to have had a prosperous rule, but Egypt found itself engaged in a war for the throne after Qa'a passed away. Thus, the death of Qa'a also meant the death of the First Dynasty.

Around 2900 BCE, Qa'a died. After his death, a war took place, and two names appear in the fight for power over the fertile lands of Egypt: Sneferka and Horus Bird, who were two supposed royals that might have had nothing to do with the First Dynasty. These ephemeral rulers are not very well known to Egyptologists, as even the way their names are read is disputable. While some historians read the name of Horus Bird to mean "Soul of Horus," others translate it as "the Heir of Horus." In the tradition established in the First Dynasty, each pharaoh was given a Horus name with their coronation. This is why it is presumed that Horus Bird was a pharaoh, although there is not much evidence on who his parents or relatives were or for how long he ruled. Both Sneferka and Horus Bird ruled for a short period, fighting over the throne of unified Egypt with the ruling First Dynasty falling apart. Along with Horus Bord and Sneferka, another royal name appears on the list of throne successors: Hotepsekhemwy. He became the first pharaoh of the Second Dynasty of Egypt after breaking up the war between Sneferka and Horus Bird. With Hotepsekhemwy as the next pharaoh, Egypt entered a new era and welcomed a new royal line. The remains of the First Dynasty are all left in Abydos in the form of royal tombs, and they remind us of the era when Upper and Lower Egypt became one.

Chapter 3 – Ancient Iran: From Early Urban Settlements to the Rise of the Elamites

Ancient Iran is home to some of the oldest known civilizations, modestly rising alongside the development of unified Egypt and Mesopotamia. Before Mesopotamia became the first empire in the history of civilization and the greatest force in the Fertile Crescent, the territory of ancient Iran saw some of the earliest urban settlements, which date to around 7000 BCE. The oldest lowland village of southwest ancient Iran, Chogha Bonut, rose in 7200 BCE. The settlement of Chogha Bonut would become the epicenter of the Elam civilization's early development, which was one of the most dominant civilizations of the Susiana Plain.

Chogha Golan, located in the foothills of the Zagros Mountains, was one of the earliest agricultural communities, where the first signs of cultivation and the domestication of plants and wild animals have been noted to start as far back as 10,000 BCE in the Middle Paleolithic period. By this time, the communities of Iran had already started to express their cultural identity through art by creating rock sculptures and ornaments. Chogha Golan was one of the first places in the Fertile Crescent where domesticated wheat was used as a food source. The people fished and hunted red deer, pigs, sheep, and goats, along with cultivating lentil, grass pea, barley, and wheat. Over time, the community of Chogha Golan flourished, growing and developing on more than just the agricultural scale. They used grinding stones and mortars to process grains, turning their crops into some kind of rough flour. This flour might have been roasted or cooked before being used for food. They also used mudbrick walls and plaster floors for buildings.

Chogha Mish, located in western Iran, emerged in 6800 BCE, and its people thrived on the domestication of pigs and horses. They dominated the Susiana region at the time.

Early connections between the Susiana Plain and Mesopotamia can be noted in the history of Chogha Mish, more specifically in pottery found in Mesopotamia and the vicinity of Chogha Mish. Up until 4400 BCE, Chogha Mish was the area with the largest population in the Susiana Plain before Susa was established as the dominant settlement in the region. The Chogha Mish settlements showed significant developments prior to the Elamites taking over as the dominant culture. Some of the earliest kilns (chambers with thermal insulation properties used for making tiles, bricks, and pottery) were found in Chogha Mish. The appearance of literacy is also noted in the settlements, as Chogha Mish and Susa used clay tokens as an accounting system. This system transformed into clay tablets using marks, which gradually became the first model of a cuneiform writing system. The people of Chogha Mish eventually migrated, and some reestablished their villages in Susa around 4200 BCE when the city was formed.

The Emerging Elamite Culture

The Elamites appeared around 3300 BCE, first taking the area on the Iranian Plateau with its center at Anshan. The center of Elam was later shifted to Awan in the mid-2nd millennium BCE.

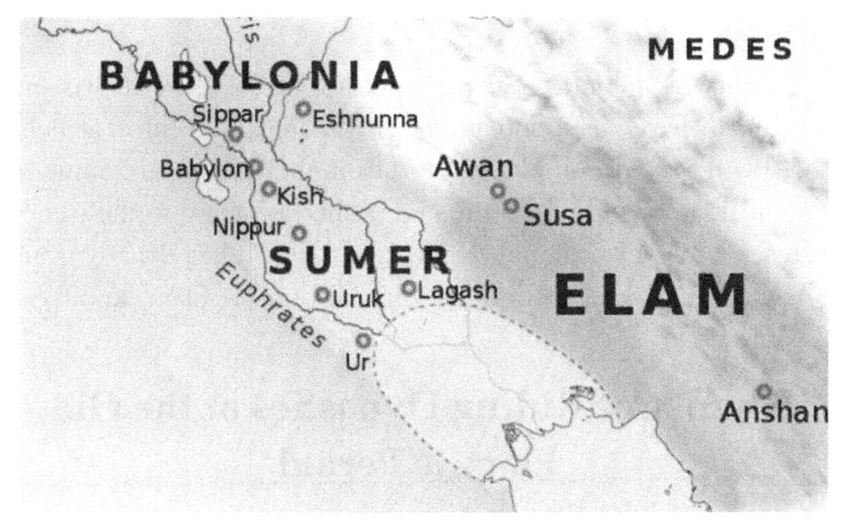

Map of Elam

File:Near East topographic map-blank.svg: SémhurFile:Elam-map-PL.svg: Wkotwicaderivative work: Morningstar1814, CC BY-SA 3.0 <https://creativecommons.org/licenses/by-sa/3.0>, via Wikimedia Commons https://commons.wikimedia.org/wiki/File:Elam_Map-en.svg

The history of Elam at the very beginning of its development was turbulent, as the power over the state was constantly shifting between Elam and Mesopotamia. Unfortunately, it appears that the powerful hand of Mesopotamian rulers was stronger than the Elamite culture and the hunger, or the lack thereof, for a powerful unified kingdom of the Elamite people.

The records of the first king of Elam emerge in 2650 BCE. Before that period, no significant historical figure appears to have carried the role of the ruler of Elam. In 2650 BCE, according to the Sumerian King List, King Enmebaragesi of Kish took over Elam and subdued the region in the name of Sumer and the First Dynasty of Kish. Elam was once again influenced by an outside culture, assimilating with the culture of Sumer and Mesopotamia. With the conquest of Enmebaragesi, Elam entered a new era in history known as the Old Elamite period, which lasted from around 2700 BCE to 1500 BCE. Enmebaragesi was allegedly killed by Gilgamesh's predecessor, although some sources indicate that the very Gilgamesh from the Sumerian *Epic of Gilgamesh* put an end to the rule of Enmebaragesi.

During this period of Elamite history, three different dynasties are said to have ruled and protected this region. With that being said, Elam was not completely freed from the influence of Sumer in the Old Elamite period. At the end of this era, Elam would witness a great return to its cultural origins, and a new ruling dynasty would emerge to mark a period in the history of Elam known as "Elamization."

The Three Ruling Dynasties of the Old Elamite Period

Elam was rich. The Elamites had easy access to some of the biggest shipping routes across the Persian Gulf, which is how the people of Elam had access to artwork, food, and other items from many different civilizations. When looking at their location, it is not hard to determine that the region was also agriculturally strong, which means that Elam didn't have to depend on others for food. Due to their wealth, Elam was a constant target of kings who wanted to bring the known world to its knees. After thousands of years of shifting power, the Old Elamite period, although it began with a Sumerian conquest, brought Elamite dynasties to the throne. Three different dynasties emerged amongst the Elamite royal rulers: Awan, Shimashki, and Sukkalmah.

The dynasty of Awan was the first known dynasty of Elam to be mentioned in the history of the Elamite people. This dynasty overcame rulers who were in constant conflict with Mesopotamian and Sumerian rulers. The first ruler of the Awan dynasty is sadly unknown to history. Some sources indicate the Awan dynasty took over the Elamite throne in 2350 BCE, while the Sumerian King List suggests the dynasty only had three rulers, who ruled for a combined 356 years. The length of their rule cannot be confirmed, though, so the list is most likely inaccurate, as the same source suggests that Enmebaragesi, the Sumerian king who invaded Elam, ruled for centuries.

While the Sumerian King List only mentions three kings of the Awan dynasty, a list of royals found in Susa, an important city of Elam, suggests the dynasty had twelve kings. The list even provides the names of these kings, although some parts of the names are missing. Archaeologists agree that the list cannot be considered completely reliable due to the lack of other evidence that would support the existence of twelve Awan kings.

The Sumerian King List mentions that the Awan dynasty came to power once the first Awan king defeated the First Dynasty of Ur. Ever since its humble beginnings, Elam had always feuded with Sumer, and the very fact that Awan defeated the First Dynasty of Ur in their territory gives the dynasty great importance. Elam and Sumer may have had a love-hate relationship, but business boomed between the two. The Elamites imported all kinds of foods, and they exported wool, slaves, cattle, silver, and many other things to the city-states of Sumer. The people of Elam also had some technological advancements, which also made them great craftsmen. There is a record of a request from Sumer for the governor of Uruk, a city in Elam, to turn tin into bronze. This indicates that the Elamites might have had more advanced technology than the Sumerians at the time.

Although Elam and Sumer might have had strong trading connections, the Awan dynasty engaged in several campaigns in Mesopotamia, trying to conquer some of the most powerful city-states of Mesopotamia at the time: Lagash and Kish. On one occasion, a party of 600 Elamites tried to plunder Lagash but were successfully defeated.

The Awan dynasty continuously feuded with Mesopotamia and its city-states. These little wars go all the way back to the Akkadian Empire and the rise of Sargon. Around 2300 BCE, Sargon was involved in a series of campaigns across the Iranian Plateau. Texts have been found that testify to Sargon's glory and success in these incursions, of which plunder was a standard part. Sargon defeated the eighth king of the Awan line, Luh-Ishan, the son of Hishiprashini. The Susa list of Awan kings doesn't quite match these texts; according to that list, Hishiprashini was the ninth king. Perhaps the names of the kings were mixed up, but there might also be some names missing from the Akkadian scriptures.

Whatever the case may be, after Sargon created the perfect conditions for Elam to be conquered, his son Rimush completed this venture with the defeat of the Awan king. This series of defeats brought the western lowlands of Elam under the ruling hand of the Akkadian Empire. A peace treaty between Elam and the Akkadian Empire came into being after Sargon's grandson succeeded the throne from his father. Naram-Sin, the third king of the Akkadian dynasty, signed a peace treaty that created conditions for Elam to not be assimilated completely. Although the Akkadian dynasty might have defeated the Awan dynasty, some city-states in Elam were never reached by Akkadian troops and thus were never vassals to that great empire.

The capital of Anshan was one such city, as it was located in the steep mountains and was geographically unreachable and secluded. The Elamites were able to preserve their cultural identity, although they were not content with the way things turned out. Over time, their hatred toward the Akkadian Empire grew. The tensions would not cease until the oppressed Elamites saw the Akkadian Empire fall to the Gutian soldiers. The Elamites helped contribute to the fall of the first empire in the ancient world, as they simply waited for their moment to strike. Even though the list of Awan kings of the Susa king list isn't a reliable source of information when it comes to the kings and their names, as well as the ruling order of the Awan dynasty, it does tell us who the last Awan king was: Puzur-Inshushinak, who ruled around 2100 BCE. He is remembered as the Awan king who brought independence to the people of Elam, people who had lived far too long under the ruling hand of the

Akkadian kings. However, every great empire meets its demise, and the Akkadian Empire was no exception. And when one empire falls, another one rises—and the Elamites eagerly seized their opportunity.

Puzur-Inshushinak, the last king of the Awan dynasty, carried the title of governor of Susa and military governor of Elam, which was the title carried by the governors of the Akkadian Empire. Puzur-Inshushinak, however, called himself the "Mighty King of Elam." This was found in the inscription known as "Table au Lion," or "Table of the Lion," a monument. To achieve independence for his people, Puzur-Inshushinak headed out on a series of conquests, conquering some of the most important cities in Mesopotamia, including Akkad, Akshak, and Eshnunna. He considerably weakened the Guti as well, chipping off a good portion of their newly conquered territory. The most likely reason why Puzur-Inshushinak became one of the most remembered kings of the Awan line was his commitment to preventing the assimilation of the Elamites by the Mesopotamians. He was dedicated to building the citadel in Susa, and the king was also a passionate advocate of the Linear Elamite script, encouraging people to use the original Elamite language when the Akkadians tried to force their cultural identity onto the people of Elam.

Although Puzur-Inshushinak strove for cultural and political freedoms and the independence of Elam, it only lasted during his lifetime. After Puzur-Inshushinak's death, the Linear Elamite script was forgotten and fell out of use. Susa fell into the hands of the Neo-Sumerian Empire, also known as the Third Dynasty of Ur. The founder of the Third Dynasty of Ur, Ur-Nammu, who ruled from 2112 BCE to 2095 BCE, was the one to put an end to Elamite sovereignty. Ur-Nammu's son and heir, Shulgi, continued his father's policies. Shulgi even went on to marry the daughters of rulers who controlled the eastern territories of Elam to strengthen his power in the region.

The Shimashki dynasty emerged around 2200 BCE, although it didn't become dominant until 2100 BCE. It began with an unnamed king, whose reign is veiled in mystery, as is the other kings of this dynasty. The Susa king list names fourteen other kings. The dates are obscure, and there is no information found about the reigns of these kings in other sources. Thus, historians suggest these were not sequential rulers and that the dynasty was an alliance of people from different Elamite cultures.

The Shimashki dynasty's rule over Elam, which lasted from around 2100 BCE to 1900 BCE, coincided with the Third Dynasty of Ur. In 2028 BCE, Ur was led by Ibbi-Sin, who would become the last ruler of the Third Dynasty of Ur. The Shimashki military ravaged the kingdom of Ur, looting its riches and destroying its capital. The Shimashki dynasty ruled over the fallen empire for a little over two decades. After the fall of the Third Dynasty of Ur, Shimashki entered more conflicts with Larsa, a city-state around twenty-five kilometers (fifteen and a half miles) southeast of Uruk, and Isin, another Sumerian city, located around thirty-two kilometers (almost twenty miles) south of Nippur. The Shimashki dynasty brought Elam on top, which was what their predecessors had wanted. Under the Shimashki, Elam became one of the richest and most powerful kingdoms in the area of West Asia. Their successors, the Sukkalmah dynasty, continued to rule over the mighty kingdom of Elam. At the time, Syria and Mesopotamia were under the influence of Elam, at least in the commercial, diplomatic, and military sense.

The Sukkalmah dynasty was formed around 1900 BCE, presumably by King Ebarat. Although Shilhaha is the name listed as the founder of the dynasty, historians believe Shilhaha and Ebarat to be the same person. There are thirty rulers recorded on the list of Sukkalmah kings, but little is known about them. Perhaps the most prominent king of the dynasty, aside from the dynasty's founder Ebarat, was King Siwe-Palar-Khuppak, who ruled around

1778 BCE. The king formed diplomatic relations with Hammurabi of Babylon and Zimri-Lim of Mari to conquer Eshnunna, a city-state in central Mesopotamia. His ambition was so great that he wanted to establish his power in Babylon as well, which is when his coalition turned against him. The others drove the Elamites from Eshnunna, putting an end to their influence in Mesopotamia. Little is known about the later kings of the Sukkalmah dynasty, even though the dynasty ended more than a century after Hammurabi turned against Siwe-Palar-Khuppak.

Culture, Government, and Military of Elam

In the earliest times of the Elamites, there was an overlord who would oversee smaller regions of the Elamite territory. Vassal princes governed these smaller regions in the name of the ruling overlord. Despite the general tradition in the lands of the Fertile Crescent, where the firstborn son would inherit the throne, power, and wealth after the king's death, the Elamites had viceroys who would fill that role. The viceroy was usually the overlord's eldest brother. If the overlord died, the viceroy would become the next ruler. If the viceroy died, and there were no brothers left to take over the role, one of the vassal princes would be named as the next overlord. If the overlord's wife became a widow, she wouldn't serve as a queen regent; instead, she would be remarried to the overlord's brother–the future overlord–or marry a vassal prince who would inherit the throne. Their son wouldn't have inheritance rights, as brothers or vassal princes were the ones to take on the power and wealth that came with the throne. In that case, the former vassal prince would be able to name his son or nephew as his successor, leaving the rule over the Elamite territory in the family and starting a new royal dynasty of overlords. This type of governance was complex and complicated when it came to checks, control, and inheritance rights, which was why the Elamites later turned to father-son inheritance, keeping the power close in the family.

The Elamites had a terrestrial army that didn't number more than over a thousand soldiers, although it is possible the Elamites just had a smaller army in the early days. The kingdom might have had its own navy; however, this presumption is not historically confirmed with any accuracy. It is also unknown whether there was a difference between the standing army and the professional one, as well as whether soldiers were fighting voluntarily or were commissioned to defend the kingdom and engage in battles.

According to some archaeologists, Susa was an extension of the Sumerian city-state of Uruk before it became the capital of Elam. Susa can be easily reimagined by visiting the site thousands of years later, as the ancient city, now dead and buried in ancient history, still offers a glimpse into its former glory. Susa still has a magnificent platform rising in the center of the city, complete with ceramic vessels that once offered sacrifices to the gods. The platform used to be a temple, and hundreds of graves rose up around the base of the building. Archaeologists suggest the founding of Susa was conditioned by the destruction of Chogha Mish, which was a nearby settlement, and the abandonment of nearby villages. Judging by the way the ceramics were painted from this period, and as concluded by the artifacts that were excavated thousands of years later, the region was strongly influenced by Mesopotamian culture and during the period before Susa became an integral part of the Uruk period in Mesopotamia. Later on, in the middle of the 4th millennium, Susa became the capital of Elam.

Unlike Mesopotamia in the late 4th millennium and the beginning of the 3rd millennium, ancient Iran didn't become literate all at once. However, lowland Khuzestan, where the people of Elam lived, developed a national identity by creating their very first alphabet. Surprisingly, even though a great part of this region was influenced by Mesopotamian culture and the Uruk period, Elamite emerged as an isolated language that can't be linked to any other language. Since Elam had a fascination with different cultures, it wasn't easy for the Elamites to develop their own language and alphabet and to form a unique identity in the ancient world. As a language isolate, Elamite language cannot be compared to any other known language, which is why its interpretation is often difficult. The Elamite language uses cuneiform, much like Akkadian; however, these languages don't share the same morphology. Out of 20,000 cuneiform clay tablets that represent the opus of the Elamite writing, the majority were economic records.

With the development of literacy and material power, Elam established federal governance. The strength of Elam was seen in its governance, as it held all these lesser states together and efficiently utilized the resources each state had.

Chapter 4 – Anatolia: The Bridge Between Asia and Europe and the Rise of the Hittite Old Kingdom

From prehistoric times, Anatolia, which made up most of modern-day Turkey, was the birthplace to many civilizations. After all, it was a strategic region, as Anatolia represented the bridge between Europe and Asia. The first serious attempt to create a civilized nation in Anatolia is noted to have occurred in the late 4th millennium BCE, which happened alongside the arrival of metallurgy in the Early Bronze Age. The Kura-Araxes, a Transcaucasian culture, brought bronze metallurgy to Anatolia. However, unlike the Fertile Crescent, which had already given birth to kings and soon-to-be emperors, Anatolia remained "trapped" in prehistoric times. This is why we don't hear stories of great wars and spilled blood among the people who lived in this region before the rise of the Akkadian Empire.

Sargon of the Akkadian dynasty is the one responsible for breaking the prehistoric cycle in Anatolia. After Sargon rose to power, he took an interest in Anatolia, as he wanted to use the region to export valuable materials for manufacturing. That is how Anatolia surrendered to a far more powerful region of the Fertile Crescent and became heavily influenced by Akkadian culture. According to the epic Mesopotamian tale of Sargon the Great, known as the *King of Battle*, a campaign was led against the Anatolian city Purushanda, located in central Anatolia, south of the Kızılırmak River. The motive behind the campaign was to protect Akkadian merchants. Although Sargon didn't conquer all of Anatolia, the Akkadian culture stuck around long after Sargon died, lasting until the Guti defeated the last ruler of the Akkadian royal line and took over the empire.

Driven by climate changes, the lack of manpower in the military, hunger, and constant discontent due to the worsening living conditions in the once-great Akkadian Empire, the Guti were able to come in and tear down the great Mesopotamian power. With that move, the influence of the Akkadian Empire in Anatolia slowly but steadily faded away. The Guti were vanquished by another super force: the Assyrian Empire. With the start of Ur-Nammu's reign, who ascended the throne in 2112 BCE as the founder of the Third Dynasty of Ur, the Guti were driven away from the remains of the Akkadian Empire. Anatolia was a part of this claim, and the Assyrians took them over during the Middle Bronze Age. The Assyrians were mostly interested in the silver that could be found in Anatolia. Up until the end of the Middle Bronze Age, Anatolia remained under the influence and rule of the Assyrian Empire.

However, empires rise and fall, and by the end of the Middle Bronze Age, a new kingdom would emerge in Anatolia to take over the region and establish a new cultural identity: the Hittite Old Kingdom. This kingdom would change the political scene in Anatolia by taking over Hattusa, making it the capital of a new Anatolian empire. The entrance of the city was framed with a sphinx gate and was surrounded by rich, lush landscapes, so it is no wonder that the people of Hittite chose Hattusa as the capital of the Hittite Old Kingdom.

However, before the Hittites arrived in Anatolia from the lands beyond the Black Sea, the Hattians lived in central Anatolia. Evidence of Hattians inhabiting this area of Anatolia date all the way back to the influence of the Akkadian Empire and Sargon, around 2350 BCE. The influence of the Hattians was so deeply established in this region that central Anatolia was known as the "Land of the Hatti." Like in the other parts of Anatolia, the Land of the Hatti was defeated and heavily influenced by the Akkadian Empire and, later, the Assyrian Empire. The land of the Hattians was organized into several smaller city-states, in which theocracy ruled. This meant the Hattians believed that their ruler was assigned by the gods or was even related to the gods. The authority of such a ruler was never questioned, as his word was considered to be the word of the gods. The Hattians and Hittites were often confused for being the same people with the same origin, even though that was not the case. This confusion might be due to the assimilation of the Hattians once the Hittites arrived in Anatolia. The Hittites also addressed their kingdom as the "Land of the Hatti," which might have contributed to the misunderstanding. The Hittites arrived in north-central Anatolia around 1600 BCE. About 200 years later, the Hittites would rule over most of Anatolia, the northern Levant, and Upper Mesopotamia.

The Rise of the Hittites in Ancient Anatolia

It is thought that the Hittites arrived from the region of today's Ukraine. To help confirm that theory, the language of the Hittites, which gradually assimilated with that of the Hattians, was a form of an Indo-European language. Although it was far different from the language the Hattians used, the language of the Hittites became a part of the culture of Anatolia.

The story of the Anatolian Hittites starts with King Anitta. King Anitta arrived in north-central Anatolia around 1600 BCE with his people and the Hittite military. The conquest of the region began with the sacking of Hattusa and the Kussara kingdom. The exact borders of Kussara remain unknown, as the city has never been found. Before that moment, Hattusa was the most powerful and richest city of Hatti, and it had stood its ground since 2500 BCE. Hattusa was even successfully defended from Sargon of Akkad and his grandson, Naram-Sin, but it didn't stand a chance against Anitta, who ruled Kussara around the 17th century BCE. King Anitta burned the city down and is said to have cursed it and anyone who ever attempted to rebuild it. The city was rebuilt a generation later by Hattusili I, the founder of the Hittite Old Kingdom, who reigned from 1650 BCE to 1620 BCE. Hattusili means "the one from Hattusa." Archaeologists once argued that the founder of the Hittite line was also known as Labarna I, in which case his son and successor would have been known as Labarna II. However, *labarna* was actually a title rather than a name.

Hattusili didn't stop at rebuilding the city of Hattusa, which happened sometime during his reign. He also decided to extend the domain of his people to the Black Sea and the Mediterranean Sea, expanding the territory of the Hittites in the first year of his reign. In his second year, King Hattusili conquered Alalakh and several other cities in Syria. Hattusili was an ambitious king, and he continued his war campaigns, arriving at Arzawa in western Anatolia in the third year of his reign.

While the king was away on his campaigns, the Hurrians occupied the cities he previously subdued in Syria. The Hurrians lived in Anatolia, Syria, and Mesopotamia, but their most powerful kingdom was known as Mitanni. The Mitanni kingdom was associated with horses, as this animal was highly respected in the Hurrian culture. King Hattusili spent the next three years retaking the cities in Syria that he had previously conquered. There is no further evidence of King Hattusili's reign, although it is known he ruled longer than six years.

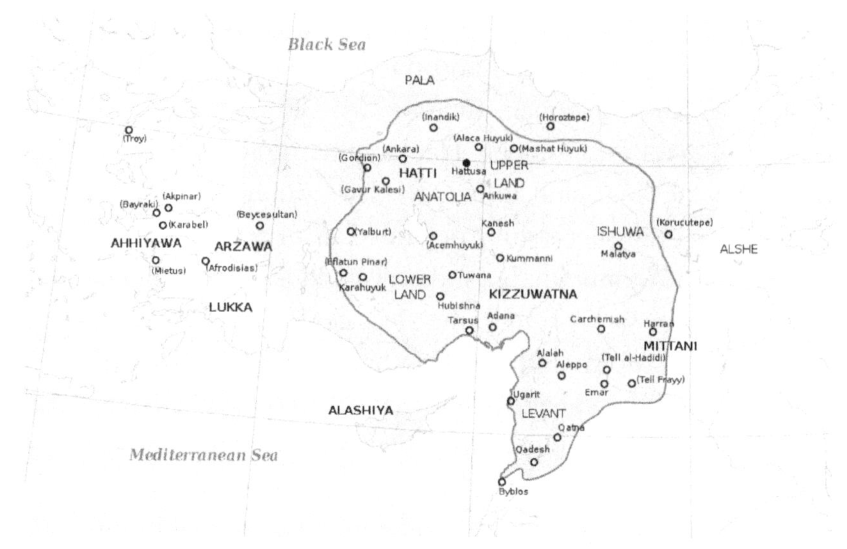

The Hittite Empire at its greatest extent

Near_East_topographic_map-blank.svg: Sémhurderivative work: Ikonact, CC BY-SA 3.0 <https://creativecommons.org/licenses/by-sa/3.0>, via Wikimedia Commons https://commons.wikimedia.org/wiki/File:Map_Hittite_rule_en.svg

Hattusili's reign was harsh, as he had complete control over the lives of his subjects. He was known for punishing deeds he considered to be wrong with the death sentence. At times, his justice was merciless, even when his children were involved.

Before we delve into that, let us look at the family life of Hattusili. Sadly, not much is known about the woman to whom the king was married. It is known that her name was Tawananna. The name of Hattusili's wife would become the title that all Hittite queens would take. Having a queen wasn't just a formality, for the queen held power in case of the king's absence. If the king was away on war campaigns, the queen would then rule the kingdom with full control over the subjects. The queen also had the role of the high priestess, while the king was the high priest. The queen could also perform diplomatic duties, but her official duties were mostly religious. However, the succession of the throne wouldn't go to the queen after the king died. Instead, the first son would become the successor to the throne. In case the first son wasn't able to take the throne, the second son would be named as the successor. In case the king didn't have any sons, he would name his son-in-law as the next ruler, in which case the king's daughter would become Tawananna.

Hattusili had named his nephew, his sister's son, as his successor. The king went off to war with the city of Halab, which was the capital of Yamhad (an ancient Semitic kingdom), destroying it so badly that Halab would never retrieve its glory. All of Hattusili's conquests took place in the first three years of his reign, while he spent the next three in reclaiming the territories from the Hurrians. However, Hattusili returned with severe wounds that could have quickly turned fatal. His nephew seemed to be uncaring about the king's predicament. Despite the king's fierce and sometimes merciless rule, he became furious about how cold his successor was. King Hattusili concluded that it was wrong to have named his nephew, who became his adopted son, as the heir to the throne, as the prince did not shed a tear over Hattusili's possible death. Instead of listening to and caring about Hattusili, the adopted prince, known to history as "Young Labarna," listened to his brothers, sisters, and mother. These people were not teaching the young heir the proper way of kingship, at least in Hattusili's eyes. The king even used to call his sister "the snake." The king couldn't take this disobedience of his adopted son any longer. He exiled him, granted him the title of a priest, and sent him to an estate.

Renouncing Young Labarna wasn't the only time the king was disappointed and betrayed by his own blood. His actual son joined the people of Tappassanda (unknown location) to conspire against the king. Hattusili's son planned the uprising, which included the demise of his own father. The people of Tappassanda joined in on the conspiracy because they would receive an exemption from taxes. The betrayal of his son and later his daughter, who conspired against him so that her son could take the throne, was what made up the king's mind to adopt his nephew and name him the heir to the throne in the first place.

Despite all of this backstabbing, the king finally found an heir he thought would be the perfect successor to the throne: one of his young grandsons, Mursili. Mursili I inherited the throne around 1620 BCE, and since he was a minor, he wouldn't go on war campaigns for three years. Hattusili appears to have chosen the perfect successor, as Mursili, once he came of age, decided to follow in his grandfather's footsteps when it came to conquest. Mursili went on to reclaim the cities in northern Syria, and he also conquered the Yamhad kingdom and its capital, Halab (modern-day Aleppo). From there, he headed out on an ambitious conquest, going forward with his military 2,000 kilometers (a little over 1,240 miles) into the very center of Mesopotamia. The goal was to attack, raid, and sack Babylon. Although the motivation behind the attack is not quite clear to historians, it is thought the king perhaps wanted to take Babylon's grain, as the Hittite crops were destroyed by the Thera eruption (a major volcanic eruption on the island of Thera around 1600 BCE). The king was so successful in his conquest of Babylon that he brought an end to the Amorite dynasty. When Mursili returned to his kingdom after sacking Babylon, he was assassinated, which happened sometime around 1526 BCE. Despite the king's exceptional conquests and war strategies, Hantili, his brother-in-law, and Zidanta, Hantili's son-in-law, sought the king's death. Hantili was also the king's cupbearer, and he was the one who would rule the kingdom after Mursili's death.

During his reign, Hantili I managed to lose the territory in Syria that Mursili had conquered, while the central rule started to lose its power. The rule of Hantili was marked with social decay and uncertainty. His military conquests, or attempted conquests, cost him territories that his predecessors had ruled. Hantili, who ruled for thirty years, was succeeded by Zidanta I, who ruled for ten years.

According to the preserved written sources, Zidanta I was not the rightful heir to the throne—at least not while Pisheni, the legitimate heir, and his children existed. Toward the end of Hantili's life, Zidanta killed Pisheni and his children so he could assure the throne for himself.

Almost as if it was a tradition, Zidanta I was also killed, and by the hand of his own son, Ammuna, no less. Zidanta was married to one of Hantili's daughters, which is how the royal line was preserved, for Ammuna was a child from that marriage. King Ammuna appears to have been even less capable in military strategy and warfare than his father. During his reign, Ammuna lost a substantial amount of territory held by the Hittite Old Kingdom. The king had a daughter, Istapariya, and a son, Huzziya. Ammuna might have had two more sons who were older than Huzziya—Hantili and Tittiya—and they had the right to the throne over Huzziya. However, the relations between Hantili and his supposed sons have never been confirmed with any certainty. Huzziya is said to have organized a series of assassinations to inherit the right to rule. So, once again, the new king came to power through murder and conspiracy.

The next successor and the last king of the Hittite Old Kingdom was Telipinu. Telipinu was married to Istapariya, Ammuna's daughter, which means that Huzziya was his brother-in-law. Telipinu wanted to stop the bloodshed, but he was still motivated by the hunger for power, and he couldn't avoid his fate by following in his predecessors' footsteps. Thus, Huzziya and his supposed brothers were all killed, together with King Telipinu's son and wife. Due to all of the murders that had taken place before his reign, as well as the great loss of territory with each new king that came to the throne, King Telipinu decided to create an edict that would prevent murder for the sake of inheriting the throne. King Telipinu was able to recover some of the lost lands from Mitanni and the Hurrians by allying with the Hurrians of Kizzuwatna. After Telipinu died, the kingdom entered a period that would last for seventy years, known as the Middle Kingdom or the "Dark Ages."

Chapter 5 – The Levant: The Kingdom of Ebla and the Cultures of the Ancient Levant

With Mesopotamia on the east and set between the Mediterranean Sea and the Arabian Desert, the "land of the rising sun" gave birth to some of the first nomadic tribes in the Stone Age. From 8500 BCE to 7000 BCE, numerous settlements were formed in all parts of the Levant, an area that included modern-day Syria, Lebanon, Jordan, Palestine, Israel, and most of Turkey. The domestication of dogs and other animals, as well as plants and grain, has been recorded in these parts. By 6000 BCE, the climate started to change, and settlements began shifting to a nomadic way of life. Groups of hunters and gatherers emerged, and they tended to be influenced by the culture of Egypt, at least judging by the pottery found in the Levant.

The Early Bronze Age corresponds to the Early Syrian Period, a period when several mighty kingdoms ruled the Levant. The First Eblaite Kingdom, the Kingdom of Nagar, and the Second Mariote (Mari) Kingdom dominated the Early Syrian Period, which is around the time when the Akkadians established numerous cities in northern Sumer, around 3500 BCE to 3000 BCE. Ebla was one of the earliest kingdoms in the region of Syria, and it began as a modest settlement in the Levant at the beginning of 3500 BCE. Although it started as a small settlement, Ebla would soon become an unparalleled trading empire. Ebla traded with Sumer, Egypt, Cyprus, and Afghanistan. Instead of borrowing a language from one of these cultures, the people of Ebla had their own language, Eblaite, which is an extinct Semitic language that had been used in the region since the 3rd millennium BCE.

Ebla might have emerged as a part of the Kish civilization that arrived in the western Levant from central Mesopotamia in the mid-4th millennium BCE. The city of Ebla was established around 3500 BCE, and it was built on an outcrop of limestone, which was how Ebla got its name, as it is thought that Ebla means "white rock." Ebla would soon become one of the most powerful kingdoms in the region.

The Rise and Fall of Ebla and Other Ancient Syrian Kingdoms

Although the names of the kings who ruled Ebla during the era of the First Eblaite Kingdom are known to history, there is very little information on some of their reigns. The First Eblaite Kingdom was founded by Sakuma, who started his reign around 3100 BCE, about 400 years after Ebla was founded as a small settlement and over 600 years before the First Eblaite Kingdom would meet its demise. Very little is known about the first king of Ebla. History knows very little about his successors as well, whose names were discovered in the mid-20th century. With the reign of King Sagisu, which commenced around 2680 BCE, more information became available on the royal names and the kings' reigns.

Soon, Ebla became a powerful kingdom with favorable connections with Mesopotamia, southern Syria, and central Anatolia. Not long after this, a hundred-year war with Mari, a Syrian city-state, would begin.

Northwest of the Euphrates riverbank, the people of Mari, under King Ansud, began preparing their attack on the First Eblaite Kingdom. Ansud would later become known as the earliest attested king in the history of the Mari kingdom. Before Mari became a military force to be reckoned with, Mari was a small settlement, much like Ebla. The settlement was abandoned around 2500 BCE for unknown reasons, possibly due to the floods in the area that couldn't be prevented with the major canals that had been previously built in the region. The people of Mari returned a half-century later to repopulate the city, after which Mari became a kingdom that was nearly as powerful as Ebla.

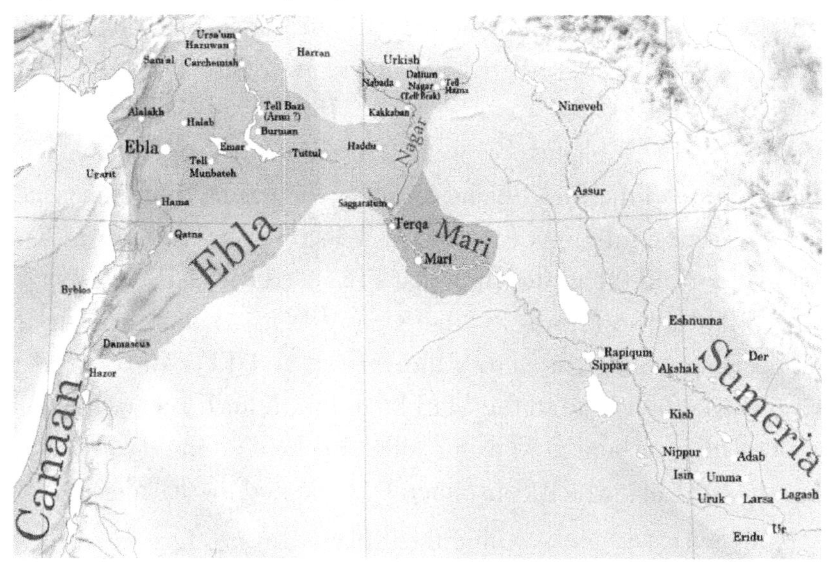

The First Eblaite Kingdom at its greatest extent including vassal states

Sémhur, CC BY-SA 4.0 <https://creativecommons.org/licenses/by-sa/4.0>, via Wikimedia Commons https://commons.wikimedia.org/wiki/File:First_Eblaite_Empire.png

Around the end of 2416, under the reign of Sa'umu, Mari would continue the war with Ebla. King Sa'umu launched a series of attacks on many cities of the First Eblaite Kingdom, which gave Mari the upper hand. Kun-Damu, who was the king of Ebla during Sa'umu's reign, managed to defeat Mari.

Kun-Damu's successor, Adub-Damu, is almost unknown to history except for his name, so little is known about his reign. However, more is known about the successor of the Mari kingdom's throne, Ishtup-Ishar, as he continued the path set by his predecessors by conquering two Eblaite cities and continuing the war. While Adub-Damu might have had troubles with defending the kingdom of Ebla, his successor, Igriš-Halam, or Igriš-Halab (š is pronounced as "sh"), led a victory against the Mari kingdom, which led to the expansion beyond the city of Halab. It is thought that his other name might be a commemoration of driving the Mari away from Halab.

However, Igriš-Halam's reign is best remembered by his capitulation to Mari. King Iblul-II was on the throne of the Mari kingdom, and he is said to have been one of the most energetic kings that the kingdom ever saw. Iblul-II was interested in conquering the Eblaites, as well as their vassals and allies. King Iblul-II noticed that the Eblaite king was increasing the military and setting out on ambitious campaigns. To stop their expansion, King Iblul-II blocked the trade route that Ebla used with Kish and Nagar. King Iblul-II, also known as "the King of Mari Abarsal," continued his ravaging campaigns across the region, and Ebla was forced to pay a shameful tribute to the Mari kingdom. Iblul-II received a great amount of silver and gold as a result, and he continued to conquer the cities of Ebla, which consequently weakened the Eblaites.

After twelve years of ruling the Eblaite throne, Igriš-Halam was succeeded by his son, Irkab-Damu, who proved to be a far more vigorous king, as he wished to retrieve the old glory of the kingdom of Ebla. Irkab-Damu succeeded the throne around 2340 BCE and ruled for eleven years. During his reign, Ebla became a dominant power in the Levant. King Irkab-Damu started his rule by settling a peace treaty between Abarsal, which was a part of the Mari kingdom, located east of Ebla alongside the riverbank of the Euphrates. The king's goal was to put an end to the tribute given to

Mari, so he planned to attack. Nizi, the successor of Iblul-II, was not nearly as skillful in combat and military strategy as his predecessor. This is how Irkab-Damu defeated the Mari kingdom and established Ebla as a powerful force in the region. During the eleven-year reign of Irkab-Damu, Ebla was expanded to its greatest extent, about half the size of modern-day Syria. Half of the kingdom was controlled directly by the king and his district administrators, while the other half was run by Eblaite vassals. The kingdom of Ebla also developed diplomatic relationships with surrounding city-states and kingdoms, which included Egypt and Hamazi (an ancient city-state whose location is unknown). A letter that was sent to King Zizi of Hamazi testifies that Irkab-Damu sent gifts to the king, asking for mercenaries in return. Irkab-Damu referred to Zizi as his "brother," which further shows the close relationship between the two kings. The gifts from the ruler of Egypt also indicate the political and diplomatic reach of Ebla.

During Irkab-Damu's reign, the vizier would become more important in the political affairs of the kingdom. This would happen mostly in the last two years of his reign, for this was when Vizier Ibrium saw his own rise to power before Irkab-Damu's son, Isar-Damu, took over the throne around 2320 BCE. Isar-Damu's mother, Dusigu, who married the king in the fifth year of his reign, was actually related to Vizier Ibrium. Since Isar-Damu inherited the throne at a very young age, probably when he was six or seven years old, the vizier would become the king's chief official. Irkab-Damu had other sons who were older, so this succession was most likely due to Queen Dusigu's interference, as she was one of her husband's favorite consorts. Her decision wasn't a mistake, for Ebla remained strong under her son's rule, which lasted for thirty-five years.

Isar-Damu continued his father's wars, but he also established a strong diplomatic system, which may have helped Ebla stay on top. While Isar-Damu was still very young, his mother and Vizier Ibrium ruled by his side, during which time the vizier led campaigns against the rebellious vassals of the kingdom. During Isar-Damu's reign, Ebla concluded an alliance with Nagar, which resulted in a marriage between Princess Tagrish-Damu, Isar-Damu's daughter, and the prince of Nagar, Ultum-Huhu. In the hopes of defeating the Mari kingdom once and for all, Isar-Damu allied with Nagar and Kish. At the head of the campaign was the son of Vizier Ibrium, Ibbi-Sipish, who became the new vizier after his father's death. After their victory near Terqa, the king and his allies attacked Armi, a rebellious vassal city of Ebla. King Isar-Damu is considered to be the last king of the First Eblaite Kingdom, although his son, Ir'ak-Damu, who was married to Vizier Ibbi-Sipish's daughter, ascended to the throne for a brief period.

The last days of the First Eblaite Kingdom were recorded to have happened around 2300 BCE when the kingdom was destroyed for the first time. Since the perpetrator(s) and the cause are still unknown, several theories exist as to what happened. Some believe it might have been Mari seeking revenge, as the destruction happened several years after the Battle of Terqa. However, based on the records of Sargon's grandson Naram-Sin, who went campaigning in the region around this time, the city of Ebla was destroyed by the Akkadians. In the inscriptions of Naram-Sin, it is recorded that the army of the Akkadian Empire destroyed the city of "Ibla," which might be a reference to Ebla. Some archaeologists argue that it was a natural catastrophe. It has been suggested that a fire broke out, as the most significant impact was limited to the palace. There were also no signs of looting, which may provide clear indications that the Akkadians weren't responsible for the destruction.

After the destruction of the city, a new period for the kingdom came about. This is known as the Second Eblaite Kingdom, which lasted from 2300 BCE to 2000 BCE. The second kingdom began with the construction of a new royal palace, which was set in the lower area of the city. A new royal line is also said to have emerged, although they were related to the line of kings who ruled the First Eblaite Kingdom. Very little is known about this period since there is no surviving written evidence on the names of these kings. The kingdom was once again burned around 2000 BCE, and it is thought that this destruction was the result of an invasion by the Hurrians, who arrived in the region around 2030 BCE. A former Eblaite vassal city, Ikinkalis, is said to have led the attack that brought the city and the Second Eblaite Kingdom to its knees. The Third Eblaite Kingdom emerged from the ashes of the burned city, and once again, a new royal palace was built, along with new temples.

The Third Eblaite Kingdom would last from 2000 BCE to 1600 BCE, starting with the rule of Ibbit-Lim. Since Ibbit-Lim is an Amorite name, it is suggested that the people of Ebla were now Amorites, as were the majority of inhabitants in Syria at the time. The Amorites were a Semitic-speaking people, who would go on to establish a powerful dynasty of Babylon. The list of kings who ruled the Third Eblaite Kingdom appears to be exclusively Amorite. However, the list seems to have severe gaps. Only four names appear on the list, despite the fact the kingdom was around for 400 years. This lack of written evidence takes us to 1750 BCE when the kingdom was ruled by King Immeya, whose full name is not known. What is known is that the king had diplomatic relations with Egypt and Pharaoh Hotepibre of the Thirteenth Dynasty. At the time of Immeya's rule, Ebla had become the vassal of Yamhad, an Amorite kingdom. After the reign of King Immeya, an unknown king came to the throne. Archaeologists have found a partial name for this ruler from a tablet found in the ruins of this city, but nothing else is known about his reign. It has been suggested that his name was Hammurabi, as the partial name is "Hammu." Indillima emerged as the last king of Ebla, and he ruled around 1600 BCE. His son, Maratewari, never had a chance to rule, as the kingdom was destroyed by King Mursili I of the Hittites. The Eblaite kingdom was destroyed, and it never retrieved its previous glory.

Culture, Military, and Government of Ebla

Although it was located near the regions heavily influenced by Sumer and Mesopotamia, the Eblaites managed to preserve their cultural identity through their unique political organization, language, and religion. The deities that were worshiped in this region were specifically related to the Eblaite culture, and women enjoyed great respect, which made the queen an important figure in political and religious affairs.

The city of Ebla had fifty-six hectares of land that were divided into four districts, with each district having its own separate gates and fortifications. The city had a lower town and an acropolis in the center, where the king's palace was built. The city also had two temples, and the kings were buried outside the city in royal tombs. The kingdom would go through many transformations and changes in terms of buildings and overall architecture with the Second and Third Eblaite Kingdoms. The government of Ebla had the king as the head of the city-state, but the king didn't rule by himself, as he had a council of elders, administrative divisions, and the grand vizier that all helped make decisions as well. Thirteen court dignitaries oversaw the administrative divisions, and each one controlled between 400 and 800 men. Since the city was divided into four districts, each district had several deputies and one chief inspector, who would oversee the district and report to the king. The king would extend his power to protect royal interests by employing agents, messengers, and collectors. The next in line for the throne, the crown prince, would be included in internal affairs, while the second eldest son was involved in foreign affairs. The queen also had an important role in the kingdom, and her title allowed her to have a vote in the kingdom's matters and internal affairs. The vassal states were autonomous, but they still had to pay tribute to the kingdom and send military assistance upon the king's request.

The settlement of Ebla started to get rich based on trade, especially due to the rising demand for wool in Sumer. The records found in the ancient kingdom testify that the king had many sheep, meaning he had abundant wool to trade. The Eblaites also produced excess food with which to trade. However, the kingdom's economy and financial prosperity were mostly in the hands of villages, which paid their share in taxes to the kingdom. The king would distribute food for all seasonal and permanent workers in the palace. The kingdom mostly lived off pastoral agriculture, while large herds of cattle were kept by the palace and controlled by the king as well.

The language of the Eblaites is known as Eblaite or Paleo Syrian, and this language belongs to the group of extinct Semitic languages. Eblaite wasn't only used within the borders of the kingdom, as a modified version of the language was also used in the kingdoms of Mari and Nagar. The majority of Eblaite writing is related to the economy and administration; however, texts with myths and proverbs were also found, as well as bilingual texts written in Eblaite and Sumerian.

Chapter 6 - The Rise of the Assyrian Empire and Babylon from the Ashes of Akkad

The Akkadian Empire fell around 2154 BCE with the arrival of the Guti, who displaced the power of Akkad in the Fertile Crescent by taking advantage of the civil wars and droughts that had created an explosive and tense atmosphere in the empire. Descending from the Zagros Mountains as a tribal conglomerate, the Guti sought the prosperity that could be found in the plains of Mesopotamia, Sumer, and the surrounding regions. The Guti conquered Akkad by demoralizing their troops, as they looted and destroyed everything with a "hide-and-seek" strategy, in which the Guti would attack a city then move onto the next one before the military could even arrive. Working in the fields and traveling became unsafe due to the Guti. All of this resulted in fear and famine in the cities of the former Akkadian Empire.

At the time, the Guti were ruled by a nameless king, and while they moved across the region, conquering and looting, some of the city-states that belonged to the Akkadian Empire managed to survive and remain untouched by the tribe from the Zagros

Mountains. Lagash was one such place, as it continued to thrive under the ruling hand of a local dynasty.

It is perhaps unimaginable for a modern-day reader to understand the horror of the Mesopotamians, who were facing famine, droughts, and internal conflicts when the Guti arrived. The Guti were described as subnormal beings without religion and an unwillingness to conform to the laws and customs of the civilized world. They are described by the Mesopotamians as animals who spoke a language that sounded much like babbling. The Guti released the domestic animals kept by the people so they could roam freely, and they knew nothing about irrigation and agriculture. This contributed to the dark ages of Mesopotamia, where everyone ruled but no one was king. The Guti weren't able to lead in a civilized world, as they knew nothing about politics or even complex canal networks. As a result, their rule was crude and disorganized. Their inability to rule a civilized world with complex organization swept prosperity away from the region, which resulted in a great number of deaths caused by famine.

After the death of Shar-Kali-Sharri of Akkad, the Sumerian King List names four different kings in only three years, indicating an intense turnover of power in the kingdom. After them, the list goes on to name nine more kings, who ruled for a combined sixty-five years. The Gutian hordes were led by nameless kings, with a total of twenty-one Gutian kings for ninety-one years. One of the Gutian kings ruled for only forty days, which perfectly describes the political climate of the Mesopotamian dark ages.

The Assyrians were subjects of the Akkadian Empire before its fall, and they managed to gain independence with the arrival of the Gutian hordes. It didn't last, for after the founding of the Neo-Sumerian Empire, otherwise known as the Third Dynasty of Ur, which happened around 2112 BCE, the Assyrian city of Ashur fell under the influence of the new Sumerian power. However, Nineveh and the far north remained untouched.

The Third Dynasty of Ur

During the Sumerian renaissance, the Guti were driven out of the region by the king of Uruk, Utu-Hengal. His son-in-law, Ur-Nammu, would become the founder of the Third Dynasty of Uruk. Utu-Hengal came to power over Uruk in 2120 BCE and ruled until 2112 BCE. Utu-Hengal defeated the last Gutian king, Tirigan, which signaled the end of the Gutian era and the Mesopotamian dark ages. Utu-Hengal is considered to be the direct predecessor to the Third Dynasty of Uruk, and he was looked upon as a great hero by the Sumerian people. Utu-Hengal even carried the title characteristic for the kings of Akkad, "the king of the four quarters," also known as the "king of the world." The king's daughter married his successor, Ur-Nammu, so the crown of Ur stayed in the royal family.

Ur-Nammu came to the throne in 2112 BCE. During this time, the Assyrians were largely under the influence of Sumer and the Third Dynasty of Ur. Although the dynasty was officially founded by Ur-Nammu, his father-in-law had set a solid ground for the development of a strong dynasty. The Guti and their reign of chaos were gone, and the cities of Sumer, including Uruk, could now reestablish their power and glory. Around half a century after the foundation of the Neo-Sumerian Empire, the Assyrians would become vassal governors of the Ur dynasty.

Ur-Nammu continued on to conquer Susa and built the wall of Ur in the third year of his reign. He would then receive the kingship from Nippur, where he would later build the temple of Nanna. The Guti weren't truly defeated until the seventh year of his reign. After completely destroying the Guti, Ur-Nammu dedicated his rule to restoring the general order in the region, focusing on trade, roads, rebuilding temples and the looted, decaying cities, and reconquering territories in central and northern Mesopotamia. Ur-Nammu also created the oldest preserved code of law, known as the Code of Ur-Nammu. This code, which was written in Sumerian, regulated the lives of the people, including slaves and free people.

Ur-Nammu ruled until 2095 BCE, after which he was succeeded by his son, Shulgi. Shulgi is said to have ruled for forty-eight years, finishing most of what his father had started during his reign and strengthening the dominance of the dynasty in the region and beyond. He even received the title of divinity in the thirty-third year of his reign. Shulgi continued with his father's work of modernizing the kingdom, which led to writing reforms, reorganizations of the army, major reconstruction projects, and tax reforms. After a long and fruitful reign, Shulgi was succeeded by Amar-Sin in 2047 BCE.

During the rule of Amar-Sin, Ushpia would become the first independent king of Assyria, although some records mention a King Zariqum, who is claimed to have been the governor of Ashur during the reign of Amar-Sin. Amar-Sin extended the borders of the Neo-Sumerian Empire to the northern provinces of Hamazi and Lullubi, and these provinces were assigned governors to protect royal interests. His reign ended in 2038 BCE. He was succeeded by his brother, Shu-Sin. Shu-Sin reigned until 2029 BCE, which was only several years before the rise of the Old Assyrian Empire in 2025 BCE. During the first year of his reign, Shu-Sin had to deal with the rebellion of his Amorite subjects, and he decided to build a fortified wall between the Tigris and Euphrates to prevent more potential Amorite offenses. He was succeeded by his son, Ibbi-Sin, who would reign from 2027 BCE to 2002 BCE.

Ibbi-Sin was the last ruler of the Neo-Sumerian Empire, as the Third Dynasty of Ur was about to fall. Over the years, the Assyrians had slowly been recollecting to form an independent kingdom. Ibbi-Sin decided to campaign against Elam, which was how he met his demise. The king didn't make it far into the Elamite lands. The Elamites defeated the king, took him captive, and ultimately destroyed the Neo-Sumerian Empire and the Third Dynasty of Ur. It was time for the Amorites, who had slowly gained power over the years, to rise up and establish their influence in Mesopotamia.

Although they first introduced a semi-nomadic lifestyle to the people, the Amorites soon built a merchant empire, establishing independent dynasties in the city-states of southern Mesopotamia, among which were Lagash, Eshnunna, Larsa, Isin, and later Babylon.

After the demise of the Third Dynasty of Ur, Puzur-Ashur I, whose name is translated as "the servant of Ashur," began his reign over Assyria, ruling until 1950 BCE. He was succeeded by his son, Shalim-Ahum, meaning "keeping the brothers safe." This name might show the determination of the Assyrians to gain back their independence and reestablish their cultural identity while defying potential attacks from neighboring city-states. He reigned until 1900 BCE and was succeeded by Illu-Shuma, his son, after which Erishum I, the son of Illu-Shuma, came to the throne. He began his rule in 1905 BCE and ruled until 1876 BCE. Erishum I expanded the borders of the Assyrian Empire while building new temples, walls, and fortifications. The king also established *karums*—"trading posts"—along the trading routes of Anatolia. Erishum also revised the code of law and established tax exemptions for the remission of debts, which could be paid in silver, gold, or even wool. He even allowed plaintiffs to be represented by attorneys.

Erishum was succeeded by his brother, Ikunum, who reigned from 1867 BCE to 1860 BCE, which was more than a half a century before the Old Assyrian Empire would meet the rising power of Babylon. The king further fortified the city of Ashur and continued to maintain the trading colonies along the Anatolian trade route. Ikunum was succeeded by his son, who carried the name of the first emperor in history. Sargon I, "the steward of Ashur," ruled for thirty-nine years until 1821 BCE. His son, Puzur-Ashur II, came to the throne at an old age, as his father ruled for almost forty years. Puzur-Ashur named his son Naram-sin, after the grandson of Sargon of Akkad, which might show the desire for the Assyrians to identify with the once-glorious Akkadian Empire. The dynasty of

Puzur-Ashur I ended with Naram-sin's successor, Erishum II. Erishum II would rule the kingdom from 1815 BCE to 1809 BCE. He was deposed by the usurper Shamshi-Adad I.

Shamshi-Adad I of the Amorites conquered the Old Assyrian Empire, Upper Mesopotamia, most of Syria, and the Levant. Shamshi-Adad ascended as the first Amorite king of Assyria, although he claimed to be related to Ushpia to legitimize his right to the Assyrian throne. His son and successor, Ishme-Dagan I, who came to the throne in 1776 BCE, wasn't a brilliant warlord like his father. Instead, he lost many of the territories his father had conquered during his reign, which included the Levant and southern Mesopotamia. These fell under the influence of the Sumerian city-state of Eshnunna and the Mari kingdom. Ishme-Dagan I was a contemporary to King Hammurabi, who managed to reinforce Babylon as an important power in the region, and the two had tolerable relations. Since Ishme-Dagan's line would continue for three more generations, his successors would witness the rising power of Babylon, which started with the First Amorite Dynasty and King Sumu-abum.

The Rise of Babylon and the First Amorite Dynasty

Before Sumu-abum, Babylon was just a city in Babylonia, which was a kingdom in Mesopotamia. Although Sumu-abum showed no interest in declaring himself as a king of Babylon, he is still known as the first king of the First Babylon (Amorite) Dynasty. He freed Babylon and a small area that belonged to the Amorite city of Kazallu. He also claimed a small administrative center in southern Mesopotamia. Sumu-abum was a chieftain of Babylon from 1894 BCE to 1881 BCE and was succeeded by Sumu-la-El, his son, who would reign from 1881 BCE to 1845 BCE. Four generations later, Hammurabi, the sixth king of the First Dynasty, would establish an empire based in the city of Babylon that would live as long as the king who founded it. Hammurabi inherited the throne from his father, Sin-Muballit, who had to renounce his position due to falling ill. Hammurabi's reign started around 1792 BCE when he was about eighteen years old, and it lasted for forty-two years, during which he transformed Babylon into a powerful kingdom.

Before Hammurabi came to the throne, Babylon was a rather small city, which, although growing more powerful by the year, was surrounded by mightier neighbors, such as Isin, Eshnunna, Larsa, and Assyria. However, Sin-Muballit conquered a small area in south-central Mesopotamia, which included Kish, Sippar, and Borsippa. When Hammurabi ascended the throne, he was the king of a small kingdom with a fairly complex geopolitical situation. Regardless of the more powerful kingdoms and their plans for expansion, Babylon didn't enter conflicts with other cities and kingdoms in the first years of Hammurabi's reign. Hammurabi took care of Babylon instead, starting a great number of public works, which included the expansion of temples and improving the city's walls for defensive purposes.

Several years into his reign, around 1783 BCE, the mighty kingdom of Elam decided to invade the Mesopotamian plains with some allies, which led to the conquest of Eshnunna and several smaller cities in the plains. That was the first time Elam invaded this region, and it met with success, partially thanks to its allies. The next target for Elam was Hammurabi's little kingdom and Larsa. Elam didn't attack the two kingdoms directly but instead tried to start a war between the two kingdoms to consolidate power. Instead of battling against one another, the king of Larsa and Hammurabi entered into an alliance to crush the Elamites. Larsa might have been an ally, but the kingdom didn't put any effort into contributing to military power. Despite this, Babylon crushed the Elamites. Hammurabi couldn't forgive the king of Larsa for failing to send military assistance against Elam. So, the king of Babylon decided to attack Larsa and expand into the southern parts of the

Mesopotamian plains. He was in control of this region by 1763 BCE.

Hammurabi continued his conquests, as his ambitions didn't stop at defending Babylon from the Elamites and conquering Larsa. Hammurabi took his army to the north, conquering Eshnunna and the kingdom of Mari, even though Mari was one of his allies in a previous campaign. Mari probably surrendered without a battle. After this, Hammurabi entered an extended war with Assyria, which was led by King Ishme-Dagan I. Seeking for a way to gain the upper hand in this war, both sides recruited allies, which included several smaller city-states in the region. Right before the death of Ishme-Dagan I, Hammurabi had finally won the war, and the new king, Mut-Ashkur, the son of Ishme-Dagan, had to pay tribute to Babylon. In only several years, all of Mesopotamia, with the exclusion of Qatna and Aleppo, was under the rule of the mighty Hammurabi. Moreover, Assyria continued to pay tribute to Babylon. Hammurabi even claimed the title "King of the Amorites" after his conquests.

Hammurabi also famously wrote a new code of law, which was fairly different from earlier Sumerian laws. This code of law focused on punishing the perpetrator instead of compensating the victim of the crime. Many of the punishments in the Code of Hammurabi resulted in death. The preface of the code states that Hammurabi was chosen by Shamash, the god of justice that was worshiped in Babylon. During the reign of Hammurabi, Babylon gained the status of being the holiest city in all of Mesopotamia.

However, despite all the might that Babylon had established in the region, the empire lived as long as its driving force. Babylon's short-lived power started to decline with the death of Hammurabi and the rule of his son and successor, Samsu-Iluna, who ascended the throne in 1750 BCE after his father died.

A few years after the death of Hammurabi, the conquered cities under Babylon's control started to rebel. Elam and Assyria were the first among many to start an uprising against the once-mighty kingdom that Hammurabi had founded. However, Hammurabi's son couldn't preserve it. There were many revolts, of which some were successfully extinguished by Samsu-Iluna. However, the chaos that emerged with the numerous rebellions was too much for Hammurabi's successor, leaving the king of Babylon with a fraction of the territory that his father had left him with.

Culture, Government, and Military of the Assyrian Empire

The Assyrian government was a monarchy, and the king was considered to be divinely appointed. The king would rule autonomously, although he wasn't alone in running the affairs of the kingdom. The king had court officials, chief ministers, and servants, who all helped take care of the court. The royal officials mostly belonged to the Assyrian aristocracy. However, some officials had different origins; some were slaves who were granted their freedom, and others had humble backgrounds. Servants were practically the arteries of the court, as they were in charge of everyday chores in the royal palace and ensured everything ran smoothly. Palace officials would control and oversee the servants to make sure everything was in proper order and matching protocols. One of the highest-ranking officials was the royal cupbearer. The cupbearer would share insight into the matters of the kingdom with the king and would certainly have his confidence. Important chief ministers included the chief of the army and the chancellor. There was also a large administrative staff that participated in internal and foreign affairs. The title of the king was hereditary, so the crown prince was proclaimed during the king's life and would be trained to become a king as to be ready when his turn came. The crown prince would learn about war, diplomacy, and politics, including both internal and foreign affairs.

The Assyrian army was based on the early standards of Mesopotamian warfare, referring to the concept of the imperialistic army that Sargon created in the Akkadian Empire. The strength of the Assyrian Empire was solely based on its army's power. Even though Assyrians looked up to the model of Akkadian military forces, the Assyrians made some warfare innovations. The Assyrian army was the first army in the world to take advantage of weapons and armor made of iron. During the Bronze Age and Early Iron Age, aristocratic soldiers were usually armed better and had chariots for more efficient warfare. However, when iron was used later on in the Iron Age, the Assyrians could efficiently arm common soldiers, as the production of iron armor, weapons, and chariots were cheap since they had accessibility to iron ore. As a result, there were more soldiers in the cavalry and infantry units. The Assyrian army also started to equip its soldiers with more horses, which made chariots moderately redundant, as horse riders were more efficient in combat. Each commander had a permanent army garrison stationed across strategic points in the empire, usually close to the vassal kingdoms to keep the vassals in check. Soldiers voluntarily served the army, and they would be trained in camps before being sent off to campaigns. Common soldiers could be awarded higher ranks based on their service, training, and war contributions.

The Assyrians used the Akkadian language in everyday life, so the early Assyrian language represents a dialect of Akkadian. Sumerian was also used during the Old Assyrian Empire, which lasted between 2025 BCE and 1378 BCE. However, Sumerian was only used by priests for liturgic and religious purposes. The language of trade was Aramaic, which was later adopted by the Assyrians in the Neo-Assyrian Empire around 911 BCE.

Culture, Government, and Military in Hammurabi's Babylon

Hammurabi brought some of the greatest reforms to Babylon. Not only was Hammurabi an exceptional military leader and war strategist, but he was also interested in reforming the law to respond to his vision of justice. This is why he created the Code of Hammurabi. The code didn't only cover the main laws of the kingdom but also addressed everyday life concerns. For instance, the code prescribed fees that needed to be paid for various professional services, such as medical services, for example. The Code of Hammurabi also regulated divorce, marriage, trading, damaged property, inheritance, building standards, and the responsibility of builders for their work. Hammurabi presented the law as given by the god of justice, Shamash, and he took on the role of a righteous king who was gladly getting involved with the legal disputes of his subjects. The Code of Hammurabi was also the first law to include the presumption of innocence, which means that the accused would be treated as innocent until proven guilty. Moreover, there was a social stratification in the laws of the empire based on which punishments, rewards, and legal provisions were made. The social stratification differentiated slaves, free men, and women.

Hammurabi also relied on administration and court officials to practice and execute the laws he had presented as the will of the god of justice. Scribes and scholars were the very basis of his administration, as they recorded everything that was going on within the empire. Running an empire was made more efficient by this and by the number of officials participating in the empire's internal matters. Hammurabi's sons also participated in the empire's affairs, specifically participating in diplomatic missions. Whenever Hammurabi would conquer a new territory, he would send a delegation of officials with one of his sons at the head to peacefully integrate the region.

Hammurabi learned from the past when it came to the way he organized and conducted his warfare tactics. He copied tactics first used by Sargon and used the same weapons and military units as well, taking advantage of composite bows. One of Hammurabi's tactics was to create alliances and then later conquer and subdue them.

Chapter 7 – The Old and New Kingdom of Egypt: Dynastic Egypt and the Rise of Power in the Banks of Nile

With the end of the Predynastic period and the First Dynasty of Egypt, a new dynastic power was about to emerge. With the rise of Hotepsekhemwy, the Second Dynasty was established, in which Upper and Lower Egypt were still unified. Although little is known about this dynasty, records indicate that this was a period of important economic and institutional development that later defined Egypt as a kingdom. Hotepsekhemwy started his reign in 2890 BCE and ruled for around twenty-five years from Thinis, the capital of the kingdom. There is little known about the first pharaoh of the Second Dynasty, but it has been suggested that the pharaoh came to the throne during political turmoil, as indicated by the word "Hotep" in his Horus name, which means "peaceful" or "reconciling."

According to written evidence and royal tablets, Nebra was the next in line. He ruled between ten and fourteen years; however, similar to his predecessor, little is known about his reign. His royal name is given to honor Horus, and it means "Lord of the sun," which signifies the beginning of sun-worshiping in the Egyptian religion. Following the rule of Nebra, the Egyptian throne belonged to Nynetjer, then Senedj, and then Khasekhemwy, who is undisputedly the most well-known pharaoh of the Second Dynasty, as well as the last pharaoh of the dynasty. Khasekhemwy ruled around 2690 BCE for eighteen years. What is important to know about this period is the presence of radical civil wars between Upper and Lower Egypt and the disbalance between the worshipers of the Egyptian deities Horus and Seth, which caused the two regions to split once more. Khasekhemwy stopped these civil wars and reunited Upper and Lower Egypt. After this, Khasekhemwy focused on masonry during his reign. He had several war campaigns during his reign but is most known for the reunification of Egypt and building forts at Abydos and Nekhen.

After the death of Khasekhemwy, the kingdom of Egypt entered a new era once again. This was the Third Dynasty, which introduced the Old Kingdom of Egypt in 2686 BCE. The Old Kingdom was ruled by the Third, Fourth, Fifth, and Sixth Dynasties, ending around 2613 BCE.

Although the records about the end of the Second Dynasty are obscure, it is suggested that Egypt might have gone through a turbulent period, for it was possibly ravaged by civil wars. Djoser was the first pharaoh of the Third Dynasty, and during his reign, the capital was relocated from Thinis to Memphis. Djoser was the son of Khasekhemwy and was also his successor to the throne, although it remains a mystery as to whether he was actually the first in the line. Djoser ended the civil war after ascending to the throne and reuniting Upper and Lower Egypt. The first pharaoh of the Third Dynasty also led a substantial number of expeditions, most notably in the Sinai Peninsula. It is said that he ended the famine in Egypt that had lasted for seven years after rebuilding the temple of

Khnum, but his most famous construction project was his step pyramid in Saqqara, where he was buried after his death. He was succeeded by Sekhemkhet in around 2648 BCE, who might have ruled for six or seven years. Very little is known about his reign. The list of the Third Dynasty pharaohs is likewise obscure, as archaeologists are unable to differentiate all the names found on the tablets. Later came Khaba, his son Huni, and then his grandson Sneferu. Sneferu would be the founding pharaoh of the Fourth Dynasty.

Sneferu founded the Fourth Dynasty around 2613 BCE under the Horus name, "Horus has perfected me." He ruled Egypt for at least twenty-seven years, although some archaeologists suggest that he might have ruled longer. He had eight sons and five daughters. Some of his daughters were married to their brothers, probably under a belief of preserving the purity of the royal bloodline. Khufu, Sneferu's successor, who was probably his oldest son, was married to two of his sisters. Khufu's brother's, Ankhhaf and Nefermaat I, served their father as viziers, and Ankhhaf was married to one of his five sisters. During his reign, Sneferu erected the Dahshur pyramids, creating a new standard for building these wondrous monuments that served as royal tombs. By this point, Egypt already had a strong cult of the afterlife, which means that pharaohs, who were believed to be some sort of deity, invested a lot of their wealth, power, and time into planning out their burial places. During the reign of Sneferu, the land became richer, which was how the three pyramids were able to be built, as they demanded substantial human labor. Sneferu made that possible by conquering Nubia and Libya, from where he took a great number of people as slaves and raw materials.

Khufu, also known as Cheops, succeeded his father around 2589 BCE, and he was the commissioner of the Great Pyramid of Giza, which has been preserved for thousands of years and is categorized as one of the Seven Wonders of the Ancient World. The name of the new pharaoh also might point out a bold change in the deity dominance, as he was dedicated to worshiping the god of creation and growth, Khnum. Some archaeologists and Egyptologists point out that Khufu was Sneferu's son-in-law and that he ascended to the throne by marrying two of Sneferu's daughters.

Khufu was blessed with nine sons and five daughters. His firstborn son, Kawab, was supposed to inherit the throne; however, he died before the pharaoh, so Khufu's successor became his second eldest son: Djedefre. In 2566 BCE, Djedefre ascended the throne. He became the first pharaoh to associate his power and the sacred right to rule with the religious cult of Ra. He introduced the title "Son of Ra," and he later married his older brother's widow. Djedefre was succeeded by his younger brother after he died. Khafra, the new pharaoh, married his brother's widow, the same wife as Kawab. Djedefre continued the tradition by building another pyramid, which would become his resting place. Khafra also built the second-largest pyramid in Giza during his reign, along with one of the most famous ancient Egyptian monuments—the Great Sphinx of Giza. However, it is not known why Djedefre was succeeded by his brother instead of one of his many sons. Khafra was described as a heretic and a cruel ruler by Herodotus 2,000 years later. The same tyrannical reputation followed his father, Khufu, as well.

The successor of Khafra, his son Menkaure, was said to be completely different. Herodotus writes that Menkaure relieved the suffering and pain that his father imposed on his subjects. His father had supposedly enslaved his own people and made them labor for his own prosperity and advantage. Menkaure ruled for around twenty years, starting his reign around 2520 BCE. He didn't have many children compared to his predecessors, as he only had three sons and two daughters. He was succeeded by his younger son, Shepseskaf, the sixth and last pharaoh of the Fourth Dynasty.

While some archaeologists suggest that there was another pharaoh after Shepseskaf, which would have made Shepseskaf the penultimate pharaoh of the dynasty, there is not enough evidence to prove that the presumed pharaoh, Thamphthis, was a pharaoh of the Fourth Dynasty. Thamphthis is recorded as being the next to take the throne, but his name does not appear in any tomb or royal monument, making it unclear who he even was. Thus, it remains uncertain whether the next pharaoh was Thamphthis or Shepseskaf's son Userkaf, who was the founder of the Fifth Dynasty. Userkaf might have been the priest of Ra, as the cult of Ra became stronger and more present during his rule. This elevation of Ra might be another indication that Userkaf wasn't related to the last king of the Fourth Dynasty. For more proof that could help testify this theory, Egyptologists and archaeologists turn to the Westcar Papyrus. The Westcar Papyrus is an ancient Egyptian text that contains stories of magic and wonders. Among these stories, there is a legend about the transition between the Fourth and Fifth Dynasties. This story takes us back to the time when Khufu ruled the kingdom. Khufu was given a prophecy that claimed that he and his heirs would be overthrown by triplets who would be born to the wife of the priest of Ra from Sakhbu.

In the early 25th century BCE, Userkaf was succeeded by Sahure, his son and heir. Sahure's reign would mark the Fifth Dynasty's political and cultural peak. During his reign, Egypt established trading connections with the coastal cities in the Levant. These naval expeditions brought slaves, cedar trees, and numerous exotic items back to Egypt. Egypt was flourishing and changing with the developing trading relations, and the Egyptian navy flourished and developed as well, which included the creation of small racing boats and fleets designed for the high seas. After Sahure's expeditions brought back myrrh, electrum, and malachite from Punt, he led a war campaign against the chieftains of Libya in the Western Desert, which is how livestock was brought back to Egypt. It appeared that the golden age for Egypt had arrived with Sahure and the Fifth Dynasty. His son and successor, Neferirkare Kakai, who ascended the throne in the mid-25th century BCE, is also said to have been a benevolent ruler, and he was succeeded by Shepseskare after ruling for twenty years, but this was only for several months. Shepseskare is believed to have been a younger brother of Neferirkare, and it is unknown if he died of an untimely death or was dethroned for some reason by his nephew, Neferefre, who became the pharaoh after Shepseskare's death. Neferefre died suddenly in his early twenties after only several years on the throne, after which he was succeeded by his younger brother, Nyuserre Ini, who came to power around the late 25th century BCE. He either ruled for twenty-five or thirty-five years. Nyuserre Ini continued with the mining expeditions, and exotic items continued to arrive in Egypt, but very little is known about the military campaigns that might have been led by this pharaoh. However, he remains the most prolific builder of the Fifth Dynasty, as he had six pyramids built during his reign. The pharaoh was succeeded by Menkauhor, his son, whose own son, Djedkare Isesi, took the throne after Menkauhor's death.

Djedkare ruled for at least three decades, and there is some strong evidence that the pharaoh ruled Egypt for forty-four years. To testify his long reign, religious, governmental, and political reforms that placed power in decentralized and provincial administrations can be traced for over four decades. He was the eighth ruler of the Fifth Dynasty, and during his reign, Egypt continued to trade across the Levantine coast. The pharaoh also started expeditions to Sinai, which would bring turquoise and copper to Egypt, and he also took incense from Punt and gold and diorite from Nubia. Djedkare became a part of a religious cult in Egypt that possibly lasted until the very end of the Fifth Dynasty. Djedkare made radical changes to the way the kingdom was governed by decentralizing the ruling control and appointing officials of the kingdom as a part of the new state administration. These reforms placed more power in the hands of officials, but some historians argue these changes brought the Old Kingdom into the dark ages.

Unas, his son, ascended to the throne after his father died in his fifties sometime in the mid-24th century BCE. Unas's reign was marked by economic collapse. The new decentralized administration of the kingdom also continued under his rule, which seemed to add fuel to the pyre of the Fifth Dynasty. Some Egyptologists believe this type of administration allowed the officials to become more powerful, which would contribute to the overall collapse of the Old Kingdom of Egypt almost 200 years later with the last ruler of the Sixth Dynasty. Despite the hardships in the economy, Egypt continued to maintain its trading relations. Unas's death marked the end of an era in Egypt, as the next ruler, Teti, would start the Sixth Dynasty. Evidence found by archaeologists indicates that ancient Egyptians didn't make a distinction between the Fifth and Sixth Dynasties, although we do today for easier accessibility.

Teti might have been married to Unas's daughter, which would have made her one of his three queens. Marrying a royal would explain how Teti came to ascend the throne. He founded what is arguably known as the last dynasty of the Old Kingdom, although some archaeologists consider the Seventh and Eighth Dynasties to be a part of the Old Kingdom era as well. This is because the administration of the later Fifth Dynasty continued in these later dynasties.

Teti had three sons, but he was succeeded by a man named Userkare, who is believed to have murdered the pharaoh to get to the throne. Userkare very well might have been a usurper to the throne since his body wasn't buried in any of the royal tombs. Another theory indicates that Userkare might have ruled until Teti's son came of age, as he succeeded the throne after Userkare. This would have made Userkare an official of the kingdom rather than a usurper.

Pepi I Meryre, Teti's son, inherited the throne in 2331 BCE and ruled for fifty years. At the end of his life, he established a coregency with his son and heir, Merenre I. The consolidation of dynastic power continued with his reign, as Merenre appointed a court official, Weni, as the governor of Upper Egypt. It seems he inherited his predecessor's fascination with Nubia, which is why he continued exploring this land. After his death, Pepi II Neferkare gained control of Egypt, with the power of the governors continuing. Pepi II maintained foreign relations, as he is mentioned in inscriptions written by the Phoenicians. However, his power and the power of the pharaoh as the ruling figure was slowly decaying due to the decentralized governance and administration of the kingdom, as it allowed for the rise of the nobility. These nobles soon started to attack one another due to their ambition to take more territory and become wealthier. Pepi II's son, Merenre II Nemtyemsaf, inherited the throne at a very old age, and he only ruled for a year. By that point, the kingdom was divided into forty-two provinces, and each of these provinces was controlled by a governor who had been appointed by the king.

The power of the pharaohs, which had been established hundreds of years before, was crumbling with the rising ambition and thirst of the Egyptian governors. Herodotus wrote about an Egyptian legend that mentions Queen Nitocris as the last ruler of the Sixth Dynasty. According to the story, she was the wife and sister of Merenre II, who is said to have been killed in a riot. The queen wanted to take revenge, so she drowned all of his murderers during a banquet.

However, there are no records that this queen ever existed, instead attesting Pharaoh Netjerkare Siptah as the last ruler of the dynasty. He is considered to have ruled for only three years before he was succeeded by Menkare. This was when the Old Kingdom came to a violent and dark end, introducing Egypt to the First Intermediate Period, also referred to as the dark ages. Political chaos, looting, the destruction of monuments and temples, and civil wars marked this era. The Egyptian kingdom was now divided into two main powers: Heracleopolis in Lower Egypt and Thebes in Upper Egypt. The kingdom saw the reunification of these two parts once Mentuhotep II ascended to the throne with the Eleventh Dynasty of Egypt, which marked the beginning of the Middle Kingdom.

Mentuhotep II ascended the throne in Thebes, Upper Egypt, while the Tenth Dynasty ruled Lower Egypt as a rivaling power. The Middle Kingdom is also known as the Period of Reunification, as Mentuhotep II sent his armies to destroy the Tenth Dynasty and conquer Lower Egypt. The conquest took place during the fourteenth year of his reign, and the main trigger for such an action was Lower Egypt's desecration of the ancient necropolis of Abydos, which not only was located in Upper Egypt but was also sacred. Mentuhotep II seemed to have realized the damage that the some-200-year-old administrative reform had brought to the kingdom, for after he defeated the Tenth Dynasty, Mentuhotep decided to rid the land of the decentralized administration. The kingdom, which was controlled from Thebes, was completely centralized, meaning the governors were stripped of the power they once had. The power was then restored to the hands of the pharaoh.

The Eleventh Dynasty had six more pharaohs after Mentuhotep II. The last king of the Eleventh Dynasty was Mentuhotep IV, who ruled from 1998 BCE to 1991 BCE. Mentuhotep IV sent expeditions to Wadi Hammamat, a dry riverbed in Egypt's Eastern Desert. These expeditions were led by his vizier, Amenemhat, who historians believe became the next pharaoh. It is entirely possible Amenemhat came to power by overthrowing Mentuhotep IV. Still, some archaeologists believe that the rule of Mentuhotep IV collided with Amenemhat I's in the form of a coregency, which would remove usurpation as an option. After ascending to the throne, Amenemhat I founded the Twelfth Dynasty—the ruling dynasty that would bring the true golden age to Egypt. Amenemhat also led a great number of expeditions, similar to his predecessors, in addition to organizing military campaigns in Nubia. He came to the throne in times of turmoil and geopolitical uncertainty, and unfortunately for him, this uncertainty was still present at the end of his reign. Amenemhat was murdered in a conspiracy that his bodyguards executed, and it was a horrible event for his son Senusret I, as described in an ancient Egyptian poem called *Instructions of Amenemhat.* The passage tells about the assassination, written as if Amenemhat is writing about his own murder:

It was after supper, when night had fallen, and I had spent an hour of happiness. I was asleep upon my bed, having become weary, and my heart had begun to follow sleep. When weapons of my counsel were wielded, I had become like a snake of the necropolis. As I came to, I awoke to fighting, and found that it was an attack of the bodyguard. If I had quickly taken weapons in my hand, I would have made the wretches retreat with a charge! But there is none mighty in the night, none who can fight alone; no success will come without a helper. Look, my injury happened while I was without you, when the entourage had not yet heard that I would hand over to you when I had not yet sat with you, that I might make counsels for you; for I did not plan it, I did not foresee it, and my heart had not taken thought of the negligence of servants.

Senusret was campaigning in Libya at the time of his father's assassination, and upon hearing the news, Prince Senusret immediately rushed back to Egypt, where he would take the throne.

Senusret would become one of the most powerful pharaohs of the Twelfth Dynasty, following in his father's footsteps when it came to conquests and expansionist politics. Nubia was still ripe for exploitation, so Senusret sent military expeditions there, and he also established the southern borders of Egypt. The pharaoh himself went on an expedition to an oasis in the Western Desert and established diplomatic relationships with several rulers in the towns of Canaan and Syria. Senusret was succeeded by Amenemhat II, who is thought to be his son. Two generations later, the Middle Kingdom would reach its peak with a warrior king called Senusret III.

Senusret III started his reign in 1878 BCE, and it was marked with conquests and military campaigns. Nubia was still the target of the ruling dynasty, and the pharaoh went on a series of war campaigns there, often leading the battles himself. After finishing his conquests, he built several massive forts to mark the border between the Egyptian kingdom and the conquered parts of Nubia. These forts were manned with scouts, who were supposed to monitor the Medjay, a nomadic Nubian group of people who lived in these parts, and send reports back to the capital. The Medjay were not allowed into the kingdom and beyond the newly established borders; however, trading was allowed between the natives and the Egyptian traders. The reign of Senusret III also records a military campaign in Palestine against Shechem, which was the only war campaign in this region during the Middle Kingdom. The pharaoh also reformed the authority of the kingdom's administration by placing more power into the hands of officials, which could have repeated the scenario of demise and chaos that took place before the Middle Kingdom.

After Senusret III, there were two more generations of pharaohs before the last pharaoh of the Twelfth Dynasty came to the throne. Queen Neferusobek, also known as Sobekneferu, is the first confirmed female Egyptian ruler, although it is believed females ruled as early as the First Dynasty. She was the sister of Amenemhat IV, the penultimate ruler of the Twelfth Dynasty. Since her brother didn't have any male heirs, Neferusobek ascended the throne, reigning from 1806 BCE to 1802 BCE.

By the time Queen Neferusobek left the throne, the golden age of the Middle Kingdom had ended. The rulers who came to power after Neferusobek were somewhat ephemeral and are deceivingly categorized as pharaohs of the Thirteenth Dynasty, even though the pharaohs weren't all related. Many of them were actually commoners. The power was divided again, and chaos reigned, although not to the extent of the period before the Middle Kingdom. After the end of the Thirteenth and Fourteenth Dynasties, the kingdom started to drift from the central authority, and four different dynasties, including a short-lived local dynasty of Abydos, sprung up, separating the power over Egypt. This period is known as the Second Intermediary Period, and it was yet another dark age for the people of Egypt before the kingdom was reborn into the New Kingdom.

The Rise of the Eighteenth Dynasty and the New Kingdom of Egypt: The Egyptian Empire

The New Kingdom began with the Eighteenth Dynasty in 1550 BCE. In this era, Egypt would become a major empire in the ancient Near East and beyond. The entire known civilized world would learn about Egypt and the pharaohs who controlled the lands bathed in the River Nile. The Eighteenth Dynasty was founded by Pharaoh Ahmose I, who was the brother of the last king of the Seventeenth Dynasty. Ahmose I was determined to expel the Hyksos rulers, who had come to Egypt from the Levant and established the Fifteenth Dynasty. Ahmose was succeeded by his son, Amenhotep I, whose reign is obscure due to the lack of written evidence.

His son and successor, Thutmose I, would compensate for his father's lack of action by leading war campaigns. Under his reign, the borders of the kingdom expanded farther than ever before, as Thutmose conquered the Levant and Nubia, entering deep into the territories of these lands. By building the Tombos fortress, the pharaoh expanded the military presence of Egypt in the surrounding regions, which were slowly becoming a part of the empire. Thutmose I was succeeded by his son, Thutmose II, in 1493 BCE. Thutmose II married Hatshepsut, his sister, to better secure his kingship. Thutmose II actually had less right to the throne than his sister-wife since his mother had a lower rank when compared to Hatshepsut's mother, who had royal blood and was closer to the dynastic lineage. During his reign, Thutmose II dealt with rebellions in the Levant and Nubia, as well as defeating a group of nomads called Bedouins. However, Thutmose II wasn't a militaristic man, so his generals won these battles in the name of Egypt.

Hatshepsut, which translates to "The Foremost of Noble Ladies," ascended the throne in 1481 BCE. Her right to the throne was indisputable, as she was the sister, wife, and the daughter of pharaohs, and she had royal blood coursing through her veins. Before her reign, the still undefeated people of Hyksos had destroyed important trading routes in Egypt. So, Hatshepsut turned to rebuilding and reestablishing the trading routes, which was how the wealth of the Eighteenth Dynasty was built. The reign of Hatshepsut is believed to have been peaceful, with only a few or no military campaigns, as she was more focused on expeditions that would bring prosperity to the land. She is still remembered as the first extraordinary woman that history didn't fail to mention.

While his mother focused on bringing economic prosperity to Egypt, her stepson, Thutmose III, was to become a conqueror. He was set on making a true empire out of the kingdom of Egypt, and he succeeded in at least seventeen recorded war campaigns during his reign. After inheriting the throne from his aunt and stepmother in 1479 BCE, the new pharaoh conquered the Niya Kingdom; by doing this, he expanded the borders of Egypt to its greatest extent so far. Since he was the ultimate commander of the Egyptian army, Thutmose III was known as an exceptional warrior, and he used a specific war tactic in his campaigns, which ultimately brought him success. His tactic was to find the weakest link, such as the least defended town, in the chosen kingdom he planned to conquer. Fragment by fragment, and with both patience and might, the pharaoh would defeat the smallest and weakest cities until the enemy kingdom was not able to defend itself.

Thutmose III was succeeded by his son, Amenhotep II, who was also his coregent in the last years of his reign. Although Amenhotep had led several war campaigns and fought for dominance in the Syrian region with Mitanni, Amenemhat, the firstborn of Thutmose III, was supposed to inherit the throne. However, after his untimely death, Amenhotep II was appointed as the pharaoh of Egypt, even though he was born from a lesser wife of Thutmose III, as she wasn't of royal blood.

Next, Thutmose IV came to inherit the power over Egypt, although his older brother was supposed to become the next successor. Although there is no proof, it is presumed that Thutmose IV ousted his brother and then later tried to justify his right to the throne by coming up with a story that was later carved into the Dream Stele. Thutmose IV claimed he fell asleep under the head of the Sphinx, which was buried in the sand. In his dream, the Sphinx told him that he would become the next pharaoh if he restored the beauty and glory of that monument, which he did. Although his right to the throne was considered disputable, Thutmose IV ruled for thirty-nine years. His younger brother, Amenhotep IV, inherited the throne next, eventually changing his name to Akhenaten, meaning "Effective for the Aten."

Monotheism in Egypt with Pharaoh Akhenaten and Queen Nefertiti

Since the very creation of Egypt as a kingdom, the Egyptians believed in polytheism, mainly worshiping Horus and Ra as the holy and sacred unifiers of Upper and Lower Egypt. Akhenaten became known as an enemy in royal archives since he wanted to change the religion to Atenism, a monotheistic religion. Atenism revolved around the god Aten, who represented the sun, much like the god Ra, who had been worshiped for hundreds of years. Egyptian pharaohs had a strong religious cult, as the people believed the rulers of Egypt were actually semi-gods employed by Horus and Ra, among other deities. These deities were represented as life-givers but were also perceived as protectors of the pharaohs in the afterlife. The extent of Akhenaten's religious reforms would haunt him after his death, as all his statues would be removed and hidden by later successors.

Akhenaten married one of the most famous queens in the history of Egypt: Nefertiti. She carried the title of "Great Royal Wife," which meant that she was the primary wife of the pharaoh. Thus, their children would have the utmost advantage when it came to the inheritance of the throne. The queen stood by her husband's side and was described as an idealist, mysterious, and revolutionary but also mad, fanatic, and heretic. The name Nefertiti is translated as "The Beautiful Woman Has Come," and since her origin can't be confirmed, it is suggested that Nefertiti might have arrived from a foreign kingdom as a beauty worthy of a pharaoh. Some evidence suggests that Nefertiti ruled in coregency with her husband in the twelfth year of his reign, which would grant Nefertiti a status that not many queens had. Some archaeologists believe that Nefertiti died of the plague, which came to Egypt with the prisoners of several war campaigns during Akhenaten's rule, while some suggest that she outlived her husband and influenced the next two successors that came to power. Aside from Nefertiti, who is said to have been the pharaoh's greatest love, Akhenaten also married one of his sisters, Meritaten, and his daughter, Mekhetaten, at least according to written evidence. His daughter most likely died due to childbirth at a very young age, either ten or twelve.

Since the Hittites were establishing their dominance in the region, Akhenaten feared that the balance in the ancient Near East would be jeopardized. Allies and vassal territories sought help from the pharaoh, but his peaceful politics hindered those who needed help. Akhenaten wasn't aggressive, and as such, he was not dedicated to military campaigns and battles, even though the geopolitical situation in the region called for such a ruler. The pharaoh's diplomacy skills, however, are praised by some Egyptologists. Akhenaten often focused on internal affairs, as he wanted to strengthen the newly established religion. He commissioned temples and statues that celebrated the god Aten, and he also moved the capital to Amama, the city he built to honor the glory of Aten. By this point, Nefertiti had yet to ascend the throne in coregency with her husband (if she ever did at all), but the queen still supported the new monotheistic deity.

In 1335 BCE, the throne would be succeeded by Smenkhkare, who continued worshiping Aten. His parentage is also unknown, as historians suggest that Smenkhkare's father may have been Akhenaten or Amenhotep III. Very little is known about this ruler; archaeologists cannot even confirm with certainty whether Smenkhkare was male or female. Since Akhenaten introduced new religious and political views during his reign, it is possible that his heir was a female ruler. Smenkhkare was succeeded shortly after by Neferneferuaten, a name that was used to describe Nefertiti in some inscriptions. This is evidence that shows Nefertiti outlived her husband and ruled as a pharaoh one generation later. It would also explain how the cult of Aten survived two more generations, as the succeeding kings returned to polytheism.

The Rule of Tutankhamun and the End of Amarna

Tutankhamun ascended the throne around 1334 BCE as the last ruler of his family to control the land of Egypt. As the son of Akhenaten, Tutankhamun gained the right to rule even though his mother wasn't the pharaoh's primary wife. Instead, he was born out of the marriage between Akhenaten and one of his sisters. Likewise,

Tutankhamun married his own half-sister upon inheriting the throne.

Although his name honors Aten, Tutankhamun decided to reform religion by returning to the old deities and retrieving monuments and rebuilding temples of gods that Egypt never forgot, even during the Amarna period, which refers to when the pharaohs worshiped Aten. Tutankhamun's birth name, Tutankhaten, is translated as the "Living Image of Aten," which signifies that he was born into the reformed religion. However, the name was later changed to "Living Image of Amun" to signify the reform that Tutankhamun himself brought to Egypt. It refers to Amun, a celebrated deity of the Old Kingdom of Egypt.

Tutankhamun was forced to use a cane due to a deformity of his left foot and crippling bone necrosis. Since Tutankhamun was only eight or nine years old when he became the ruler of Egypt, he reigned under the viziership of Ay, who would later become his successor. Tutankhamun and his sister-wife had one stillborn child and one who died shortly after being born, both of which were girls. This left him with no blood-related successors.

Aside from Ay, the pharaoh had other advisors. Horemheb was one of the most notable, as he was Tutankhamun's general. Tutankhamun's father had neglected relationships with allies and neighboring kingdoms, essentially creating a period of economic turmoil. Tutankhamun tried to resolve this with successful diplomatic and war campaigns, and he especially wanted to restore the relationship Egypt had with Mitanni before the reign of Akhenaten. However, it is unlikely that Tutankhamun led any of the war campaigns by himself, as he was severely ill and had major health issues. King Tut, as he is often referred to today, died at the young age of nineteen in 1325 BCE.

After discovering Tutankhamun's intact tomb thousands of years after he was buried and mummified, archaeologists found a serious fracture on his left leg, which might have caused his death in combination with the other health issues he suffered from. A rumor of the pharaoh's curse emerged after the opening of King Tut's tomb, as there were several deaths related to the moving of Tutankhamun's mummy.

Tutankhamun was succeeded by Ay, who only ruled four years before the throne fell into the hands of Horemheb. Horemheb was the last ruler of the Eighteenth Dynasty.

The Peak and End of the New Kingdom – The Warrior Kings

Horemheb didn't have any children, but he did choose someone to inherit his power: his vizier, who took the royal name Ramesses I. Ramesses founded a new dynasty in Egypt, the Nineteenth Dynasty, in 1292 BCE. Ramesses's reign is significant, as he not only founded a new dynasty, but he also brought the New Kingdom to its peak, which continued after his death with his son and grandson.

His son, Seti I, ascended the throne around 1290 BCE, with his name celebrating the god Set (or Seth). Seti's main goal was to reaffirm the old gods that had been worshiped in Egypt before Akhenaten reformed religion during the Amarna period. Seti I also wanted to reestablish control over Canaan and Syria, where the Hittite kingdom was placing great pressure on the sovereignty of Egypt. Seti didn't fear war or battles, so he used any opportunity he had to attack the Hittites. Although he didn't break apart their kingdom, he did retrieve the hegemony over the disputed territories. Seti I also relocated the capital of the kingdom back to Memphis. He accomplished much during his reign, but his glory would be overshadowed by his son and successor, Ramesses II.

Ramesses II became known as Ramesses the Great, and for good reason. The pharaoh is often regarded as the most powerful and most successful ruler of the New Kingdom. In the early years of his reign, Ramesses II started building monuments and temples, as well as rebuilding cities. Later on, he led war campaigns in Nubia, Syria,

Libya, and the Levant, and he also reestablished control over Canaan. He prevented havoc from spreading across the Egyptian side of the Mediterranean coast by defeating the Sherden pirates. Ramesses would allow the pirates to attack their intended targets while placing his troops in strategic locations along the coast. He would wait for the pirates to think they had successfully made off with the loot and then attack them, catching the pirates by surprise.

Amid all the battles and campaigns that Ramesses II led during his reign, the pharaoh signed a peace treaty with the Hittite kingdom after the deposed king, Mursili III, fled to the kingdom of Egypt. Ramesses also commissioned a massive temple complex, known as the Ramesseum, and relocated the capital to Thebes, probably because he wanted to be closer to the Egyptian territories in Canaan and Syria. Ramesses II lived for ninety years, and he ruled for an impressive sixty-seven years, the longest of any Egyptian pharaoh. He outlived most of his wives and children and left behind many riches from the conquered lands as his legacy.

After Ramesses's death, his thirteenth son, Merneptah, came to the throne, as his older sons were all dead. The new pharaoh was quite old himself, ruling at the age of seventy years old. Merneptah continued his father's policy, employing the Egyptian army to move against Libya and the Sea Peoples, a mysterious group of seafaring people. However, he could never match the reputation of Ramesses II. He was succeeded by his son Seti II, whose right to the throne was challenged by Amenmesse, who was supposedly his half-brother. Amenmesse usurped control of Thebes and Nubia in Upper Egypt during the fourth year of Seti's reign. Seti II retrieved Upper Egypt back in the fifth year of his reign, removing all statues made in honor of Amenmesse. Amenmesse's remains were desecrated, but the circumstances surrounding his death remain unclear.

Seti's son, Siptah, ascended the throne after his father's death. After his short reign, Twosret succeeded the throne. She was probably Amenmesse's sister and the second wife of Seti II. She died in 1189 BCE, and with her, the New Kingdom and the Nineteenth Dynasty died as well. The kingdom once again entered a period of turmoil and uncertainty. This period was known as the Third Intermediate Period, and it officially lasted from 1133 BCE to 717 BCE, which was when Egypt entered a new era known as the Late Period. During the Third Intermediate Period, Libyan settlers took over the Nile Delta around 1000 BCE, and their autonomy grew stronger. King Piye and the Kushites also took Thebes around 791 BCE. Egypt began its recovery with the Twenty-fifth Dynasty, which oversaw both the Kingdom of Kush and Egypt. Under Pharaoh Taharqa, the empire became as large as the one in the New Kingdom. Other pharaohs from the Twenty-fifth Dynasty worked on restoring buildings, monuments, and cities across the Nile Valley. However, near the end of this period, Egypt's prestige and riches started to decline, as foreign neighbors had fallen under the influence of the Assyrians, who were preparing to invade Egypt. The war between the Assyrians and Egyptians began around 700 BCE during the reigns of Taharqa and his successor, Tantamani. The Assyrians pushed the Kushites back to Nubia, and although Egypt won several battles against the Assyrian forces, the Assyrians occupied Memphis and sacked Thebes.

The Late Period was marked with the rise of a new dynasty, that of the Twenty-sixth Dynasty, also known as the Saite Period. The dynasty was actually formed by Assyrian vassals, who had gained control in Egypt thanks to the Assyrians themselves. The Saite kings turned to Greek mercenaries who had naval forces, as they wished to rid themselves of the Assyrians. Greek influence became evident in Egypt with this turn of events, and the capital was moved to the new city of Sais (hence the name "Saite Period"). Egypt once again enjoyed a thriving economy and culture, but it was only for a brief period of time, as the Persians arrived in 589 BCE, ready to attack and conquer the land of the pharaohs. Egypt wouldn't gain their independence back until 466 BCE, after joining forces with Phoenicia and Cyprus. The Thirtieth Dynasty of Egypt would be the last dynasty with native pharaohs, as the Persians would establish a new dynasty with themselves in charge. Mazaces, the last ruler of the Persian dynasty in Egypt, would hand Egypt over to Alexander the Great without putting up a fight in 332 BCE.

With Alexander the Great, a period of Hellenistic rule commenced in Egypt, known to history as the Ptolemaic dynasty. Alexander the Great was observed as a savior in the eyes of native Egyptians, and he made sure to honor Egyptian traditions and culture after his effortless conquest. This period would last for 300 years before the arrival of the Roman Empire.

Culture, Government, and Military of Egypt

In the ancient world, the government of Egypt was based on the theocratic monarchy. This means the Egyptian pharaohs were appointed by the gods and were intermediaries between the gods and people. The central government was officially established with Pharaoh Narmer and his unification of Upper and Lower Egypt around 3150 BCE. However, historians suggest there was a form of government in Egypt even before this unification. Sources from the Predynastic period also note the existence of monarchs, although it is not known how they operated.

The way the Egyptian government was organized often changed through the centuries. From 3150 BCE to 2890 BCE, the central authority belonged to the pharaoh, while the second-in-command was the vizier. An interesting sidenote about pharaohs is that the term wasn't used until the New Kingdom, although today we refer to all the Egyptian dynastic kings as pharaohs. There were other important government officials as well, such as scribes, tax collectors, and regional governors, and every city had its own mayor. Priests administered temples, which were commissioned by pharaohs in honor of the gods. From 1782 BCE, Egypt would also have a police force as a part of the government.

Egypt's economy was based on agriculture. Low-class peasants would farm the lands that belonged to landowners. Some of the crops and produce were kept by the peasants, while a greater portion was given to the landowners. Landowners would give some of the produce to the government, which the king would use for trading purposes. The king would personally control the wealth of the kingdom, traveling across the districts to assess their riches rather than believing the regional governors. That way, the pharaohs also demonstrated their presence and power to the people. Tax collectors would inspect each province and district after the king and take a certain amount of goods, which was given to the central government. By the end of the Old Kingdom, this type of government was slowly crumbling, as provincial governors had been given greater authority with the decentralization of the government. And as they were getting richer, they cared less about the pharaoh's authority. This change might have led to the collapse of the Old Kingdom in combination with other malevolent circumstances.

Egypt started using official military units in the Old Kingdom around 2686 BCE; however, a military hierarchy wasn't established until the Middle Kingdom around 2055 BCE. By the time the New Kingdom was formed around 1550 BCE, the Egyptian military was divided into three branches: the infantry, the chariotry, and the naval forces. The army was divided into two parts, located in the north and the south, and these armies would be further divided into four. The four armies would be named after the gods Ptah, Sutekh, Ra, and Amen. Mercenaries were also used in times of war with the native Egyptian army. Captains would usually be lower-ranked princes of noble houses or highly educated officials with strong political or educational backgrounds who were chosen by army commanders. Egyptian armies also used projectile weapons in combat, such as slings, javelins, spears, and throwing sticks.

The administration wouldn't haven't even existed if it wasn't for literacy. The Egyptian language was an Afro-Asiatic language, and it was spoken within the territories of the ancient Egyptian kingdom. The earliest stage of the language was attested in 3300 BCE, at a time when hieroglyphs weren't fully developed. The most extensive texts date as far back as the Old Kingdom, and they were written on the walls of pyramids, tombs, and temples across Egypt. Aside from writing on walls and clay tablets, Egyptians used papyrus, a form of thick paper dating from the Old Kingdom. Papyrus was perishable, so many Egyptian texts are believed to have been lost.

Chapter 8 – The Middle and New Kingdoms of the Hittite: The Dark Ages and the Glory of the Hittite Empire

The Old Hittite Kingdom ended around the mid-15th century BCE with the reign of Tahurwaili. The end of the Old Kingdom introduced a new era known as the Middle Kingdom, which corresponds to the Hittite Kingdom's dark ages. This period was brief and is obscure, as not many surviving records of the Middle Kingdom survived, for the Hittites were constantly weakened by attacks. The kingdom mainly suffered attacks from the Kaska, who arrived from the shores of the Black Sea.

Telipinu was the last ruler of the Old Kingdom, and he was succeeded by Tahurwaili. This happened in the mid-15th century, but the exact date is not known. Tahurwaili was Telipinu's first cousin, which made him the direct successor to the throne, as Telipinu had no sons who could inherit his position. Telipinu had previously exiled Alluwamna, his son-in-law; however, Alluwamna returned after his death to take over the throne. It is not known if he ruled before Tahurwaili or after, but it is believed he ruled very briefly.

The next king of the Middle Kingdom was Hantili II. He was the son of Harapseki, Telipinu's daughter, and King Alluwamna. As with other kings in the Middle Kingdom, little is known about Hantili's reign, including when he succeeded the throne. Hantili II was succeeded by Zidanta II, who was probably his nephew. Zidanta II ascended the throne in 1450 BCE and probably ruled until 1440 BCE. Huzziya II followed; however, the relation between the two kings, the date of his accession to the throne, and the length of his reign is not known. What is known is that Huzziya II was killed by his own royal bodyguard, Muwatalli. Muwatalli I may have even been Huzziya's brother, which might have facilitated his right to the throne.

Muwatalli I's reign was also violently interrupted, as he was killed by Kantuzili, who was the overseer of the Gold Chariot Fighters, and Himuili, the chief of the royal servants. Muwa, who was the chief of the royal bodyguard and probably the brother of Muwatalli, fled the kingdom and asked for help from the Hurrians, possibly to get to the throne. In the meantime, one of the king's assassins, Kantuzili, joined forces with Tudhaliya. The Hurrians agreed to help Muwa, although the terms of the agreement remain unknown. Muwa and the Hurrians clashed with Kantuzili and Tudhaliya. The latter won, and the Hurrians were pushed back. This is how Tudhaliya came to the throne around 1430 BCE. Tudhaliya might have been a grandson of Huzziya II, a Middle Kingdom ruler, making him the direct successor to Muwattalli I. However, as with many other rulers, it is not known for sure how Tudhaliya was related to the king.

This victory helped Tudhaliya reconfigure the alliance with Syria and also led the Yamhad king to change sides and provide support to Tudhaliya. Such political change didn't last long, as Halab (the capital of Yamhad) was once again conquered by the Hurrians.

That didn't stop Tudhaliya from expanding the borders of his kingdom to the far eastern parts of Anatolia. He made Zippasla a vassal territory of the Hittites and conquered Assuwa, which was a confederation of twenty-two Anatolian city-states created sometime before 1400 BCE. Some historians consider Tudhaliya I to be the first king of the New Kingdom. However, other scholars think this honor belongs to King Suppiluliuma I, who will be mentioned later in the chapter. It is more likely that Tudhaliya I was the first king of the New Kingdom, as the Hittite kingdom slowly recovered from the period known as the dark ages.

The Legacy of Tudhaliya I: The New Kingdom and the Rise of the Hittite Empire

One of the most important legacies that the kings of the dark ages left to their successors was their ability to make treaties and alliances with the neighboring lands. The Hittite settlements were slowly forming into an empire, which is why the New Kingdom is also known as the Hittite Empire period. The Hittites started to make settlements in southern Anatolia, making treaties to establish their presence and expand their growing empire. The king started to be referred by the citizens as "My Sun," as the kingship was gaining strength.

Tudhaliya I was succeeded by his son-in-law, Arnuwanda I. Arnuwanda ruled in coregency with Tudhaliya in the early 14th century BCE. Arnuwanda I had two sons, Asmi-Sarruma and Tudhaliya, who became the next king in 1422 BCE. Tudhaliya II was nothing like Tudhaliya I, as he wasn't very successful in keeping the empire intact. During his reign, he lost a part of the conquered territories in Anatolia, and the capital of the Hittite kingdom burned to the ground. He was succeeded by Tudhaliya III, who may not have even ruled, as there are no dates or records attesting his reign. The supposed king Tudhaliya III was killed by a group of officers in a conspiracy. His successor, Suppiluliuma, who was most likely his brother, was involved in the assassination. Suppiluliuma I ascended the throne in 1408 BCE and ruled until 1386 BCE. As mentioned above, some historians believe the New Kingdom started with Suppiluliuma I. This is because Suppiluliuma turned out to be a warrior king and a successful statesman, who even dared to challenge the Egyptian empire. Before he became the king, Suppiluliuma I was the army general and the chief advisor of Tudhaliya II. Suppiluliuma knew the importance of diplomatic relationships, so he married a sister of the Hayasan king and married his own daughter off to Maskhuiluwa, the ruler of the Arzawan state of Mira. The king also married a Babylonian princess. Suppiluliuma reconquered some of the Arzawan territories and defeated the Mitanni kingdom, which was reduced to a small city-state.

Although his victory over the Mitanni kingdom testified his military glory, Suppiluliuma I made his mark by taking advantage of the situation in Egypt during the period of Amarna and the reign of Pharaoh Akhenaten. Akhenaten's rule brought serious religious reforms and turmoil to Egypt, and Suppiluliuma took advantage of this by conquering the Egyptian territory in Syria. This conquest caused many of the Egyptian vassals to revolt. Although Suppiluliuma was victorious in war, he didn't neglect the need for diplomacy and alliances. He decided to send a letter to the widow of Tutankhamun, asking her to marry one of his sons, who would then rule with her as the Egyptian pharaoh. Dakhamunzu, King Tut's widow, agreed to this, so Suppiluliuma sent Prince Zannanza to Egypt. Unfortunately, Zannanza never made it to Egypt. He died on his way there, so Suppiluliuma assumed that Pharaoh Ay, who had seized the throne of Egypt in the meantime, had something to do with his son's death. That was the main motive behind the war between the Hittites and Egyptians. Angry that he wasn't able to secure the Egyptian throne or gain closure for his son's death, Suppiluliuma unleashed his army on the vassal states of Egypt in northern Syria and Canaan. Victorious King Suppiluliuma brought many Egyptian prisoners to his kingdom.

What Suppiluliuma didn't know was that the prisoners he took back home would be his demise. The prisoners were infected with the plague, which ravaged the Hittite kingdom, killing Suppiluliuma and his successor, Arnuwanda II. He came to the throne after his father's death in 1386 BCE, but he died only a year later. He was succeeded by Mursili II, his brother, who was the next in line to inherit the throne. Mursili II was the king of Hittites until 1359 BCE.

The Hittites had many enemies. During this period, the most notable were the Arzawan kingdom and the Kaska. According to Mursili's annals, his enemies considered him to be a child and an inexperienced king, who only came to the throne because of the sudden death of his brother. However, despite the scorn of his enemies, Mursili II turned out to be an adequate statesman, as he was able to secure the territory of his kingdom. He successfully stopped the invasion of the Kaska, all while securing the northern borders of the kingdom. The Arzawan king, Uhhaziti, threatened the Hittites from the west, and he tried to win over some of the Hittite allies, but Mursili managed to put these efforts down. Although he was probably unprepared for the throne, Mursili II was a successful ruler. He was succeeded by his son, Muwatalli II, after his death in 1359 BCE.

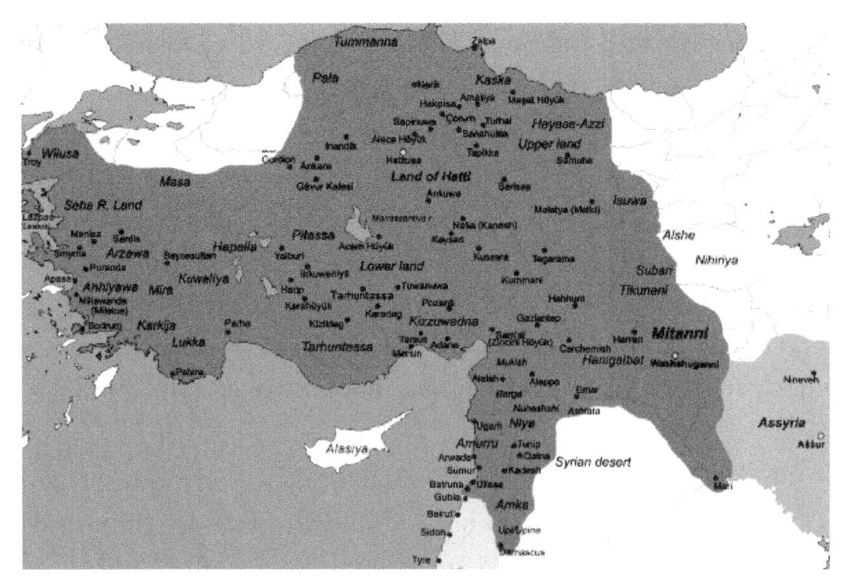

The Hittite Empire at its greatest extent under the reign of Suppiluliuma I
https://commons.wikimedia.org/wiki/File:Hittite_Kingdom.png

Muwatalli II changed the capital of Hattusa to Tarhuntassa, whose exact location remains unknown. Scholars believe the king moved the capital farther south because Hattusa bordered the Kaska. Muwatalli II is best known for his role in the Battle of Kadesh, which took place sometime around 1338 BCE. It was fought against Egypt, which was ruled by Ramesses II, who was seeking to reclaim territory the Hittites had taken. Muwatalli II first sent his scouts to find the exact location of the Egyptian troops, as he knew they were approaching the Hittite lands. The scouts found the Egyptians when they were nearing Kadesh, and they pretended to be deserters from the Hittite army. The scouts told Ramesses's men that Muwatalli's troops were far away in Aleppo, which was hundreds of miles from Kadesh. Soon afterward, several other Hittite scouts were caught, and Ramesses II then figured out what was going on. Muwatalli wasn't near Aleppo; he was right outside of Kadesh with his troops, ready to attack. Muwatalli didn't waste any time attacking the Egyptian troops outside of Kadesh. Ramesses II had only one of his two divisions, as the second had yet to arrive. Muwatalli took advantage of this. While he directly attacked the first division, he also sent charioteers to attack Ramesses's camp. Ramesses managed to fend off the attack, which he saw as a victory, proclaiming that he won the battle the next day. However, Muwatalli's records show that he also proclaimed victory over Ramesses and the Egyptians. Although both sides claimed victory, historians believe they both suffered great losses and that the battle led to a reduction of military power.

In 1336 BCE, Muwatalli II died, and he was succeeded by his eldest surviving son, Mursili III, who would rule until 1329 BCE. Mursili III decided to move the capital back to Hattusa. After this move, Mursili lost Hanigalbat in northern Syria to the Assyrians, which consequently weakened his legitimacy as a ruler. In the seventh year of his reign, Mursili III realized his uncle Hattusili was a threat to his reign, as he was a powerful man with a connection to the throne. To deal with this problem, Mursili attacked his uncle's strongholds in Nerik and Hakpissa, which were a part of the kingdom's borders. Hattusili wrote about the way he was affected by his nephew's attack, stating that after serving the crown for seven years, he would no longer submit to the king. According to Hattusili, if Mursili had never taken his fortress in Hakpissa from him, Hattusili would never have started a war to challenge the throne. It appears Mursili created a scenario for his own demise by fearing the power of his uncle. Hattusili gathered a sufficient military force to remove his nephew from the throne. He was known throughout the kingdom for his participation in the Battle of Kadesh, and he recruited allies from the strongholds that had been taken by his nephew. Hattusili's forces even included the Kaska, who were enemies of the Hittites. Thanks to his experience in military strategy and his allied forces, Hattusili was able to seize the throne from his nephew. Mursili wasn't killed, and he fled to Egypt, yet another enemy of the Hittite, to attempt to convince Ramesses II to help him retrieve his throne back. The newly crowned Hattusili III wrote to the pharaoh, asking him to extradite his nephew. The two forces were once again close to starting another war, but thankfully, a treaty between Egypt and the Hittite kingdom was established. The treaty also contained a clause of extradition, after which all traces of Mursili III are lost. Some evidence suggests Mursili was banished by Hattusili III to the land of Nuhasse, where he was given fortified towns on the edge of the empire to watch over.

Hattusili III the War King and the Demise of the Hittite Empire

When Hattusili III usurped the throne, driven by anger and disappointment in his nephew, he was immediately faced with problems concerning the dominance of the kingdom over the vassal lands in the west. The vassals had sworn to the Hittite king to attack any usurper, which Hattusili III was. Thus, the vassals found themselves in an uncertain situation. Every vassal state could technically attack Hattusili under the excuse of attacking the usurper and defending the interests of the Hittite kingdom. Ahhiyawa, in western Anatolia, might have been the greatest threat, as it rivaled the Hittites. This vassal state had sided with King Mursili III, but they did not actually help him in the civil war against Hattusili III. Ahhiyawa was slowly taking control over some of the Hittite allies, which included the Lukka lands in the far south of Anatolia.

Hattusili III knew he ascended the throne in an uncommon way. Although assassination was a fairly common way of inheriting the throne in the Hittite Empire, Hattusili III was the first king to use an army to gain power. Hattusili wanted to justify his deeds, which he tried by writing his version of the story in what is known as *The Apology*. The king explains how Mursili did him wrong, which made him rebel against him. He emphasizes that no one got hurt and that his motive was to unify the kingdom.

Once he affirmed his rule as the "Great King," Hattusili decided to upgrade the palace of Buyukkale by completely rebuilding the citadel's platform, creating three gates at the southern peak of the palace. Despite affirming his right to the throne, Hattusili III was soon faced with a major threat coming from the west: the vassal kings. The Lukka warriors decided to take advantage of the oath they had made to Mursili to attack the Hittite kingdom. The Lukka warriors arrived at the Hulaya River Land (an unknown area in western Anatolia), where another district of the kingdom, centered in the city of Hawaliya, revolted against the Hittite usurper. Other cities, whose names are not well preserved, also revolted in the western part of the kingdom, challenging Hattusili's potential to preserve the kingdom's borders. Hattusili couldn't control these incursions, which led to more attacks from other enemies. The city of Millawanda, with Piyama-radu at its head, invaded the Hittite lands. Hattusili III sent a messenger to Piyama-radu, questioning his deeds and urging him to stop. It seems Hattusili's message didn't have a particularly strong impact on Piyama-radu. Instead, it showed weakness. If Hattusili couldn't handle the first wave of attacks by the vassals, then it wouldn't take much to break him. Piyama-radu went on to conquer the entire Hulaya River Land and a part of the Lower Land (today's Turkey). He even arrived at the land of Nahita, located in the east of the kingdom. Hattusili needed to act and take back control over these territories. He made a good start by regaining the Hulaya River Land and a great part of the Lower Land, even though it seems he didn't reestablish his control in the coastal territories. Hattusili needed to find a way to regain control over the vassal kingdoms, so he decided to make a vassal out of Tarhuntassa, where the capital had been under Muwatalli II. Hattusili created a new kingdom there and placed his nephew, Ulmi-Tessup, the son of Muwatalli II, as the king. The new king of Tarhuntassa was encouraged to reclaim the lost territories with his own resources, as specified by a treaty created between Ulmi-Tessup and Hattusili. It was expected of Ulmi-Tessup to expand his dominance to the southern and southwestern borders of the kingdom, and he did not fail this task. By the end of Hattusili's reign, the territory of Tarhuntassa would be expanded to the Kastaraya River (Asku River) in the west and the Mediterranean Sea in the south.

As the imperial strength of Hattusili's kingdom grew, he could focus on building and maintaining relations with neighboring kingdoms. One of the most important treaties made by Hattusili III was with Egyptian Pharaoh Ramesses II. This was known as the Eternal Treaty or as the Treaty of Kadesh. Although the Treaty of Kadesh is one of its names, this treaty was signed fifteen years after the battle. Relations between Ramesses and Hattusili were fairly close, as the pharaoh and king frequently exchanged correspondence. In fact, the idea for Ramesses to marry Hattusili's daughter emerged from this correspondence. Hattusili promised to give a great dowry ("greater than the dowry of a Babylonian princess"), telling the pharaoh that his daughter would bring servants, cattle, horses, and sheep to the land of Aya, which was the border of the Hittite kingdom. However, Hattusili's daughter was delayed from making her journey, as Hattusili had troubles with collecting everything for the dowry. Hattusili's daughter finally arrived in Egypt in around the thirty-fourth year of Ramesses's reign, but she still married the pharaoh. Soon afterward, Hattusili married another daughter to the elderly pharaoh. Diplomatic relations continued, and Egypt even sent grain to the Hittite kingdom to resolve the problem of famine. These friendly relations continued even during the reign of Hattusili's successor, his youngest son, Tudhaliya IV, who came to the throne in 1301 BCE. Hattusili and Tudhaliya ruled together in a coregency for the first years of Tudhaliya's reign.

In 1273 BCE, Tudhaliya died, and the throne was succeeded by his son, Arnuwanda III. Arnuwanda only ruled for two years and was succeeded by his brother, Suppiluliuma II. He was the last king of the New Kingdom era. Suppiluliuma II ruled from 1271 BCE to 1242 BCE. A year before he became king, in 1272 BCE,

Suppiluliuma commanded a fleet against the Cypriots, who came from Cyprus. This is the first recorded naval battle in history. During Suppiluliuma's reign, the Sea Peoples invaded the Hittite kingdom, first taking Cyprus and Cilicia, then cutting off the Hittite trade routes. The capital of Hattusa was burnt to the ground, which marked the end of Suppiluliuma's reign and the end of the Hittite Empire. Some claim the king "vanished," while some believe he was killed in the chaos. The Kaska most likely moved in to take over the region.

Culture, Military, and Government of the Hittite Kingdom

According to scholars, the Hittites might have had the first constitutional monarchy when they transitioned to the New Kingdom. In the Old Kingdom, kings had too much power and ruled as absolute monarchs. The king was the only entity in the kingdom who had the right to make decisions and rule as he pleased. In the New Kingdom, the king's power could be constrained to some extent, as the *pankus* (a general assembly) would take care of the kingdom's legal matters and were utilized for other decisions as well, such as helping the king pick his successor. The Hittites didn't establish a clear line of succession, which is how the youngest son could inherit the throne even if the eldest son was alive and able to succeed. That is perhaps why assassinations were so common. The *pankus* also had judicial duties. The law of the Hittites was well established, and it even recognized the difference between accidental and intentional law breaches.

The Hittite culture was greatly influenced by neighboring kingdoms throughout their history, such as the Egyptians, Akkadians, and Hatti, so their clothes and art often resembled these civilizations. The language of the Hittites belonged to the family of Anatolian Indo-European languages, and they used Hittite cuneiform and Luwian hieroglyphs for writing.

The Hittite Empire would have never taken the true form of an imperialistic force if it weren't for weapons and warfare. In the Battle of Kadesh, King Muwatalli II led an army that numbered between 17,000 and 20,000 men. The fact that Muwatalli managed to gather such a large force is supported by the king's ability to utilize and employ the manpower provided by vassal kingdoms and city-states. The army had archers, infantry, and chariots. The Hittite infantry used medium-length spears, axes, and sickle swords, and they were equipped with scale armor, helmets, and leather boots. The most noticeable part of their equipment was the shield, which was designed in the form of the number eight. The thin waist of the shield made it light enough to carry while still offering solid protection. The chariotry in the Hittite army was the decision-making unit, as this unit was the first to attack.

Chapter 9 –Beyond the Wars and Thrones: The Everyday Life of Common People in the Ancient Near East

The history of the ancient Neat East goes beyond the wars for succession and battles for territory. To really get an insight into the ancient Near East, one must ask about the everyday life of the common people. Different civilizations had different ways of life and habits, and these civilizations often clashed and assimilated with one another to a certain extent.

Everyday Life in Mesopotamia

There were not many distinct social classes in ancient Mesopotamia. There were the wealthy and the poor. The official classes were the royals, nobility, priests and priestesses, upper class, lower class, and slaves. A poor Mesopotamian would begin his day with the women in the house preparing breakfast, which could have been soup, porridge, or bread with beer. In the homes of the rich and wealthy, servants prepared breakfast, which could have contained fruit and nuts alongside staple foods such as beer, bread, onions, and porridge made out of different types of grains, such as barley and wheat. There were usually two meals, one in the morning before work and another in the evening after work. Sometimes, Mesopotamians would bring some bread and beer as a snack to work to replenish themselves during the day. On special occasions, they cooked meat—mostly lamb.

Most women took care of their families and stayed home as homesteaders; however, some women worked as bakers, potters, tavern keepers, and weavers. Men worked in a variety of occupations, including farming, construction work, jewelry making, goldsmithing, and carpentry. Men could also work as musicians, tavern owners, metallurgists, artists, basket makers, and brick makers. Women and men alike could also become prostitutes. Professions like perfume markers, jewelry makers, and prostitutes could be considered elite jobs in cases of exceptional skill and being in favor of the king. Interestingly, women were the first doctors and dentists, as well as the first tavern keepers and brewers in ancient Mesopotamia. However, these professions were soon dominated by men, as they proved to be lucrative occupations.

The everyday life of Mesopotamians was greatly influenced by religion. They offered sacrifices to the gods before and after erecting buildings and temples, as well as daily and before meals.

Homes were usually built out of mud bricks. Poor citizens lived in buildings with several stories, usually in narrow streets far from the city center, and with no windows. They used to sleep on their roofs during hot days, as there was no other way to cool down from the high temperatures. Wealthy people lived closer to the palace in the center of the city and usually in houses with gardens. They had servants and windows for extra light and fresh air. They also used sesame oil lamps, while the poor went to bed when it became dark to save on oil or due to the lack of lamps altogether. Interestingly, even though there were strictly defined social classes, the lower class could earn their way and become upper-class citizens.

Slaves could buy their freedom and weren't only used for manual labor. They could also be tutors, accountants, or jewelry makers. They could even manage the estates of the wealthy. One could become a slave if they were kidnapped, sold to pay off their family's debt or their own debt, or as a punishment for a crime.

Everyday Life in Ancient Egypt

In ancient Egypt, slaves, servants, and farmers working on the estates of the king and nobility were at the bottom of the social class pyramid. The middle-class status belonged to soldiers, builders working on temples and royal buildings, artists, and sailors. Above this class were the scribes, accountants, and doctors, who enjoyed great respect in Egypt. They were followed by the upper class—the nobility. At the top of the social pyramid was the royal family, who were considered to be immortal and in direct contact with the gods.

Magic was a great part of everyday life in ancient Egypt, as it was believed the gods acted through a divine, somewhat magical force. Egyptians believed in balance, which is why everyone was encouraged to live in peace, as it would bring about prosperity. The Egyptians enjoyed festivals and festivities, and spending time with family and friends was very important to them. They also enjoyed sports, reading, and games.

Rich or poor, an Egyptian would be considered incomplete if they remained unmarried. Boys were advised to marry at a young age and have as many children as possible. Sons usually inherited their professions from their fathers, and they would spend much time together so the son would be well prepared when he entered the workforce. Cooking, cleaning, and caring for the children were greatly appreciated skills of which women were in charge. Egyptian art depicts women as pale caretakers staying at home to provide for the home and children, while the men are painted with darker skin, indicating they would have spent more time outside working. Women had the same rights as men and were allowed to own property by themselves and without a male legal guardian.

Ancient Egyptians mostly lived in prosperity regardless of their social class, although slaves lived in more modest conditions and had restricted rights. This was probably why Egyptians believed the afterlife was a continuation of life on earth. Ancient Egyptians lived in a fertile land, so they had food and water in abundance. A common family would enjoy fish, vegetables, fruit, bread, and grain on a regular basis, as well as the occasional small game. The nobility and upper class ate more meat on a regular basis; however, food wasn't lacking in any social class. Everyone drank beer and wine was present only in the homes of the rich and wealthy, which included the royal family. Egyptians wore simple garments, although the royals had more "festive" white pleated garments. Common Egyptians wore clothes made of linen, shawls, and woven sandals. They would patch their garments until they were no longer wearable. When that happened, these garments would be used as mummy wraps.

Thanks to mummification, doctors of ancient Egypt could learn more about the human body, but they still didn't understand how exactly the human body works. They believed the body was comprised of a series of canals, such as nerves and veins, that all led to the center of the body—the heart. If any of these canals flooded, Egyptian doctors believed it was the cause of some illness. They would often pierce holes in the aching parts of the body, hoping to unclog these canals and remove the source of the illness. Still, Egyptian doctors were considered to be the best in the Mediterranean, combining magic and rituals with medicinal knowledge and diagnoses.

The royals, nobility, and court officials all lived in prosperity. Scribes also enjoyed a comfortable lifestyle, as it was believed they were chosen by the gods to record events through the written word. All priests and physicians were scribes, but not all scribes were involved in those fields. Men and women alike could become physicians and scribes by getting a higher education. However, these professions were predominantly male occupations.

Lower-class peasants were mostly farmers, who had small private gardens that their wives tended to while they were working the noblemen's fields. They kept some of the crops for themselves as compensation for their labor, and the rest was given to the landowners. The lowest social class with the least amenities were the slaves. Slaves were usually people who had broken the law, had to pay a debt, or were foreigners captured in war. Slaves could gain their freedom after paying their debts or performing a labor sentence.

Everyday Life in the Hittite Kingdom

If you lived in the Hittite kingdom around 3,500 years ago in the area of central Anatolia, chances are you would have been an ethnic mixture of Luwian, Hurrian, Hittite, and Hattian, maybe even Greek and Canaanite. The mortality rate of children was high, so any parent was lucky to see their child survive past the age of five. Many families had more than six to seven children, especially upper-class families, as they could afford physicians and good medical care for their infants. Girls and boys were welcomed to the world equally and given female, male, or gender-neutral names. Youngsters would begin to learn and train for their profession at the age of seven, usually learning their family craft. Common boys would typically learn how to farm or make pottery, while girls learned from their mothers how to cook and weave. Children would also learn to write cuneiform letters for hours.

Women are depicted in ancient Hittite art with long dark hair, and men are shown with shoulder-length hair and a perfectly shaved face. Men wore kilts with tunics and belts made of leather, while women wore long dresses. All clothes were either made of wool or linen. Married women would also wear veils. The Hittites dyed their clothes, using blue, red, white, green, black, and yellow. The wealthy could show off their affluence with purple dye, which was imported from Lesbos or the Levant, and wore jewelry.

The kingdom was often raided on the outskirts, so one would consider themselves lucky if they lived in the heart of the kingdom. The majority of people lived in small villages surrounded by trees and thick forests. As in Mesopotamia, people often ate before work and after work, while some brought snacks to work, like bread and beer. Bread was usually made out of barley and wheat, but it could also be made out of lentils and beans. The Hittites ate moon bread, spear bread, fig bread, flatbread, and honey bread. Honey was a common food in the kingdom. The diet of an average Hittite would include dairy products, vegetables, fruit, and meat. Commoners of the Hittite kingdom might have eaten meat more often than commoners in the neighboring civilizations of Egypt and Mesopotamia. They ate peas, cucumber, carrots, leek, dates, onion, garlic, grapes, pomegranate, beans, olives, lentils, milk, butter, and cheese. The popular types of meat were goat, sheep, cow, and sometimes wild game. Many dishes were flavored with cumin and coriander, and some of the most popular meals were porridge and stews with meat and veggies. The Hittites drank water, milk, beer, and wine, and they even had a drink that was a combination of wine and beer.

There were three distinctive social classes: upper, lower, and slaves. The upper class included royals, the nobility, court officials, and people with lucrative occupations. Upper-class men were district leaders, and they worked and lived in the royal court or owned property. The lower class was mostly comprised of peasants. Slaves were considered to be the lowest social class, and they had little to no freedom to make their own choices. Slaves were made through conquests and punishments, as in other cultures of the ancient Near East.

Everyday Life in Hammurabi's Babylon

Hammurabi's Babylon was probably one of the most beautiful cities in the ancient Near East. Hammurabi wanted to honor the patron god Marduk with a glorious city proportionate to the power of this deity. At the time, every city in the Babylonian Empire had its own patron deity, and the center of the empire, Babylon, was protected by Marduk. The city had tall, strong walls framed with rich greenery. The summers were hot and dry, so people spent time on the rooftops in the evening and in the mornings to try and get some refreshing breeze. They even slept and cooked on the roofs. The wealthier could afford sheltered roofs with four walls to create a shade from the sun, and they usually cultivated grape arbors for food. Even the poorest in the city had three levels of living space. The rooftop was perhaps the most important level of the house. Each house had a small or large garden, where women kept poultry, sheep, or a few goats, alongside with cultivating fruit and vegetables.

The city had tall walls and narrow streets, and everyone's front doors were accessible from the street. The streets were used for garbage as well. People used to just throw their trash away in the streets, in front of their homes. The smell was probably horrific, and this problem would be solved from time to time by having a layer of clay added across the city's streets. As a consequence, the level of streets became higher, which called for stairs leading down to the front doors.

The Hanging Gardens, one of the Seven Wonders of the Ancient World, were in Babylon, although it is not known for certain if they even existed at all. It is believed to have been created by Nebuchadnezzar II, who wanted to make something beautiful for his wife, as she was homesick. In the center of the city stood a stele with Hammurabi's law engraved in stone. This stele provided laws that had to be honored to keep the balance in the crowded but peaceful city.

With proper law regulations came prosperity, and Babylon thrived. Soon, it became a major trading center, and people could buy anything from coats and jewelry to cheese, milk, fish, meat, and fresh vegetables and fruit. Date wine was one of the most popular drinks in Babylon. Bread was the main staple food in the city and the Babylonian Empire in general.

According to the Babylonian law code, there were three distinctive social classes: *Awilu* (the upper class, i.e., nobility), *Mushkenu* (the lower class), and *Wardu* (the slaves). Unlike in Egypt and the Hittite kingdom, women and men weren't treated equally, and the law prescribed different punishments depending on the perpetrator's gender.

Chapter 10 – The Birth of Religions in the Ancient Near East: The Cradle of Civilization and the Gods

The Fertile Crescent wasn't only the Cradle of Civilization. It was also the birthplace of religions that are still alive today, with gods who are still worshipped. Wars, hunger, droughts, floods, death, the sun, the moon, night, and day—all of these experiences, events, and natural phenomena needed to be explained, and the origin of these things was often identified as the will of the gods or a manifestation of the gods themselves.

Polytheism was deeply rooted in the lands and civilizations of the Fertile Crescent. The Assyrians and Babylonians believed that the gods were protectors of humankind. Still, these deities were believed to be capable of anger as well. Ancient civilizations believed that if something bad happened to them—for instance, war, famine, or drought—they must have done something to anger the gods.

Religions in Mesopotamia

The Mesopotamians had hundreds of gods and deity cults, as there were different deities for every profession and every city. The gods who protected the Mesopotamian cities were considered patron deities, and there were also major gods who controlled important realms of life in the ancient world, such as the sky, the sun, and the air.

Anu was the father and creator of all gods, and he was the god of the sky, from where he ruled over the universe. Utu was the god of the sun and also the facilitator of justice and truth. Other major deities were Enlil, the god of the air; Inanna, the goddess of love and war; Nanna, the god of the moon; Enki, the god of freshwater, magic, and wisdom; and Ninhursag, the goddess of the earth. The major deities were worshipped by the kings, while the commoners of Mesopotamia paid more attention to personal gods, who they considered their guardian angels. Kings would show their devotion to the major deities by commissioning temples, and each temple had its own deity.

The civilizations of Akkad, Sumer, and Assyria shared some of their religious beliefs and mythology, although there were minor changes in the story of Earth's creation and the births of the gods and their names.

Religions in Ancient Iran

The cultures of ancient Iran had many different spiritual beliefs and religions, which included Yazdanism, Mandeanism, and Zoroastrianism, among others. The people of Mitanni, who came into conflict with the ancient Egyptians on several occasions, practiced Zoroastrianism, which is one of the world's oldest continuously practiced religions. Zoroastrianism was founded by the spiritual leader Zoroaster, who is also known as Zarathustra. His central writings are contained in the Avesta, which is a compilation of religious texts. The main deity is Ahura Mazda, translated as the

"Wise Lord." Ahura Mazda is proclaimed to be the supreme creator of the universe, and he is divided into three: the earth, atmosphere, and heaven. The opposite of the Wise Lord would be Angra Mainyu ("evil thought"), who is actually the embodiment of a destructive spirit. Ahura Mazda gave people free will so they could choose whether to worship the Wise Lord or give in to the influence of Angra Mainyu. This religion tells a story about the world of good and evil, combined with the ideology that good will always prevail.

Religions in Anatolia

Before Judaism, Christianity, and Islam were formed as major religions in Asia and Europe, Mesopotamian mythology and polytheistic religion dominated Anatolia. The civilizations of Akkad, Sumer, and Assyria shared some of their religious beliefs and mythology, although there were minor changes in the story of Earth's creation and the births of the gods and their names. The Hittites also used some elements from Mesopotamian religion, combined with the Proto-Indo-European religion. Proto-Indo-European religion represents a collection of mythology that includes Greek, Roman, Slavic, Celtic, Baltic, and even Hittite. There are many similarities between the mythologies of civilizations, especially regarding creation, the underworld (otherworld), life after death, and the main deities. The spiritual beliefs of the Hittites were also influenced by the Hurrians, a neighboring civilization. The mythology and religion of the Hittites remain incomplete to this day, as not all religious scriptures survived the ravages of time. What is known today about their religion is that deities were commonly shown on the backs of different animals, while some gods were shown as animals. Hittites worshipped their gods through Huwasi stones, which were considered to be sacred and were placed in temples or among trees and plants. Two main Hittite deities known to history are the God-Sun and the God-Storm. Moreover, the Hittite kingdom was known as the kingdom of a thousand gods, as their religion assimilated with the Mesopotamians, Hurrians, Canaanites, and Hattians.

Religions in the Levant

In the Levant, the dominant religions were Yahwism and the religion of the ancient Canaanite people. Yahwism, a monolatristic religion, dates back to the Late Bronze Age or the Early Iron Age. Yahwism was considered to be related to the Canaanite culture until Yahwism separated its spiritual identity from the supposed Canaanite heritage thousands of years later in the 6th century BCE. Yahweh began as a deity in control of wars and storms. He was in control of a heavenly army as well, leading his sacred warriors to battles against the enemies of the Israelite kingdom. Yahweh was worshipped with a number of other gods and goddesses, who all signified different phenomena, local protection, professions, and celestial bodies, similar to the religion in Mesopotamia or Egypt. It is unclear when Yahwism arrived in the Levant, although it is presumed this religion might have been attested in the early 11th century BCE. The Canaanite gods were worshipped alongside Yahweh for centuries—for at least 500 years—while Yahweh became the national deity of the Israelite kingdoms in the Iron Age.

The Canaanite religion is considered to be one of the earliest forms of ancient Semitic religions, and it represented a complex line of deities who were related to each other. They ruled the humans and the skies. El and Asherah were the primary deities. The literal meaning of El is "deity" or "god," and he was the father of the other gods. Asherah was the mother goddess and is also mentioned in writings of the Hittites and Akkadians. The Canaanite religion may also be categorized as a monolatristic religion, as it consistently prescribes worshiping a single deity while recognizing that other gods and goddesses also exist. While the Canaanite religion is not the same as Yahwism, Yahwism evolved from the Canaanite religion, later on transforming into Judaism. The transformation of these religions is unclear, but it may have started with prophecies and religious amendments made by Prophets Elijah, Josiah, and Hezekiah.

Religions of Egypt

Some religions, however, like ancient Egyptian, for example, couldn't complete an imposed transition from primarily polytheistic spiritual beliefs to a monotheistic religion. The Egyptians believed their world was created by the gods, and as such, they could either be in their favor or an object of their wrath. Pharaohs dedicated their reigns to building and commissioning temples to major deities, which changed throughout time. They also spent their lives building monumental tombs and employed complex funerary rituals to assure immortality for their souls in the afterlife.

Egyptians believed their pharaohs had divine powers gifted from the gods. Pharaohs even acted as intermediaries between the common people and the gods, and it was believed the gods spoke through the words and deeds of the rulers. Ancient Egyptians had to make offerings and perform rituals for these deities, as they were convinced this was the best way to maintain sacred connections.

Akhenaten tried to convert the Egyptian religion to monotheism with his wife, Nefertiti. They established a religious cult that revolved around worshiping a single god called Aten, who was represented as the sun disc. However, this transformation didn't last long. After several generations, the polytheistic religion was fully revived by one of the greatest rulers of the New Kingdom: Ramesses II.

Popular deities, however, changed from one dynasty to another and even from one pharaoh to the next. The cult of Horus had the strongest presence with the first dynasties. Other popular deities were the god creator Amun, the sun god Ra, the mother goddess Isis, Set, Anubis, Horus, and the monotheistic deity Aten. There were even cults where two gods became one, like Amun-Ra, for instance. Egyptians also believed that the gods could be manifested through animals, so they had animal cults. Many of their deities are represented as half-human, half-animal.

Chapter 11 – Politics and International Relations in the Fertile Crescent

Wars tend to set the weak and the strong apart, and the warrior kings and pharaohs who led their armies into battle were praised as great heroes before and after their death. And they had many opportunities to prove themselves. The empires and kingdoms in the ancient Near East were ravaged by rebellions and civil wars, not to mention the wars they led on each other. The earliest civil war, a battle for the throne, took place in ancient Egypt before the unification of Upper and Lower Egypt around 3000 BCE. The Mesopotamian cities of Lagash, Uruk, and Kish fought for hegemony in the region in 2500 BCE. These conflicts came to an end with the arrival of Lugal-zage-si, who conquered several Sumerian city-states and overthrew rulers of smaller cities. Wars quickly changed the political and geopolitical scene in the ancient Near East, as kingdoms and empires soon began to form.

War wasn't the only option, although there were many throughout the period of the ancient Near East. Peace was also needed for prosperity, and some rulers appeared to be more skilled in diplomacy than in waging wars. However, almost every ruler led war expeditions. This could have been to expand their empire, but wars were also conducted to gain valuable and unique goods from other regions. This would have included exotic items, food, building materials, and ores. Trading and preserving resources were often the main motives behind treaties, as wars emptied the treasuries of kingdoms. By settling on peaceful terms, rulers would be able to conserve their riches and also receive goods that were not indigenous to their region.

There were many important relationships between the kingdoms of the ancient Near East. One such relationship was between Mesopotamia and Egypt. This started in the 4th millennium BCE in the period of Prehistoric Egypt and the Uruk period in Mesopotamia. The two cultures established a trading route and exchanged goods and arts, and the influence of both cultures was visible in Egypt and Mesopotamia. During the Hyksos period, Egypt established a diplomatic relationship with the Hittites and Crete, and later on, the kingdom established a diplomatic relationship with Mitanni as well.

The relationships between the Mesopotamians, Babylonians, and Assyrians greatly varied with the Levant. War, trade, and diplomatic relationships were common throughout the centuries. Parts of the Levant were even subdued by Babylon and Assyria as a part of the expansion of these kingdoms.

Wars were often interweaved with diplomatic relationships and treaties, leading to prosperity and peace in the lands that had been ravaged by battles. However, wars brought prosperity to the victors as well, as they brought back treasures to their kingdoms. Kingdoms and city-states that had been weakened by famine, floods, and other catastrophes were easy prey to imperialistic kingdoms, and at times, such kingdoms were forced to usurp other territories to resolve their problems while utilizing the last of their resources on acquiring solutions. Alliances were formed to repel stronger and mutual enemies, and political marriages were arranged to form stronger relationships between kingdoms and city-states.

The relationships in the ancient Near East were dynamic and greatly depended on the rulers and how they wanted to approach the situation. These relationships were what made the Fertile Crescent the Cradle of Civilization.

Conclusion

All of the mighty empires known to history started as humble settlements that later transformed into something spectacular. They were powerful and influential, but in the end, they experienced turmoil and crumbled. The changing dominance over the banks of powerful rivers in the ancient Near East brought life and prosperity to some, while others suffered. The mighty and the mightier were constantly warring for power and dominance. However, the driving force behind the rise of these civilizations was the fertility of the region.

From nomadic groups to small settlements that formed complex governance to the first city-states, the Fertile Crescent in the ancient Near East witnessed the rise of the first empire. It watched as religions developed for thousands of years, influencing and becoming some of the major religions today. Gods and kings were born, and gods and kings died. However, these gods and kings assured their immortality through the written word. This is what separates the civilizations of the ancient Near East from the many peoples who inhabited the region.

Our knowledge of these times comes from written sources, art, statues, monuments, and religious, ritual, and everyday objects. Just like the countries today, these civilizations waged wars, suffered from droughts and famine, and traded and crossed paths with each other. Even millennia later, it still feels as if we are walking in the footsteps of those who came before us.

Part 2: Ancient Anatolia

A Captivating Guide to Ancient Civilizations of Asia Minor, Including the Hittite Empire, Arameans, Luwians, Neo-Assyrian Empire, Cimmerians, Scythians, Persians, Romans, and More

Introduction

Map of Anatolia

Spiridon Ion Cepleanu, CC BY-SA 3.0 <https://creativecommons.org/licenses/by-sa/3.0>, via Wikimedia Commons https://commons.wikimedia.org/wiki/File:AnatolicLimits.jpg

What sparks curiosity about ancient Anatolia, which makes up most of modern-day Turkey, in the minds of history lovers is the diversity of its peoples throughout its territories and time. This book seeks to present the most current view on the events that unfolded through the centuries of the Bronze and Iron Ages of Anatolia. The reader can follow the rise of some of the most famous empires in the world, as well as learn about the circumstances that led to their fall. From early settlements of nomadic tribes to the creation of vast empires, Anatolia changed its face numerous times throughout history. Not just territories and kingdoms changed, but the people inhabiting it also did so as well, in their language, culture, and religion.

Even though they were faced with a lack of evidence for certain periods of ancient Anatolia, or for certain peoples, historians seek to accurately paint the picture of the lives in all the various kingdoms of Anatolia. This book follows the Hittite Empire in its rise and fall. It discusses the Arameans and the influence of their culture on the civilized world, as well as the influence of the Luwians and their dispersion throughout Anatolia. Even if they were never able to organize a united Luwian Empire, they changed all the kingdoms they came in contact with. The effects of this ancient civilization can still be felt today as certain dialects of the Luwian language still exist in Anatolia.

Furthermore, this book follows the rise of one of the largest empires of the Iron Age, the Neo-Assyrian Empire. The reader will get to know the accomplishments of the Assyrian kings and generals and the decisions they made that led to its fall. The vacuum of power that was left after the fall of the Assyrian Empire was filled with the deeds of the Cimmerians and the Scythians, nomadic peoples who fought for their right to exist in Anatolia.

The story doesn't end with them, however. Another great empire of the Iron Age, the Persian Empire, also expanded its territories through Anatolia. This book will discuss the Achaemenid dynasty and introduce the reader to Xerxes the Great, who fought at the famous Battle of Thermopylae where 300 Spartans, among others, lost their lives defending all of Greece.

The end of the book is reserved for the Romans and their own influence on the Anatolian kingdoms, as their politics gradually led to the creation of new territories, territories which had once been known as great empires but were now reduced to being provinces of Rome.

Ancient Anatolia was as diverse in its landscape as in the cultures that inhabited it, from the mountainous regions perfect for nomadic tribes and their herds to the rich valleys of rivers that were the fertile grounds for the births of great civilizations. Anatolia is rich in archeological findings, and the human effort to lift the veil of mystery that encompasses it is still ongoing.

Chapter 1 – The Hittite Empire

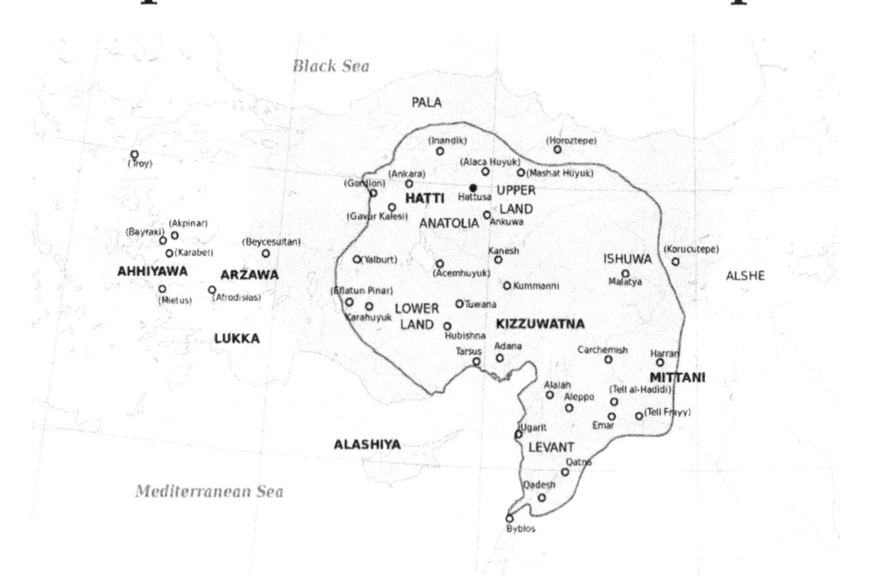

Map of Hittite Empire at its greatest extent, circa 1350 to 1300 BCE, represented by the green line

Near_East_topographic_map-blank.svg: Sémhurderivative work: Ikonact, CC BY-SA 3.0 <https://creativecommons.org/licenses/by-sa/3.0>, via Wikimedia Commons https://commons.wikimedia.org/wiki/File:Map_Hittite_rule_en.svg

The name "Hittite" refers to the people who were the inhabitants of north-central Anatolia. This land was called Hatti, and it was referred to even in the Bible. It is still unknown where the origin of the Hittite people lies, but it is known that they came to Anatolia before 2000 BCE. It is speculated that they came from the lands around the Sea of Azov in today's Ukraine because of the Indo-European language similarities.

The arrival of the Hittites in Anatolia was intrusive for the native culture there, as the Hittites brought Indo-European elements along with them. It is unknown if the means of this intrusiveness were due to conquest or the gradual assimilation of the natives into the new culture of the recently arrived Hittites.

For several centuries after their arrival, there were some difficulties in establishing a single nation. Separate groups of Hittites were centered around some major cities, and strong leadership was needed to bring these groups together in order to conquer a large part of central Anatolia and establish a kingdom with its capital, which would be known as Hattusa.

The empire was founded by King Labarna I, probably in early 1600 BCE. The only original sources we have from this period come from copies of tablets from the 17th century BCE. The copies are Akkadian in origin and were made in the 14th and 13th centuries BCE; therefore, some of the information remains unclear. It is unknown whether the founder of the Hittite Empire was actually Labarna I or Hattusili I, who also had Labarna in his name, as it was used as a title. Some historians think these two figures are actually the same person, but Hittite chronologies treat Labarna I as the predecessor of Hattusili I, who would then be known as Labarna II.

Labarna I is considered the traditional founder of the Hittite Old Kingdom, and his wife was known only by her title Tawannanna. This title was passed down to a new queen upon the death of the current queen. Even a successor's wife wouldn't obtain the title as long as the old queen lived. This means that if Tawannanna died before the king, the title would have been passed either to her daughter or to the new wife of the king. Tawannanna had the duty of ruling the kingdom while the king was absent, usually fighting in battles. She was also a high priestess of the empire, and the king was considered to be the high priest. Very little is known about King Labarna I, other than the fact that he established rule over the Hittite empire until the early years of the Iron Age.

However, Hattusili I is remembered for his military campaigns that expanded the kingdom. He conquered the areas south and north of Hattusa, and he also took his armies west, into the Arzawan lands (western Anatolia), and southeast into the Syrian kingdom of Yamhad. But only his successor and grandson, Mursili I, managed to successfully finish the campaign in Syria. In 1595, Mursili I sacked Aleppo, which was at that time the capital of the kingdom of Yamhad. During the same year, he took his army down the Euphrates River and captured Mari (located in modern-day Syria) and Babylonia. He also ransacked the city of Babylon in 1531 BCE. Instead of joining Babylonia to the Hittite Empire, Mursili I chose to give control over it to his Kassite allies, who would rule it for over 500 years. However, internal disagreements in the Hittite state made Mursili retreat with his army. The remaining years of the 16th century BCE were filled with dynastic quarrels and the war with their eastern neighbors, the Hurrians. Mursili was assassinated shortly after his retreat from his conquests, and this event marked a period of chaos in the Hittite Empire. The Hurrians, people who lived along the upper Tigris and Euphrates Rivers, took the opportunity and conquered Aleppo and the surrounding areas. They also conquered the coastal part of Adanuya, which they renamed to Kizzuwatna.

There is very little evidence of what happened following these events inside the Hittite Empire itself. It is considered that after strong leadership came a series of weak ones, and this pattern of conquering and losing lands repeated itself multiple times during the next 500 years of the Old Kingdom. The structure of Hittite kingship may be the reason for this pattern to occur so often. The king wasn't regarded as a living god by his subjects but rather as the first amongst equals. However, between 1400 BCE and 1200 BCE, the kings became stronger and centralized their power.

The next prominent king of the Old Kingdom was Telipinu, who reigned from circa 1525 until 1500 BCE. Soon after taking the throne, his son and wife were killed by his rivals. At first, the assassins were sentenced to death; however, the new king wanted to put a stop to the internal feuds, and so, he decided to banish the assassins and his rivals rather than sentence them to death. In the following years, Telipinu made an alliance with the Hurrians from Kizzuwatna, and with their help, he took back some of the former Hittite lands. This king is mostly known for drawing up the edict of Telipinu, which set up laws of succession for the throne. Up to this point, the laws were vague, and the Hittite Empire had constant conflicts between the southern and eastern branches of the royal family. The edict was clear that the firstborn son should always be the successor. In case of his untimely death, the second-born son would succeed the throne. If a king had no sons, a daughter's husband would become king. However, after Telipinu's death, the Hittite Empire entered what is known as the "dark age," which would last for approximately seventy years. Historians do not know why exactly this occurred as they do not have any sources from which to draw any major conclusions.

With the death of Telipinu in 1500, the Old Kingdom ceased to exist, and a period known as the Middle Kingdom started. In this period, the Hittites were under constant attack, mainly by the Kaskas, who settled along the coast of the Black Sea. During this period, the Hittites had to move their capital, first to Sapinuwa and then to Samuha. During the Middle Kingdom, the Hittites developed skills of international politics and diplomacy. They were the first known people who practiced making alliances and conducting treaties. During this period, the Hittite religion went through some changes, and they adopted several new gods and rituals from their Hurrian neighbors.

With King Tudhaliya I in the early 14th century BCE, the Hittites entered another period known as the New Kingdom. During this time, another set of changes in the kingdom were made, and kings became more powerful by establishing themselves as being more than human. People started referring to them as "my Sun." This is also the period when kings took the role of high priests, and they started conducting festivals and their yearly tours of holy places. Tudhaliya I expanded the kingdom to the west, encroaching on the territory of Arzawa. He also defeated the Hurrians in their states of Aleppo and Mitanni. But after his death, one more last weak period came when the Hittites lost most of their lands, with even Hattusa being raided.

However, with King Suppiluliuma I, the Hittite Empire recovered its former glory. He was the son of Tudhaliya II and Queen Daduhepa, and he ruled between 1344 and 1322 BCE. Suppiluliuma was famous for being a proficient warrior and statesmen, and he is known for challenging the Egyptian Empire that was dominating Asia Minor at the time. Suppiluliuma I bound himself to the neighboring states by marrying his sister to the king of Hayasan and his daughter to the king of the Arzawan state of Mira. He himself married a Babylonian princess named Malignal and gained control over Arzawan territory. One of the source texts mentions Suppiluliuma's first wife, Queen Henti, who was banished by her husband so he could marry the Babylonian princess for the state's advantage. This Queen Henti is considered to be the mother of all the sons King Suppiluliuma I had. He was victorious in the war against the Hurrian kingdom of Mitanni, which he made a client state and gave to his own son-in-law, Shattiwazza.

At that time, in Egypt, Pharaoh Akhenaten led a turmoil government. Suppiluliuma I seized the opportunity and took control over Amurru, an Egyptian territory in Syria. This was actually not achieved by war but by the decision of Amurru's ruler to join the Hittites instead of shedding blood on the battlefield. This event was enough to destabilize the vassal kingdoms of Egypt and to incite revolts. Suppiluliuma I was so strong that even the Egyptian queen of Tutankhamen, who had recently died, sent him a letter, asking him to send one of his sons to Egypt to marry her and rule as king. She did this to avoid being married to a mere "servant of the kingdom," which was thought to either be the Egyptian general Horemheb or Tutankhamun's vizier Ay. Suppiluliuma sent ambassadors to investigate the truthfulness of the letter, and upon their confirmation, he sent his son Zannanza to Egypt, who unfortunately died on his way there. This marriage alliance with Egypt never came to pass, and Suppiluliuma exchanged angry letters with the new pharaoh of Egypt, Ay, who Suppiluliuma blamed for the death of Zannanza. Soon after, Suppiluliuma I died of the plague, which is believed to have been introduced in the Hittite Empire by Egyptian slaves.

Suppiluliuma I was succeeded by his eldest son, Arnuwanda II, in 1322, who, like his father, soon died of the plague. After him, the throne was occupied by Mursili II, his younger brother, who ruled between 1321 and 1295 BCE. Early in his reign, he faced various rebellions from his own people, as well as contempt from his enemies. The most serious rebellions were in the mountain regions of Anatolia, initiated by the Kaskas, and in the southwest of Asia Minor, in the Arzawa kingdom. The general opinion was that Mursili II was an inexperienced ruler who only became king because of his brother's death. Even though he was young, he was certainly not a child. He had two older brothers who would have inherited the throne if Mursili wasn't of the right age to rule on his own. His brothers were serving as viceroys of Carchemish and Aleppo.

When it came to military campaigns and diplomacy, Mursili proved himself to be more than competent. He secured the northern borders of his kingdom by defeating the Kaskas in just the first two years of his reign. Immediately after, he had to fight

Unhaziti, the king of Arzawa, in the west, as he tried to separate the Hittites from their allies. Mursili also attacked a city called Millawanda, which would later be known as Miletus. The annals surviving from Mursili's time are revealing as they show there was a solar eclipse in the tenth year of his reign, and it was regarded as an omen, as he was preparing to attack the Kaskas one more time.

After Mursili II, the throne went to his eldest son, Muwatalli II, who ruled from around 1295 to 1272 BCE). Not long after he came to power, Muwatalli II decided to move the capital from Hattusa to a city he named Tarhuntassa. He appointed his brother, Hattusili, as the governor of Hattusa. The reason for this change is unknown, but based on texts written in the time of Hattusili III's reign, there could be two possibilities.

The first is that Muwatalli decided to move the capital because Hattusa was near the northern border, which was under constant military threat due to Kaskian skirmishes. This move to the southern territory of the kingdom could mean safety from the turbulent northern border, but it would also be a good strategical position for the fight against Egypt over Syria, which was about to start.

The second theory as to why Muwatalli moved the capital involves religious reasons. He implemented some changes to the state religion; more specifically, he worshiped a new storm god, whose cult's seat of power was farther to the west. He introduced this god of storms, named Umarmungsszene, in his new royal seals, and all the kings that came after him used the same motif on their seals.

Muwatalli II is best known as the Hittite king who battled against Ramesses II in the Battle of Kadesh around 1274 BCE. Kadesh was a city on the Orontes River, near today's Lebanon-Syria border. This battle is important as it is the earliest recorded battle, which included details of tactics and army formations. It was probably the largest chariot battle ever fought; the estimation is that there were

5,000 to 6,000 chariots fighting in the battle.

At the time of this battle, the Hittite's economy was largely dependent on the control of trade routes. Northern Syria was one of the most important routes for trade, as well as a source of metal for the entire empire, and this is why it needed to be protected against any possible attacks. The defense of this important Hittite area was put to the test by Ramesses II, as he wanted to expand Egypt's territories. In the spring of 1274, Ramesses II launched a military campaign with the intention of restoring territories Egypt had possessed almost a century before. To stop Ramesses, Muwatalli marched with his army to the south to confront him.

The Egyptian army consisted of four divisions: Amun, Re, Seth, and a newly created division called Ptah. There are mentions of one more troop named Nrrn or Ne'arin, which were most likely mercenaries loyal to Egypt, but they were left behind in Amurru to defend the port of Sumur. They would later play a critical role in the Battle of Kadesh. Another group of mercenaries in the Egyptian army was the Sherden troops, who were a group of Sea Peoples, possibly Akkadian. It is worth mentioning that the Sherden people's first mention in history was found in a text from the records of Ramesses II, who fought them in defense of Egypt's Mediterranean coast and later incorporated them in his personal guard.

On Muwatalli's side, the Hittites gathered all of their allies, with King Rimisharrinaa of Aleppo among them. Records of Ramesses II mention nineteen allies who helped the Hittites in the great Battle of Kadesh. The extent of Hittite influence is observed here, as such a large number of allied states came to help them.

The tactics Muwatalli used in this battle are very interesting since it is the first time historical records show the use of deception as a military tactic. Muwatalli ordered two of his spies to act as deserters and run to the Egyptian side. Once they gained Ramesses' ear, they told him Muwatalli and his army were still at Aleppo, far away. Muwatalli was actually camped at Kadesh, waiting for Ramesses in ambush. Soon after, Ramesses learned about Muwatalli's trickery and managed to defeat the division that attacked his camp. However, the rest of Ramesses' army was still farther south, fighting Muwatalli's second division. The following day, the Egyptians won the battle.

Ramesses II gave special attention to this battle and created two versions of it. One is considered poetic, as he depicts himself as a powerful military leader who made Muwatalli shrink in fear. But the other one, in the form of bulleting, tells a story of the struggles the Egyptian army went through during the battle. Muwatalli was forced to retreat inside Kadesh's fort, but the Egyptians didn't have enough resources to maintain a siege. The battle ended up badly for both sides, and both Muwatalli and Ramesses claimed victory.

After the Battle of Kadesh, Muwatalli continued to expand into Syria, while the Egyptians had to stop their planned expansion. Because of this, it is believed that the Battle of Kadesh had significantly reduced Egypt's army, meaning they were incapable of continuing their military campaign. Historians agree that the Battle of Kadesh ended up in a draw, but the tactical victory belongs to Egypt. Ramesses II managed to avoid being captured or killed in an ambush, and the innovation of using lighter and faster two-men chariots gave him a slight advantage.

Muwatalli II continued to conquer as far south as the Egyptian province of Upi. He captured these lands and gave them to his brother Hattusili to rule. Egyptian influence was then reduced to Canaan only (today's Israel), and even there, a rebellion started. Ramesses II had to start a series of military campaigns in order to stop major uprisings from happening.

It took another fifteen years and a few more conflicts between the Hittites and the Egyptians before they finally signed a peace treaty, which would later be known in history as the Eternal Treaty. Before that happened, though, King Muwatalli II died in 1272 and was succeeded by his son, Mursili III. But he only reigned for about seven years, as he was deposed by his uncle, Hattusili, who became Hattusili III, and Mursili III fled the Hittite Empire, seeking refuge in Egypt. Hattusili demanded Ramesses II to deliver his nephew to him, but Ramesses claimed he didn't know Mursili's whereabouts. War almost broke out between the Hittites and the Egyptians over this dispute, but Ramesses decided to pursue an agreement with Hattusili. The document both sides signed is the first peace treaty known in history. It was written in two languages, Egyptian hieroglyphs and Akkadian. What is interesting about this fact is that one version is not simply a translation of the other. The wording is completely different, and while the Hittite version claims the Egyptians begged for peace, the other one claims it was the Hittites who did so. The treaty was concluded in 1258 BCE, and it contains eighteen articles that call for peace and describe how the gods themselves demand peace between Egypt and the Hittite Empire. One of the terms of this peace treaty was the marriage of Ramesses and one of the Hittite princesses. Hattusili chose his own daughter, Maathorneferure, for this role.

It is believed that Ramesses and Hattusili both wanted peace because of the growing threat the Assyrians posed. While the Egyptians and the Hittites were occupied with their own conflict, the Assyrian king, Shalmaneser I, expanded his kingdom into Anatolia, Babylonia, ancient Iran, Aram (Syria), Canaan, and Phoenicia. Assyria became a big threat to the trading routes of the Hittites, just as much as Egypt was.

Hattusili's son, Tudhaliya IV, was the last strong king of the Hittite Empire who was able to keep the Assyrians from fully occupying his lands, though he did lose a great deal of territory to them. However, he was defeated in the Battle of Nihriya in 1230 against Assyrian King Tukulti-Nnruta I. This battle is regarded as the peak of hostilities between the Assyrians and Hittites. After the battle, Tudhaliya IV had to fight to regain authority over his own kingdom, but he managed to stop any internal revolts from spreading. The Hittites and Assyrians fought for another five years before they finally negotiated peace.

The last known king of the Hittite Empire was Suppiluliuma II, son of Tudhaliya IV. He ruled between 1207 and 1178 BCE and is known for commanding a fleet that defeated the Cypriots, the native people of Cyprus. This is the first recorded naval battle known to historians. It is believed that Suppiluliuma II commanded a fleet of Ugaritic ships, named after a port in Syria. The records of his time report a major political instability in the Hittite Empire, as Suppiluliuma had to fight the former vassal states of the empire, which lasted for the entire duration of his reign.

His predecessors had returned Hattusa to the status of being a capital city, but Suppiluliuma decided to abandon it once more, thus inducing the end of the Hittite Empire. Hattusa was burned to the ground around 1180 in a series of combined attacks by the Kaskas, Phrygians, and Bryges. Their enemies took advantage of this weakened Hittite Empire and ransacked its lands. Much of the Hittite territory was soon taken by the Assyrians, and thus, the great Hittite Empire ceased to exist.

Although the Hittite Empire didn't exist anymore, by 1160 BCE, a number of small successor Hittite kingdoms emerged. The most well known are Carchemish and Milid, but none of these new kingdoms ever reached the former glory of the empire. Eventually, even these Neo-Hittite kingdoms fell under the Neo-Assyrian Empire, which fully assimilated them somewhere between 722 and 705 BCE.

Chapter 2 – The Aramean Confederation

The Arameans were a tribal confederation of Northwest Semitic people. Their origin is found in the Aram region in today's Syria, which includes Aleppo. This region was known under the name Amurru from 2335 to 1750 BCE. During the Neo-Assyrian Empire, the Neo-Babylonian Empire, the Achaemenid Empire, which combined spanned between 911 and 330 BCE, Aram was referred to as Eber-Nari.

The Arameans never had an empire or even one great kingdom. They were, in fact, an alliance of small, independent kingdoms that were spread all around the Near East. These kingdoms occupied the territories of today's Syria, Lebanon, Israel, and parts of the Arabian Peninsula and south-central Turkey.

The Arameans appear for the first time in history during the Bronze Age Collapse (1200 to 900 BCE). What caused the abrupt collapse remains unknown; however, many historians believe that it was a turbulent event. This collapse caused a movement of people across the Middle East, Asia Minor, the Caucasus, North Africa, Iran, Greece, and the Balkans. New tribes and peoples emerged from these movements.

The first reference to the Arameans can be found in an inscription of the Assyrian king Tiglath-Pileser I (ruled 1114 to 1076 BCE). This inscription mentions the conquering of the Ahlamu-Aramaeans, but soon after, this term was replaced with just Arameans in other Assyrian scripts. This is evidence that the Arameans were a dominant force amongst the nomadic peoples. They established themselves in Syria by the 12th century BCE but were subjugated by the Middle Assyrian Empire.

After the death of the Assyrian king Ashur-bel-kala in 1056, the Arameans gained their independence and pressed against the northern Assyrian border in hordes. During the late 11th century, they took complete control over the lands of Eber-Nari, and from this point, the region was referred to as Aramea. The Aramean kingdoms included Aram-Damascus, Hamath, Bit Adini, Bit Bahiani, Aram-Bet Rehob, and many more, as well as tribal polities such as Gambulu, Litau, and Puqudu.

The Arameans are mentioned in the Bible as well, which tells us that Saul, David, and Solomon, the biblical kings of Israel and Judah, fought against them during the 11th and 10th centuries BCE. Also, the biblical Book of Judges claims that Israel was under Aramean rule for eight years during the early 11th century. The same source mentions Othniel, the first of the biblical judges, who defeated the Aramean forces under the command of Chushan-rishathaim, the king of Aram-Naharaim, or northwest Mesopotamia. While the biblical sources aren't considered entirely accurate, and they are often difficult to prove, they do offer some historical insight on the Arameans, of which very little is factually known.

During this same period, in the north, the Arameans took control over the Neo-Hittite city-state of Hamath, which lies on the Orontes River. However, soon after, they separated themselves from the Indo-European Neo-Hittite kingdom. The Arameans also conquered Sam'al, a Luwian-speaking Neo-Hittite territory, which soon after became an Aramean kingdom called Bit Agushi. This kingdom encompassed the territories from Arpad (northwestern Syria) to Aleppo. At this time, the Arameans were also moving to the east of the Euphrates. There they came in such large numbers that the territory was renamed to Aram-Naharaim, which means "Aram of the two rivers." Some of the eastern Aramean tribes settled in Babylonia, where one of their own was crowned as king of Babylon. He was known under the name of Adad-apla-iddina, but he was considered a usurper.

The Aramean and Assyrian armies often fought in the period between 1050 and 911 BCE. However, the Assyrians had to keep their trade routes open; therefore, they had to send several military expeditions into Aramea, Babylonia, Iran, and Asia Minor. Ultimately, the Aramean kingdoms were conquered by the Assyrians. This conquest started with the Neo-Assyrian king Adad-nirari II in 911, who fought off the Arameans attacking his borders and started a new expansion of the Assyrian Empire in all directions. Assyrian King Ashurnasirpal II and his son, Shalmaneser II, continued destroying the numerous Aramean tribes and managed to conquer the whole territory of Aramea. In addition, King Tiglath-Pileser III conquered Aram-Damascus in 732. The Assyrians changed the name of the Aramean kingdoms they conquered, but in Scripture, they were always referred to as Arameans. Furthermore, they forced deportation on the Arameans, thus moving them to Babylonia and Assyria, which already had small Aramean colonies. The result of this deportation was the birth of the Eastern Aramean dialect, which later became the common language in the entire Neo-Assyrian Empire, including Babylonia. A form of this language still survives to this day amongst indigenous Assyrian Christians in Iraq, Syria, Turkey, and Iran.

After the fall of the Neo-Assyrian Empire in 609, Aramea was ruled by the Neo-Babylonian Empire (626 to 539 BCE). The regions of the Aramean people became a battleground for the wars

Babylon fought against Egypt. Even after the fall of Babylonia and throughout the later rule of the Persians, the Aramean region kept its name Eber Nari, and imperial Aramaic was still the official state language. It was during the Seleucid Empire that the name of the Aramean region was changed to Assyria. This name was commonly used to refer to the Assyrians and to the Arameans west of Aram, even though these two peoples were separate ethnically and historically. This name controversy is present even in modern times, as scholars cannot agree on the origin of the name of Syria. Today, most scholars agree that Assyria and Syria have the same etymological origins and that Syria is actually derived from Assyria.

Chapter 3 – The Luwians

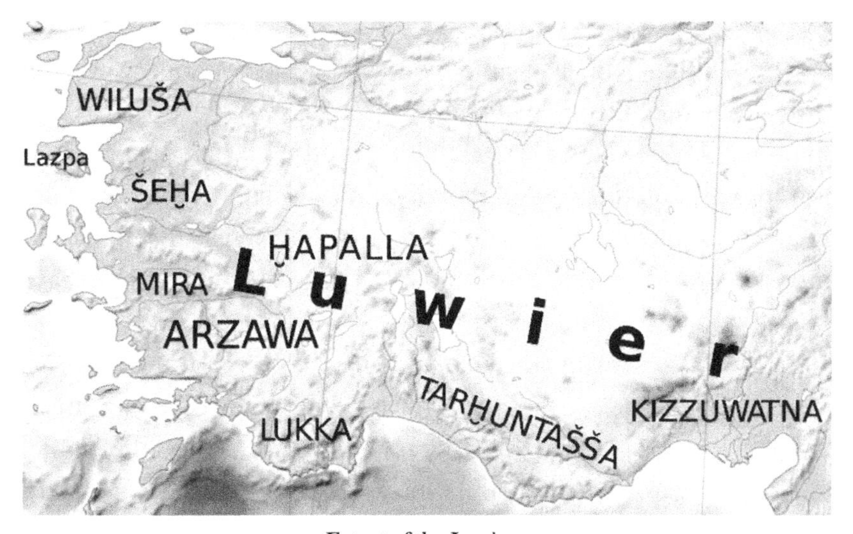

Extent of the Luwians

Near_East_topographic_map-blank.svg: Sémhurderivative work: Al-qamar, CC BY-SA 3.0 <https://creativecommons.org/licenses/by-sa/3.0>, via Wikimedia Commons https://commons.wikimedia.org/wiki/File:Luwiya.svg

Even though the Old Hittite Kingdom laws from the 17th century BCE mention the lands of Luwiya, there is no evidence for a unified state of Luwians or even a polity. When we speak about the Luwians, we speak about a group of people who spoke the common Luwian language of Indo-European origin and who were most likely a nomadic or semi-nomadic group of people. The origin of the

Luwians remains a mystery. Perhaps they came from the Balkan regions or from the territories of the Lower Volga. However, we do know that they settled in the southern and western parts of Anatolia and that most likely their political center was in Purushanda, an ancient city-state. Purushanda has not yet been discovered, but we know of its existence from Cappadocian texts and Hittite texts discovered in Kanesh (central Turkey). From these texts, it is known that there was a king ruling in Purushanda and that he defended the city against the Hittite invasion led by King Anitta. The Hittites won and gave Purushanda the status of a privileged vassal state. But soon after, Purushanda was absorbed into the Hittite Empire and was no longer mentioned under that name again.

The Luwian language and hieroglyphic inscriptions were used throughout the history of the Middle and New Kingdoms of the Hittites. The kings in Hattusa used Luwian hieroglyphic inscriptions, and this system of writing was used even after the fall of the Neo-Hittite states and into the Neo-Assyrian Empire. It is impossible to conclude anything about the extent of Luwian lands based on the use of their inscriptions, but it is clear that the Luwian culture was present in ancient Anatolia. However, Luwian writing and their language are not enough to define their ethnicity. In this context, the Luwians are all the peoples that spoke the Luwian language, regardless of their ethnicity. It is important to make a distinction between Luwian and Hittite languages. Even though the Luwian language and inscriptions were present within the Hittite Empire, this does not make the Hittites a Luwian people. In fact, the Hittites had their own everyday language, also of Indo-European origin, which was officially known as Nesite, after the city Nesa, i.e., Kanesh.

Old Assyrian Empire documents from 1950 to 1700 BCE support the theory that the Luwians and Hittites spoke two different languages. In these documents, Luwian personal names and names of places appear for the first time. The Assyrians also borrowed many Luwian words and used them in their everyday language.

There are preserved Luwian religious texts that provide us with the knowledge of their culture, but they were inserted into Hittite documents and offer no insight into the Luwian people's history or origin. Everything known about the Luwian people is derived mostly from Hittite documents. There are some exceptions, though, such as correspondences between Egypt and Arzawa during the reign of Pharaoh Amenhotep III or the mention of the Lukka people, a group of people that spoke Luwian and settled in southwestern Anatolia, in correspondences between the king of Alasiya and Pharaoh Amenhotep IV. There is no strong evidence that supports any fact of the Luwian people's history, states, or political development. However, it is worth taking note that the Hittite reports do mention some dynastic quarrels and coups amongst the Luwian people, but no details were given as they did not involve the Hittite Empire directly.

The Hittites saw the Luwians as enemies, or at least as potential enemies occupying strategically important lands. They even went to the extent of describing one of the Arzawan vassal rulers as a treacherous, disloyal subject, which makes historians wonder whether he was a hero to the Luwians, as he fought for independence from their Hittite overlords. However, at this point, everything is just speculation as there are no Luwian or Arzawan texts that survived. Even when it comes to the correspondence letter between the Hittites and Arzawa lands, only the Hittite letters survived, or rather copies of the letters survived.

In western Anatolia, there were five states, or kingdoms, occupying the region known as the Arzawa lands. This region was populated by large numbers of Luwian-speaking peoples. The initial Luwian appearance in Anatolia may be due to migration through the northwestern regions, which would explain the early settlements in the Arzawan lands and establishments of a number of small kingdoms. These five kingdoms were known as Arzawa Minor, Mira, the Seha River Land, Wilusa, and Hapalla. The history of these kingdoms is known from surviving Hittite texts, amongst them a treaty from the 13th century BCE between the king of the Hittites, Muwatalli II, and the king of Wilusa, Alaksandu. Since the Arzawa lands entered Hittite documents under this name, the term Luwiya suddenly disappears from the records.

Once the Hittites conquered all of the Arzawan lands, four of the five Arzawa kingdoms became vassal states of the Hittite Empire. Arzawa Minor is not even mentioned in this treaty drawn by Muwatalli II, which is most likely due to this state being completely dismembered during the war campaigns led by King Mursili II. After two years of fighting, Arzawa Minor was probably destroyed, and a large piece of it was claimed by the Kingdom of Mira. Deep in the lands of Arzawa Minor, there is a statue depicting a king of Mira named Tarkasnawa, who ruled in the 13th century.

A number of Hittite texts, as well as some Egyptian documents, mention the Lukka people. But these texts do not mention any political or administrative organization amongst these people. There is no evidence of Lukka kings ever existing, and no Lukka state has ever existed by that name. It is possible that while the Arzawa lands were forming their smaller states, certain populations wanted to maintain their independence and therefore resisted the newly created kingdoms. This might be how a group of Luwian people, united under the name Lukka, attracted the attention of the Hittite Empire. Hittite documents state that the Lukka people became subjects of the Hittite kings after they spread their empire across the territories of Arzawa. The impression these Hittite documents leave is that the Lukka people were hostile toward their new king and were not easily controlled. They are also mentioned as seafarers, often indulging in buccaneering campaigns against Mediterranean coastal cities. In Hittite documents, there is also a mention of Lukka lands, which leads to the conclusion that the Lukka region did exist, at least as a place that they could call a homeland, as they were scattered throughout southern and western Anatolia. Historians presume this Lukka homeland must include at least part of the coastline, as we have evidence they were seafarers. A probable territory that could fall under the Lukka homeland is a western region of the Taurus Mountains and its rugged coast, which later became the country of Lycia (now known as the provinces of Antalya and Mugla in Turkey). It is even possible that the Greek name for this region, Lycia, is directly derived from the Bronze Age name Lukka. A bronze tablet discovered in Hattusa offers further evidence of this region being known as Lukka. It is a treaty document from the 13th century drawn up by Hittite King Tudhaliya IV. In terms of borders, this treaty mentions the city of Parha (later known as Perga), a name which was in other documents used in the same context as the Lukka lands.

The first mention of the Arzawan lands are found in records about the raids led by Hittite King Hattusili I. He records his various military campaigns in a span of six years, and in the third year, he notes taking cattle and sheep from the Arzawan lands. Hattusili is known for his war campaigns against Syria and eastern Anatolia, and it is very interesting that he even recorded a raid to the west, which only had the purpose of plundering. This recorded raid was probably not the only one, as it was more likely that there were a number of such raids on neighboring Arzawan lands, which alludes to further Hittite expansion at the expense of the Luwians. An early text from the palace chronicles suggests that during the rule of King Hattusili I, part of the Arzawan territories fell under the rule of the Hittite kingdom. This text speaks of a city called Hurma and its surrounding regions, which are known to be part of the Arzawan lands.

The first solid records that shed some light on Hittite-Arzawa relations come from King Tudhaliya I's annals. Two military campaigns are recorded in these annals, both under the direct leadership of King Tudhaliya himself. The first campaign was against several countries, including Arzawa Minor, the Seha River Land, and Hapalla. All three states are identified as Luwian lands. The annals speak of the victory King Tudhaliya won in the first military campaign against the western kingdoms, but shortly after, he had to reorganize his military forces for further actions in the same region. In his second campaign, the king encountered resistance in the form of an anti-Hittite coalition, which numbered 22 nations. Wilusa, a Luwian state, is also mentioned in the texts that refer to the second military campaign. The coalition was defeated, however, and the Hittites were victorious. It is not known whether the coalition or one similar to it was ever formed again.

Even though the Hittites won and destroyed the coalition, they did not establish a permanent authority in the Arzawan lands. The Luwians probably managed to keep their independence since there is no evidence of the western kingdoms becoming Hittite vassals. Tudhaliya I was probably just trying to pacify a region that presented a threat to his kingdom. The Hittites needed peace on their western borders so they could concentrate on their military expansion in the north and southeast.

A document known as the *Indictment of Madduwatta* offers more information about Arzawa-Hittite relations. This document reveals that Madduwatta, the king of Arzawa (ruled in the 14th or 13th century) was exiled from his lands, somewhere in western Anatolia, and that he sought refuge with King Tudhaliya I. He was accompanied by his family and military troops with chariots, which is a sign of his importance. Tudhaliya gave him the lands of Zippasla to rule as a vassal king, but later on, he expanded Madduwatta's new kingdom by including the Siyanta River Lands. It is unclear where Madduwatta's kingdom was, but the documents describe it as being on the periphery of the Arzawan lands. Tudhaliya instructed Madduwatta not to try to expand his kingdom, but Madduwatta was quick to violate this agreement, and he attempted to conquer parts of the Arzawan lands ruled by Kupanta-Kurunta. Madduwatta's army was destroyed, but Kupanta-Kurunta wasn't satisfied just with defending his territory. He launched a counterattack on Madduwatta's kingdom, forcing him to flee. Tudhaliya came to help and drove Kupanta-Kurunta back to his own lands. He then restored Madduwatta as a vassal king, giving him the spoils of war. It is unknown why Tudhaliya was so generous toward his vassal when he obviously violated the agreement and tried to expand his lands. Soon after, Madduwatta concluded a peace treaty with Kupanta-Kurunta, giving him his own daughter as a bride. In correspondence with an unsatisfied Tudhaliya, he explained this peace was just a trick in a larger scheme devised to kill Kupanta-Kurunta. This is where the text becomes fragmented, so it is not known what happened next and how these affairs ended.

These texts are clearly filled with a bias toward the Hittites, but they do offer insight into Hittite-Arzawa relations. They reveal Arzawa as being an independent land under the rule of Kupanta-Kurunta, who was hostile toward the Hittite Empire. It is believed that he was the king of Arzawa Minor because it is the only Arzawa state close to the western border of the Hittite Empire while adjoining Madduwatta's vassal state of Zippasla.

Hapalla was the only Arzawan land the Hittite Empire claimed sovereignty over. Madduwatta tried to take Hapalla for his own kingdom; however, Hittite King Arnuwanda I did not approve of this, and he asked Madduwatta to return it. Madduwatta didn't want to antagonize his Hittite overlord, but he did take and keep some other lands that might have been of interest to Arnuwanda. Some of these were well within the Lukka territory.

In the Late Bronze Age, the Luwians were the largest population in Anatolia. They were also rapidly spreading their influence over western and southern Anatolia. They even formed kingdoms in the west, joined various alliances, and had a significant army at their disposal. However, they were the enemies of the Hittite Empire, with Arzawa Minor being the most influential in this hostility. It was also the largest kingdom led by Kupanta-Kurunta, who entered into conflict with the Hittites twice, and even though he lost both times, he did succeed in occupying some of the Hittite vassal states. His actions were a clear sign to the Hittite kings that Arzawa Minor would constantly pose a threat to their plans of expansion to the west.

At one point in history, Arzawa Minor had an opportunity of becoming a major power in Anatolia. During the reign of Tudhaliya III, the Hittite kingdom was invaded and sacked. Arzawa joined the invaders and attacked the Hittites from the southwest. Even the capital of Hattusa was sacked during this invasion, and the royal family had to seek shelter in the temporary stronghold of Samuha. These events opened a way for Arzawa Minor to become a dominant power in Anatolia. The Arzawan ruler Tarhuntaradu was observed as the next Great King of Anatolia, even by the Egyptian pharaoh Amenhotep III, who asked him for one of his daughters in marriage. But under the new king Suppiluliuma I, the Hittites managed to drive the usurpers from their lands and also set a goal of destroying Arzawa. His first task was to defeat the Arzawan troops in the Lower Land, from where they attacked the Hittite kingdom in the first place, and even though he succeeded, Arzawa remained a constant threat to the borders of the Hittite kingdom for as long as Suppiluliuma ruled.

The Arzawan leader Anzapahhaddu at one point gave asylum to some Hittite refugees but refused to deliver them back to Suppiluliuma. Under the command of a certain Himuili, the Hittite forces were tasked with retrieving refugees, but Anzapahhaddu defeated them, forcing Suppiluliuma to come out on the battlefield and give in to his demands.

During these upheavals with Arzawa Minor, Hapalla managed to finally gain independence from the Hittite kingdom. However, Suppiluliuma appointed his most able commander, Hannutti, as the new governor of the Lower Lands, and he launched an attack on Hapalla in hopes of restoring it to Hittite sovereignty. After Hannutti's army plundered Hapalla of its livestock and people, it was once again restored under Hittite rule.

The Arzawan lands were becoming a constant burden on the southwestern border of the Hittite Empire, and it was just a matter of time until they had to be dealt with. However, the Hittite throne was now occupied by a young and inexperienced king, Mursili II, who was crowned after his father's and brother's sudden death due to the plague. His empire was drowning in rebellions, and he received threats of war from neighboring kingdoms who thought him to be too incompetent to rule. After two years of pacification campaigns throughout his own kingdom, and after dealing with the Kaska rebellion in the north, Arzawa Minor drew its attention to the west. Under the leadership of Uhhaziti, Arzawa Minor became an instigator of an anti-Hittite movement in the region. Uhhaziti was a king in Arzawa Minor and an ally to Mursili's father, Suppiluliuma, but he turned against the Hittites when Mursili II became its king. Uhhaziti allied himself with the king of Ahhiyawa, a kingdom of mainland Greece that possibly had the city of Mycenae as its seat of power. The state of Millawanda (classically known as Miletus) joined this alliance, and it was probably this act that made Mursili act against Millawanda, as it was then conquered by the Hittites.

However, this did not stop Uhhaziti in his anti-Hittite campaigns. He mocked the Hittite king, calling him a child, and instigating a war. Mursili's brother, Sharri-Kushuh, the viceroy of Carchemish, joined the fight, which lasted for two years. The deciding battle took place at the Astarpa River in Walma, a natural border of the Hittite Empire and the Arzawan lands. Mursili won against Arzawa's king and pursued his army to the city of Apasa, which he took without any resistance. However, he failed to capture King Uhhaziti, who managed to escape the city. Puranda was the last city to be conquered, and with its fall, the Arzawan resistance was officially dealt with.

Only one Arzawan kingdom remained a potential threat, and that was the Seha River Land. It is unclear whether they were already a vassal state of the Hittite Empire, but what is certain from surviving documents is that the king of the Seha River Land, Manapa-Tarhunta, owed his position to the Hittite Empire, as they had backed him when he fought his brothers for kingship. Later, he turned against Mursili, helping Uhhaziti in his rebellion instead. However, when Mursili threatened to attack, Manapa-Tarhunta begged Mursili to spare his people. Initially, Mursili refused and came close to the city gates, where the king's mother begged him again to spare them. The Seha River Land were taken without any further resistance, and from this point on, they officially became a vassal state. Mursili II managed to take over all of the Arzawan lands and turned them into vassal states to the Hittite Empire. After the fall of Puranda and the death of King Uhhaziti, who died in exile, there is no mention of Arzawa Minor as a separate state, at least under that name, which leads to the conclusion that this was the point when it ceased to exist.

The peace after Mursili II claimed Arzawa Minor did not last long. From Kupanta-Kurunta's treaty (not to be confused with Arzawa King Kupanta-Kurunta, it is evident that in Mursili's twelfth year of rule, he, once again, had to turn his forces to the west and deal with an uprising in the Luwian lands. This uprising was led by a man of unknown origin. Mashuiluwa, the king of Mira, who was previously loyal to the Hittite Empire, joined this rebellion. Mursili turned west and brought an army, but he still called Mashuiluwa to appear before him, probably hoping to avoid open war. However, Mashuiluwa decided to run and seek sanctuary in the land of Masa. Mursili asked the authorities of Masa for his deliverance, and they obliged. Mashuiluwa was exiled from his own kingdom, but he was given a permanent residence in Hattusa.

After their king fled, the people of Mira took a pro-Hittite stand, and the nobles officially dissociated themselves from Mashuiluwa's actions. Mursili granted the throne of Mira to Kupanta-Kurunta, Mashuiluwa's nephew, but he also had support from the nobility. After this episode, there is no more evidence of uprisings or rebellions in the Arzawan lands during the rest of the rule of King Mursili II. Mursili was succeeded by his son, Muwatalli II, whose first years of rule were also free of Luwian unrests.

The peace in western Anatolia lasted approximately for two decades. A new round of unrest, which started around 1280, suggested the involvement of a highborn man named Piyamaradu, who started building a new power base in the regions of the Hittite vassal states. At this time, Millawanda was under Ahhiyawa's control, and so, Piyamaradu joined forces with the Ahhiyawan king. The result of this alliance was that Piyamaradu somehow gained control over Wilusa.

It is known that Wilusa was a Luwian kingdom in northwestern Anatolia, a landmass that geographically is in the vicinity of Troy. A Swiss scholar, Emil Forrer, who lived during the 1920s, started a debate that stated that linguistically Wilusa and another Arzawa state, Taruisa, are similar. This statement caused debate that is still ongoing amongst historians, but the majority now agrees that evidence identifying Wilusa as Iliad is not to be ignored. This could very well mean that Trojans between the 17th and 15th century BCE were, in fact, a Luwian-speaking group of people, as well as perhaps their predecessors.

Piyamaradu was soon after defeated and removed from Wilusa. A legitimate king, Alaksandu, was now on the throne, and he returned it to become a vassal state of the Hittite Empire once more. Piyamaradu himself managed to escape being captured by the Hittites, most likely seeking refuge with the Ahhiyawan king. He remained an anti-Hittite propagator in western Anatolia for many years to come. Piyamaradu was actually linked to Kupanta-Kurunta in Mira, but surviving texts are insufficient to indicate what their relation was. At this time, Mira was a loyal vassal state to Muwatalli's Hittite Empire, and most likely, they were hostile toward Piyamaradu.

Muwatalli was succeeded by his son, Mursili III, who had to fight a civil war with his uncle Hattusili. This war had a destabilizing effect on the entire Hittite Empire and very likely involved the western vassal states occupied by the Luwians. The king of the Seha River Land supported Hattusili, but the kings of other Arzawan lands remained loyal to Mursili III, amongst them being Kupanta-Kurunta. Hattusili won the civil war and gained the throne before any of the vassal states were directly involved in the conflict. The only surviving document regarding the Luwian lands that is not of Hittite origin is a letter Pharaoh Ramesses II sent to Kupanta-Kurunta. This letter was obviously a reply to a non-surviving letter of Kupanta-Kurunta in which he asked Ramesses whether he supported Hattusili or Mursili. Ramesses' response was probably the reason why Kupanta-Kurunta chose to stay loyal to the Hittite Empire, as the pharaoh was in open support of Hattusili.

During the same period, in southeast Anatolia, there were also great numbers of Luwian-speaking people. Stretching along the Mediterranean coast and farther inland, they are known as the Kizzuwatna and Tarhuntassa (see the map at the beginning of this chapter for reference). From the plain of Adana to the Anti-Taurus Mountains, covering a region of classical Cilicia, laid Kizzuwatna. It had cult centers in the cities of Kummanni and Lawanatiya. Other known cities of the Kizzuwatna territories were Sinuwanda, Zunnahara, Arana, and Sinahu. The two dominant groups of people in this region were the Luwians and the Hurrians, although there may have been a small Semitic community presence as well. A mixture of personal names in Kizzuwatna suggests the mixture of Luwian and Hurrian cultures throughout these territories. The first known Hittite treaty was with Kizzuwatna's king, Iputahsu. Their successors also drew up treaties, which suggest that there were frequent conflicts between the Hittites and Kizzuwatna. The conflicts involved the sacking and even destruction of border cities on both the Hittite and Kizzuwatna territories.

Kizzuwatna was on the main communication route with Syria, and its strategic importance made the Hittites willing to work on a permanent alliance. However, Kizzuwatna often switched sides, as they were also threatened by the Hurrian kingdom of Mitanni and their vassal king, Idrimi of Alalakh. During the reign of the Hittite king Tudhaliya I, Kizzuwatna's King Sunassura signed a treaty that would permanently bind them to the Hittite Empire.

Tarhuntassa, another region that was occupied by a Luwian-speaking people, adjoined Kizzuwatna to the west. Its name is purely Luwian, as it suggests the Luwian storm god Tarhunt. The existence of this kingdom was first noted during the reign of the Hittite king Muwatalli II. It also seems to have been created by Muwatalli himself, who incorporated the Hulaya River Land in its territory. This kingdom was given to Kurunta, the second son of Muwatalli, to rule. Because of its strategic location, Tarhuntassa played a great role in the final decades of the Hittite Empire. It is believed that the port of Ura was within its borders, if not next to Tarhuntassa, and it was this port that ships from Egypt brought grain to the Hittite Empire. It was of great importance to keep the port city of Ura away from hostile territories. A hieroglyphic inscription discovered in Hattusa suggests that during the reign of Suppiluliuma II, the conquest of southern Anatolia occurred, and Tarhuntassa was annexed. This means that, at that time, Tarhuntassa had a policy of being hostile to the Hittites.

During the Late Bronze Age, the Luwian people were dispersed all around Anatolia. They were constantly moving, as they lived a nomadic life; however, they were also forcefully moved by the Hittites, who waged wars against them and captured them as slaves and workers throughout the Hittite territories. As a result of the war campaigns of Tudhaliya I, Suppiluliuma I, and Mursili II, there must have been thousands of Luwians in the Hittite lands when the Hittite New Kingdom ended. Because of the Luwians' nomadic nature and their slave/worker status within the Hittite kingdom, they probably mostly inhabited the peripheral farm territories of the Hittite homeland. The Luwians quickly assimilated to the new Hittite culture, but the Hittites had a policy of incorporating all the new gods of conquered peoples into their own pantheon. Thus, the Luwian culture survived in one of its shapes, namely religion, which had an impact on Hittite cultural development.

However, the Hittites had little to no cultural influence on their newly conquered western lands. Arzawa was mainly under Mycenaean and Minoan Greek influence, especially during the late 14th century.

From Hattusili III's Tawagalawa letter, it is evident that the Mycenaean world had a substantial number of Luwians. Hattusili complains how around 7,000 Luwians from the Lukka lands had been transported to Ahhiyawa as a labor force for construction, the textile industry, and domestic service. Aside from being a labor force, the Mycenaeans were also interested in the raw materials western Anatolia had to offer. During the Late Bronze Age, Anatolia was rich in timber, copper, gold, and silver, and these were, undoubtedly, the items that attracted the Mycenaeans to Anatolia in the first place.

An inscription on the wall of the temple of Karnak (Luxor, Egypt) speaks of the Luwian "sea-people" who attacked the Nile Delta during the reign of Ramesses II's son Merneptah (ruled 1213 to 1204). The names mentioned in this inscription are Sherden, Shekelesh, Ekwesh, Lukka, and Teresh. The linguistics of these names suggests they were all Luwian-speaking peoples, and since the mention of Lukka is amongst them, it practically confirms this theory. This invasion was considered to be just a prelude to the great invasion of the Sea Peoples. The magnitude of this invasion was witnessed by the territories they passed through, and there were many of them. The mentioned destroyed lands include Arzawa, Hatti, Qode (possibly Cilicia), Carchemish, and Alasiya. Looking at the list of kingdoms, it is evident that the spread of the Sea Peoples extended across nearly the entire Near East.

After the fall of the Hittite Empire, the Luwian people and the elements of Luwian culture survived through the centuries. The Luwians had a strong influence on the kingdoms that developed on the territories that used to belong to the once great Hittite Empire. These elements mostly appear in the southern regions of Anatolia. The Luwian names throughout the southern regions of Anatolia in the first millennium BCE indicate their existence up to the Hellenistic and Roman imperial periods. These onomastic elements of Luwian origin are found in the documents of Lucia, Pisidia, Pamphylia, Isauria, Lycaonia, and Cilicia. Cilicia Aspera (Tracheia) and Lycia are two regions where Luwian names are concentrated in great numbers. Because of this concentration of names, the conclusion is that these were the centers of Luwian occupation in southern Anatolia after the fall of the Neo-Hittite kingdoms. Both of these regions are mountainous and are not easily approachable by land or by sea. This isolation might be what offered the opportunity for the Luwian people to survive the various upheavals and foreign intrusions during the Late Bronze Age. But this isolation had its drawbacks in a historical sense. The Luwians who inhabited the mountainous regions are rarely mentioned in surviving texts and documents. With the exception of those names, nothing else survived; therefore, historians lack concrete details about these people.

Surviving local inscriptions in Lycia are evidence enough that this region was mainly inhabited by Luwian-speaking people for the first six centuries of the Iron Age. But Cilicia Aspera has no such surviving inscriptions. However, similarities in names used in Lycia and Cilicia may lead us to the conclusion that Cilicia was also inhabited by a large population of Luwians. Cilicia was divided into two parts, Cilicia Aspera, which encompassed the mountainous regions, and Cilicia Campestris, the fertile plains in the east. In Cilicia Campestris, a Phoenician hieroglyphic bilingual inscription was found. It appears at the north and south gates of the fortification of Karatepe-Aslantas. The inscription was commissioned by a local ruler named Azatiwada, who claimed to have brought peace to the land of Adana and that it was he who established the royal family on the throne. In the same inscription, Azatiwada mentions the name of Muksa, which historians believe to be a Luwian seer called Mopsos, who was the leader of the Luwian people who emigrated from western Anatolia to Cilicia. Azatiwada mentioned that Muksa is also the founder of the ruling family in Cilicia.

Lycia, a country in southwestern Anatolia, is the best example of Luwian presence in the first millennium BCE. Lycia is, in fact, a region that was called Lukka lands in Hittite texts and documents. This region remained unaffected by the fall of the kingdoms during the Late Bronze Age. It is speculated that the Lukka lands received Luwian refugees from other kingdoms that were a part of the Arzawan lands or other western Anatolian regions. Lycia was also surrounded by a mountainous region, which served as a natural isolating border that may have helped this territory to preserve its Luwian elements.

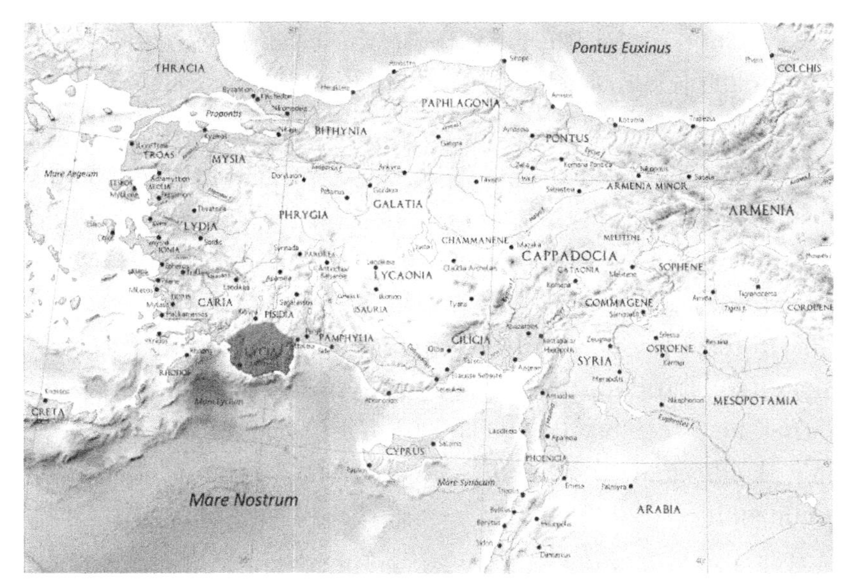

Anatolia in the Greco-Roman period

Caliniuc, CC BY-SA 4.0 <https://creativecommons.org/licenses/by-sa/4.0>, via Wikimedia Commons https://commons.wikimedia.org/wiki/File:Map_of_Lycia.jpg

Lycia is the Greek name for the country first found in Homer's *Iliad.* However, the inhabitants of Lycia called their country Trmmisa. The Greek name is obviously a transcription of the Bronze Age name Lukka, although some historians have tried to explain the name using Hellenocentric evidence, claiming that the name Lycia is purely of Greek origin. As for the name Trmmisa, there might have been a strong political and cultural presence in Lycia of another group of people, possibly Cretan immigrants, who called themselves Trmmili. This would explain how the term became synonymous for all the peoples inhabiting the lands of Lycia.

Since Lycia was inhabited mainly by a Luwian-speaking people, it is presumed that they continued their nomadic way of life. This means that they were scattered throughout the mountains, pasturing herds and flocks during the hot summer months. However, there were a number of permanent settlements, mainly religious or political centers. The Xanthos valley was probably the main area for settlement in Lycia. The land there was fertile, rich in crops and orchards due to the River Xanthos, whose banks were an area for some of the very first settlements in this region.

Lycia appears for the first time in foreign texts, in Rhodes, to be specific, during the first millennium. It appears the Rhodians were hostile to Lycia. The Rhodians settled on the southern Anatolian coast, a region that would later become eastern Lycia. However, apart from conflicts with Rhodes, Lycia remained uninfluenced by other foreign powers, probably due to its isolation from the rest of Anatolia. Herodotus, an influential Greek historian who lived during the 5th century BCE, claimed that Lycia and Cilicia were the only lands that remained free of King Croesus of Lydia's occupation.

But in 540, Lycia finally succumbed to a foreign power. Harpagos, a Median general who worked for the Persians, campaigned in these regions, and he confronted a small Lycian army, which he easily defeated and then took over Xanthos. Herodotus writes that when the Lycians saw they were defeated, they gathered their wives, children, slaves, and all the property they could move inside Xanthos and burned it all to the ground. They made one last attack against the Persian army, but they were unsuccessful and were all killed. Lycia finally became a vassal state of the Persian Empire, and the city of Xanthos was rebuilt and repopulated. Around 516/515 BCE, the first ruling family was established in Xanthos, probably with great influence from the Persian Empire. Lycia became a loyal ally to the Persians until the fifth century when it became a part of the Delian League. However, Lycia broke away from this confederacy, probably during the Peloponnesian War, which started in 431. Soon after, it resumed its alliance with Persia. In 367, Lycia participated in a satrap rebellion against Persia, but this rebellion was crushed after nine years, and Lycia was once more the subject of the Persian Empire, thus losing much of its autonomy. This new status didn't last long as in 334/3, Lycia was invaded by Alexander the Great and was never again under Persian rule.

Reconstructing the history of the Luwian-speaking groups of people proves to be a difficult task due to the lack of evidence. What is known about the regions they inhabited is mostly from inscriptions left by hostile neighbors. These inscriptions are also very biased and must be taken with an ounce of suspicion when it comes to their factual accuracy. The only texts that are originally Luwian are of religious nature, and they were inserted into Hittite documents. They do provide some evidence of Luwian culture, but there are no such texts that provide historical information of these people. The Luwians of the Bronze Age are mostly known from texts or correspondence between Hittite rulers, whose interests in the lands inhabited by the Luwians were limited.

The Hittites were a dominant force in Anatolia during the Bronze Age period, so it is known that the Luwians had a relationship with the Hittite Empire. They saw each other as enemies, or at least as potential threats to each other, and much of the surviving Hittite texts that concern the Luwian lands are propaganda against them.

After the Bronze Age, Luwian history is based on the assumption that the appearance of Luwian inscriptions means there was an actual presence of Luwian-speaking people in southern Anatolia. In fact, there is a big chance the Luwians were only a minority in these regions, as the dominant culture at the time was Hurrian. It is also known that the Luwian hieroglyphic system was adopted by other ethnicities as a simpler and more effective way of writing. The Hittites were the first to adopt Luwian hieroglyphs and replaced their own cuneiform script with it. This may as well have happened during the Early Iron Age, and therefore, the inscriptions found in Luwian might not be of actual Luwian origin at all.

A significant number of Luwian names in certain regions, as well as the usage of the Luwian hieroglyphic script, confirms the existence of Luwian-speaking populations, but they do not attest to any Luwian influence on culture or politics in these lands. On the other hand, we have a cluster of Luwian names in Cilicia and Lycia, but there's a lack of Luwian hieroglyphic inscriptions. This is why historians speak of the existence of Luwian elements rather than the Luwian people themselves. However, the change to a Hellenistic-oriented world might have had some influence on the choice of writing in southern Anatolia, and it might not have had anything to do with the existence, or non-existence, of Luwians in Cilicia and Lycia. The Luwian-based language was still in use in Lycia during the sixth to fourth century BCE when the Greek alphabet was in use. This is an indicator of an almost certain Luwian presence in Lycia.

Regarding Syria, there is no evidence of a Luwian-speaking people having a settlement there. Even though there are a number of inscriptions found in Syria that use Luwian hieroglyphs, they are of Neo-Hittite origin. Same as the title of "The Great King," the Luwian script was passed on amongst the royal families of the Neo-Hittite kingdoms. There may not be enough evidence of a Luwian settlement, but the use of the Luwian script speaks of the magnitude of their influence on ancient Anatolia.

Chapter 4 – The Neo-Assyrian Empire

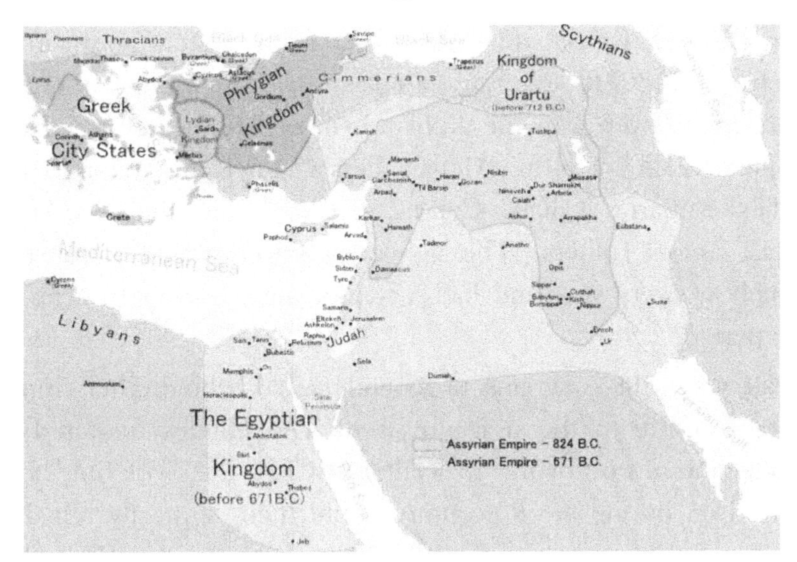

Map of Neo-Assyrian Empire

https://commons.wikimedia.org/wiki/File:Map_of_Assyria.png

The Neo-Assyrian Empire was the largest empire in the world during the period known as the Iron Age. It lasted from 911 until 609 BCE and succeeded the Old (2025 to 1378) and Middle (1365 to 934) Assyrian Empires of the Bronze Age. Its official language was Aramaic, but many other languages were common, including

Hittite, Hurrian, Egyptian, and Phoenician. This is due to the Assyrian practice of relocating the people of newly conquered territories to the old nucleus of the empire.

During its height, the Neo-Assyrian Empire spread from the Zagros Mountains in the east to the Levant (today's Syria-Palestine) and a large part of Egypt to the west, and from the Persian Gulf to the south to the source of the Tigris and Euphrates in Anatolia. This massive territory is what made the Neo-Assyrian Empire the largest empire that the Iron Age ever knew and also one of the most enduring since it lasted for around 300 years.

The first emperor of the Neo-Assyrian period was Ashur-dan II, who ruled between 934 and 912 BC. He began to reclaim and expand the territories of the Assyrian Empire, a practice that was embraced by his successors. His son, Adad-nirari II, was the one who ensured Assyria would be recognized as a great power in the known world. He led war campaigns against Egypt, where he managed to overthrow the Nubian dynasty. He then proceeded to conquer Elam, Urartu, Media, Persia, Canaan, Arabia, Israel, Judah, Samarra, Cilicia, Cyprus, Chaldea, and the Neo-Hittite states, among others. The Assyrians waged wars against their neighbors every year and had a well-organized, modern army for this period.

However, the Assyrians, in general, lagged behind other empires when it came to the usage of iron. The Hittites mastered the production of iron by the 13th century BCE, but Assyria only began using iron during the 9th century. Until then, it mostly relied on bronze for weapons and tools. Even between the 9th and 8th centuries, Assyria used only the iron obtained as spoils of war from the defeated Hittites. However, by the late 8th century, they began extracting it and working it themselves. This delay in iron use didn't affect Assyrian military success. In fact, many of the technological improvements and innovations of the Early Iron Age are attributed to the Assyrians. For instance, they were the ones who developed advanced chariots with a platform that could support three or even four men: a driver, bowman, and shield-bearer. In addition, they improved battering rams, invented earthen ramps, and employed sappers (combat engineers).

When it comes to the political structure of the Neo-Assyrian Empire, it relied on the heritage of the Middle Assyrian period. The king was regarded as someone who had an intimate relationship with the god Ashur, and he was the one who enforced the divine will. The kings had absolute power over the state and were also in charge of managing an efficient government. Furthermore, they were the ones who were responsible for the religious life of the empire and who had to provide the maintenance of shrines. However, in the Neo-Assyrian Empire, no formal legal code existed. The kings were the supreme legislators and chief justices. Most common legal matters were regulated by customs, but the king had the right to involve himself in any legal matter he thought would need his intervention.

The Assyrian kings were not regarded as immortals; instead, they were supreme human beings who were very much mortal. The kings were also the military leaders, as Assyria was a military state, but they didn't always lead the army in person. The army was usually led by priests carrying the statues of their gods in front of religious processions. For them, wars were religious actions, and they were always seen as the will of Ashur.

The administration of the empire made a clear distinction between the core Assyrian provinces, northern Mesopotamian provinces, which paid different taxes, and the vassal states of the Assyrian Empire, which had to pay a special tribute to the empire. Each province had a governor who was named by the king himself, while the vassal states had their own ruling families who were loyal to Assyria.

There is not enough information preserved about the everyday life of the common people. The majority of the population consisted of farmers and workers. Clans lived together in villages, taking care of the agricultural holdings in the vicinity. Each village had a mayor who was their representative before the state officials and who was also, in some cases, the local judge. There are no recorded rebellions of the common people against Assyrian rule. The only rebellions ever recorded were the ones of noble families fighting the empire. The state was the owner of everything that was produced; however, the king was responsible for providing the infrastructure, construction, and the expansion of agricultural lands, including trade, though trade sometimes employed private contractors. The state was the largest employer of labor, free people, semi-free people, and slaves.

The Bronze Age Collapse (1200 to 900 BCE), also known as the Dark Age of the Near East, did not affect the Middle Assyrian Empire for at least the next 150 years. While kingdoms crumbled around them, the Assyrians seemed to be completely unaffected. However, after the death of King Ashur-bel-kala in 1056, the decline of the empire began. During the span of just one century, Assyria lost all of its territories and ended up controlling only areas in the immediate vicinity of Assyria itself.

Semitic peoples, the Arameans, Chaldeans, and Suteans, inhabited the areas west and southwest of Assyria, including parts of Babylonia in the south. East of Assyria, the lands were inhabited by the Persians and Parthians. In the north, the Phrygians conquered the Neo-Hittite kingdoms. In eastern Anatolia, the Hurrians organized a new kingdom named Urartu. Even though Assyria lost all of its territories, at its heart, it remained a strong and stable state. This stability would allow Iron Age kings to retake all of their lost territories and expand their empire even more.

King Adad-nirari II (ruled 911 to 891 BCE) succeeded his father after some minor dynastic struggles. He is often considered to be the first king of the Neo-Assyrian Empire, but some historians argue that it was his father, Ashur-dan II.

Adad-nirari II started his rule with a military campaign to conquer the territories that already had the status of vassal states. In 910, at the junction of the Khabur and Euphrates Rivers, he defeated the Arameans. After taking their lands, he deported the Arameans, strategically making it impossible for them to cause any trouble in the future. Furthermore, he led regular military campaigns and conquered the Neo-Hittites and Hurrians in the north. He even attacked and defeated the Babylonian king Shamash-mudammiq twice, taking the lands and cities of central Mesopotamia. Later during his reign, he waged war against Babylonia's next king, Nabu-shuma-ukin I, and took even more territories. In the west, Adad-nirari conquered the Kabur River region as well as the Aramean cities of Kadmuh and Nisibin.

His son and successor was Tukulti-Ninurta II (ruled 891 to 884), who continued with the expansion of the Neo-Assyrian Empire by conquering lands in Asia Minor. His reign was short, but he confirmed Assyria's power in the region. He led a war campaign against the Aramean state of Bit-Zamani, forcing its king to sign a treaty that prohibited them from selling horses to Assyrian enemies. Bit-Zamani became an Assyrian ally with this treaty, but not much later, it gained the status a of vassal state. Tukulti-Ninurta II was known for developing the cities of Nineveh and Assur, and he also reinforced the city walls and built palaces, temples, and gardens.

After Tukulti-Ninurta, the throne was occupied by his son Ashurnasirpal II (ruled 883 to 859), whose reign was filled with conquests. He also started a very aggressive expansion program, which led to some revolts that were quickly crushed. Ashurnasirpal was known for being a brutal king who used war captives to build the new seat of power, a city called Nimrud, located in Mesopotamia. But he also added to the wealth of Assyria and invested considerably in art. Instead of depending on local rulers of the vassal states, Ashurnasirpal installed his own governors, thus gaining better control and even more power over the Assyrian

Empire.

Ashurnasirpal campaigned against the Arameans and the Babylonians, just as his predecessors. However, his biggest accomplishment was the war against the Neo-Hittite states. Before his military campaign into the Hittite lands, Ashurnasirpal had to deal with a rebellion that occurred in 877 in the Middle Euphrates region. Apparently, the lands of Laqe, Hindanu, and Suhu broke their allegiance to the empire and formed a coalition that became hostile toward Assyria. In order to crush this rebellion, Ashurnasirpal marched his army to the Euphrates, where he had to ferry the troops using an unconventional strategy, namely using inflated goat skins. The Assyrian king crushed the rebelling forces, destroyed their cities, and deported their population. The Aramean state of Bit Adini supported this anti-Assyrian rebellion and thus had to answer for it. Ashurnasirpal launched yet another campaign, this time in the territories of Bit Adini, probably the very next year (the exact date is unknown). He destroyed the fortress city of Kaprabu, massacring and enslaving its population. Ashurnasirpal did not strive to conquer Bit Adini; he just wanted to pacify the region. However, he did receive a significant tribute from its ruler, Ahuni. It seemed that Ahuni accepted the Assyrian victory, and he remained at peace with them for the time being. But later, during the reign of Ashurnasirpal's son Shalmaneser III, he would lead another uprising in this region and witness his state being run into the ground.

After pacifying these Aramean lands, Ashurnasirpal was ready to begin his campaign in Syria. His first objective was Carchemish, the capital city of the Neo-Hittites. Its ruler was a man named Sangara, who, upon the arrival of the Assyrian army, surrendered the city without resistance. Carchemish was, during this period, one of the most prosperous Hittite cities, and its capture brought enormous riches to the Assyrian king. The city paid tribute to Ashurnasirpal, giving him 20 talents of silver, 100 talents of bronze, 250 talents of iron, as well as furniture, thrones, elephant tusks, a couch and a chariot made completely out of gold, 200 girls, and the entire army of the city, which included infantry, chariotry, and cavalry. With this payment, Sangara ensured that the Assyrian army would not destroy the city. After the surrender of Carchemish, Ashurnasirpal declared that all the kings of this region now bowed to him, which might indicate that they were intimidated by the fall of Carchemish and, as a result, surrendered. They probably paid handsome tributes to Ashurnasirpal and ensured even more troops for his expeditions deeper into Syria. To make sure newly conquered lands would stay submissive to his rule, Ashurnasirpal took seventy hostages from them. These hostages had to accompany him on his march toward the Mediterranean.

Ashurnasirpal then began conquering Syria's coastal states, which took him to the northernmost parts of the Neo-Hittite kingdoms. Here, he conquered Patin, a Luwian Neo-Hittite state that the Assyrians called Unqi. Control of Patin ensured Ashurnasirpal had dominion over the entire Levantine coast.

Luash was the first state in Syria that gathered an armed resistance against Ashurnasirpal's army. However, they were no match for the Assyrian army, which destroyed its cities and massacred its people. The defending forces were impaled in front of the ruins of the cities to serve as a warning to any other state that contemplated resistance against the Neo-Assyrian Empire. News of Luash's fate traveled well before Ashurnasirpal while he marched to Mount Lebanon. The rulers of the Phoenician cities of this region complied with Assyrian demands in order to avoid the destruction of their lands. Upon reaching the Mediterranean, Ashurnasirpal declared his victory over the Levantine coast. Many of the riches gathered during this Syrian campaign served as building materials for the construction of Ashurnasirpal's new capital of Kalhu, better known as Nimrud. Conquering the Syrian lands, Ashurnasirpal opened trade routes toward the west. Western states had to pay

Assyria a tribute to ensure their freedom. As long as they kept paying, Ashurnasirpal promised he wouldn't lead military campaigns into their lands.

Ashurnasirpal also conquered a number of Phoenician/Canaanite cities, but he chose not to destroy them. Instead, he collected a yearly tribute, which he used to equip his army as well as to invest in the further development of the Assyrian capital. The only failure was the siege of Tyre, but this Phoenician city decided to pay tribute to Assyria to ensure no further attacks on its walls. Tyre was the main trade route to Rhodes and Miletus, and due to its tribute, it became a significant source of raw materials for the Assyrian Empire.

Shalmaneser III, the son of Ashurnasirpal II, ruled the Neo-Assyrian Empire between 859 and 824. He continued his father's practice of yearly military expeditions during his long reign. He warred against the eastern tribes, Babylonia, the nations of Mesopotamia and Syria, and the Anatolian kingdom of Kizzuwadna and Urartu. He also subdued the kingdoms of Hamath and Aram Damascus. Thirty-four of Shalmaneser's military campaigns were recorded, with nineteen taking place across the Euphrates in the Hittite regions. There, he encountered a much more serious resistance than his father because the western states had formed a coalition. Their common enemy, the Assyrian Empire, had brought together the Neo-Hittite kingdoms and their rulers. Upon Shalmaneser's entrance in Syria, he received tribute from Hattusili, the king of Kummuh, and Muwatalli, king of Gurgum; however, his next target proved to be more resilient. In the Aramean kingdom of Sam'al, he encountered the allied forces of Bit Adini, Carchemish, Sam'al, and Patin. Individually, none of these kingdoms stood a chance against the might of the Assyrian army, but together, they proved to be a bigger challenge. Assyrian records tell the story of a great victory Shalmaneser achieved, but reality might be different. He was victorious against the allied kingdoms, but he did not destroy their lands or slaughter their armies. Shortly after, he once again had to encounter the same allied forces on the battlefield. Shalmaneser defeated them a second time, and in tribute to himself, he erected a great statue inscribed with the records of his victory. But this victory seemed to have achieved little, for yet another anti-Assyrian alliance was called together by King Suppiluliuma of Patin. The kingdoms of Adanawa, Hilakku, Yasbuq, and Yahan answered Suppiluliuma's call and gathered their forces near the city of Alimush. Despite the size of the newly formed alliance forces, they were no match for the well-trained and organized army of the Assyrian Empire. Shalmaneser was victorious yet again, and he gained complete control of the Syrian states.

By taking northern Syria, Shalmaneser opened the way to conquer the richer states and cities to the south. He launched a new campaign into the valley of Orontes, where he attacked Hamath, which was ruled by King Irhuleni, and completely destroyed the northern cities of Adennu, Parga, and Argana. The central and southern parts of Irhuleni's kingdom were still intact, and the king chose to call for a new alliance against Assyria rather than to succumb under its rule. This is where Shalmaneser encountered a second coalition, but this one included eleven states. Shalmaneser's scribe recorded between 50,000 and 60,000 infantry units, 4,000 chariots, 2,000 cavalry units, and 1,000 camels belonging to the enemy forces, but these numbers might be exaggerated due to propaganda. However, even if the armies are scaled down to their more probable numbers, the forces Shalmaneser encountered were considerable. The main leaders of the allied forces were King Irhuleni of Hamath and King Hadadezer of Damascus.

The Assyrian army confronted the allied forces in the city of Qarqar in 853. The Battle of Qarqar is a point in history where the Arabs are, for the first time, mentioned in scripts. Details of the battle are unknown, but Shalmaneser boasts how he defeated his enemies and fought them from the city of Qarqar to the city of

Gilzau. Furthermore, he proclaims that he slaughtered 14,000 troops and also speaks of making a bridge over Orontes with the bodies of enemy soldiers.

Shalmaneser's victory proved that numbers alone were not enough to defeat the Assyrian army. The diversity of allied forces may have, in fact, hindered the coalition as they were not disciplined or accustomed to fighting together. However, all the leaders of the alliance survived with the chance to fight another day, because their coalition would reform once again in the future and defy Shalmaneser one more time.

In just two campaigns, led in 851 and 850, Shalmaneser conquered parts of Babylonia. This conquest started due to Babylonia being divided between two brothers, Marduk-zakir-shumi I and Marduk-bel-usati. The elder brother, Marduk-zakir-shumi, asked Shalmaneser for help in subduing his brother. He risked unleashing the Assyrian hordes in his own lands in hopes he would subdue his rebellious brother, so he must have been in great need for help since he asked not just for some troops but for the whole Assyrian army and King Shalmaneser himself as their leader. Marduk-bel-usati stood no chance against the Assyrians, and his rebellion ended. But it took two campaigns to finish what was started with the invitation of the Babylonian king. The city of Gannanate, where Marduk-bel-usati himself was hiding, resisted the first attack. However, in the second year of the Babylonian campaign, Shalmaneser managed to conquer Gannanate, plundering its treasures and massacring its population. Marduk-bel-usati escaped the city and hid on the mountain Arman, but there, his luck ran out, and he was caught and killed.

After finishing the campaigns in Babylonia, Shalmaneser once again turned his sights to the west, where an uprising against Assyria was brewing and where he would have to face the coalition of eleven states for the second time. In 848, Shalmaneser marched to meet his enemies in the land of Hamath. He claimed he conquered ninety cities during his march to finally confront the combined forces of the Syrian-Palestinian lands. The alliance suffered a heavy defeat, but several years later, they regrouped and challenged the Assyrian king once again.

Three years later, in 845, Shalmaneser returned to put an end to the Syrian-Palestinian coalition. However, the leader of the allied forces, King Hadadezer, died at an unknown date between 845 and 841, and so, the coalition fell apart, leaving Aram-Damascus to fight Assyria alone. In 841, Shalmaneser claimed victory over Aram-Damascus, but Hazael, the new king, fled to the city of Damascus, where the Assyrian army blockaded him. Even three years later, Shalmaneser could not take Damascus, even though he destroyed its surroundings, blocked trade routes, and destroyed its fields and orchards. However, Israel and a number of Phoenician cities sent tribute to Shalmaneser, accepting his rule.

In 839, Shalmaneser decided to attack the lands of Adanawa in southeastern Anatolia. The motive to attack here can be found in the invitation the king of Sam'al, Kilamuwa, sent to Shalmaneser, who wanted the Assyrian king to come and help him take the lands of the Danunians (Adanawa). In the first campaign in the Adanawa lands, Shalmaneser claimed he conquered three fortified cities called Lusanda, Abarnanu, and Kisuatnu. It took three more military expeditions to finally subdue Adanawa in 833. However, previously in 836, Shalmaneser conquered the territory of Tabal, which, together with Adanawa, marked the end of the Assyrian expansion under the rule of King Shalmaneser III. Any other military campaign led by him was purely against uprisings and rebellions in his own lands against his son Assur-danin-pal.

The eldest son would almost destroy the Assyrian Empire, as 27 cities joined Assur-danin-pal. But the rebellion wasn't against the king himself but rather because some of the governors took too much power. This rebellion was quashed by Shalmaneser's younger son and successor, Shamshi-Adad V, who would rule from 824 to

811 BCE.

The reign of Shamshi-Adad V was marked by his campaigns against Mesopotamia. In 814, he launched several campaigns into Babylonian territory, with the main battle taking place at the city of Dur-Papsukkal. This city was located in the Diyala region (part of today's Iraq) in eastern Babylonia. Opposing Shamshi-Adad was the son of Marduk-zakir-shumi I, Marduk-balassu-iqbi. The Assyrians claimed victory in this battle, but it seems that the result was somewhat inconclusive because Shamshi-Adad launched another campaign against Babylonia in 813, this time with the main battle taking place near Der, another city in the same region. Marduk-balassu-iqbi was captured and taken as a prisoner to Assyria. In the next year, the Assyrians had to return to Babylonia and confront their new king, Baba-aha-iddina, who, like his predecessor, was taken prisoner to Assyria as well. Babylonia was left in chaos and anarchy for the next sixty years until 747 when King Nabonassar took control.

Shamshi-Adad's son, Adad-nirari III, ruled between 810 and 783. He turned his attention toward the west, across the Euphrates, where their neighbors were enjoying a brief moment of peace. Adad-nirari started his campaigns to the west in 805, where he confronted a coalition of states, just like his grandfather had. Eight kings formed an alliance, which was led by Attar-shumki, the king of the Aramean Kingdom of Arpad (Bit Agusi). Adad-nirari was victorious over this coalition, but he did not manage to break up the alliance. For the next ten years of his rule, this alliance would continue to defy him. During his reign, though, he managed to invade the Levant and conquer the Arameans, Phoenicians, Philistines, Israelites, and Neo-Hittites there. He even conquered Damascus, but he left the royal family of Ben-Hadad III to rule it. Instead, Adad-nirari satisfied himself with taking a yearly tribute from him. He continued his conquests in Iran, where he subjugated the Persians, Medes, and Mannaeans, and he continued his conquest all the way to the Caspian Sea. Adad-nirari's final military expeditions were to the southern Mesopotamian region, where he conquered the Chaldean and Sutu tribes and imposed a vassal status on their states. However, his premature death in 783 was the beginning of a stagnation period for the Neo-Assyrian Empire when it came to their expansion policy.

An interesting fact of Adad-nirari's campaign to the west was the presence of his mother, Sammuramat, who followed her son on military expeditions and who claimed some military victories in her own name. She is a persona that is mentioned in history but also in the myths that are part of the classical tradition. In various Assyrian inscriptions, she is mentioned often as a "palace woman" of King Shamshi-Adad V and the daughter-in-law of the great Shalmaneser III. In legends, she is known as Semiramis, and she shows up in Greek sources as well as in various texts from Near Eastern states. The victory of Bactria was attributed to her, but she was also known for building the walls of Babylon and some other prominent monuments around the country. Armenian sources mention her as a conqueror of Urartu. Whether the sources are accurate or just an exaggeration of her persona is unknown. However, the king's mother following her son on military expeditions must have been an unusual sight. She was undoubtedly a person of unprecedented importance in the Assyrian Empire, as she is mentioned in various important scripts and documents, and she also had a royal stele of her own.

The period of stagnation of the Neo-Assyrian Empire lasted from 783 to 745. It is commonly believed that the successor to Adad-nirari III, Shalmaneser IV, was a weak ruler, and any military conquests during the time of his rule were accredited to his general, Shamshi-ilu.

In 772, Ashur-dan III took the throne, but he also proved to be a weak ruler. He had to deal with rebellions in some of his cities, including Ashur, Arrapkha, and Guzana. He tried to gain more

Babylonian and Syrian territory, but he failed in his military campaigns. Shortly following his footsteps was yet another weak king, Ashur-nirari V, and his reign was marked by internal state turmoil and rebellions.

Finally, in 744, Tiglath-Pileser III ascended to the throne and brought reassurance to Assyria. It is common belief that he was a member of the same dynasty, but Tiglath-Pileser supported the uprising against Ashur-nirari V. Some historians claim he was even his son, but there is no evidence to support this claim. Some historians see Tiglath-Pileser as a usurper who took advantage of the uprisings against the previous king in order to claim the crown for himself. Whatever his path to the throne was, he became king at just the right time. The internal struggles of the Neo-Assyrian Empire were so turbulent that they could have crushed the empire had it not been for Tiglath-Pileser.

During the stagnant period in Assyria, the Kingdom of Urartu took some of the northern Mesopotamian territories and conquered some former Assyrian tributaries. However, Tiglath-Pileser didn't wait, and in the second year of reign, he launched a military expedition to regain the lost territories. He started with the land of Namri, which was located in the upper Diyala River Valley. The Assyrian army was merciless in subjugating these lands, and other states east of the Euphrates were quick to submit to the new Assyrian king. In 743, Tiglath-Pileser turned westward and tried to regain control of kingdoms across the Euphrates, but he had to face a combined force of the Kingdoms of Arpad and Urartu. This alliance was led by Sarduri II of Urartu, but the Neo-Hittite king of Malataya joined, as well as Gurgum and Kummuh. Tiglath-Pileser reports his victory in the battle fought in Kummuh's territory. Sarduri was brutally defeated and had to retreat back to his own lands in Urartu. The kings of Malataya, Gurgum, and Kummuh accepted their defeat and submitted themselves to the Assyrian king. They were all pardoned and became tributaries to the

Assyrian Empire.

Arpad still had to be dealt with, and this state was of particular interest to Tiglath-Pileser as it was Urartu's strongest ally. However, its capital city resisted the Assyrian siege for three years until it finally fell. There are no detailed records of the siege itself, just a mention of the city's fall in the Eponym Chronicles. An Assyrian governor was installed in this region, making Arpad an Assyrian province. This event paved the path for the provincialization process Tiglath-Pileser undertook regarding western vassal states. In 739, his attention was drawn toward the east, where the Kingdom of Ulluba was planning an invasion on Assyrian territory and had the support of neighboring Urartu. However, Tiglath-Pileser reacted immediately and was successful in his campaign against Ulluba, which was then converted into a province of the Assyrian Empire.

The process of turning former tributary states into Assyrian provinces continued, as this was the way Tiglath-Pileser III consolidated his power over the conquered territories. To further secure his dominion over these regions, Tiglath-Pileser relocated the local populations into other regions of the empire and then replaced their numbers with people from other regions. Another purpose for these relocations was to break any possible alliances between former neighbors and to secure the new borders of the Assyrian Empire. At this time, the Assyrian army became a professional one, with each province sending a military contingent. The changes the Assyrians went through with Tiglath-Pileser as its king are often referred to as the "Second Assyrian Empire."

The first Neo-Hittite kingdom that became an Assyrian province and underwent the process of population relocation was Patin in 738, which was called Kullani. The rest soon followed. In the same year, Tiglath-Pileser decided to invade Israel and impose a large tribute on King Menahem. He also did the same to Azariah, the king of Judah, and Azriyau, the king of Sam'al. Furthermore, in 732, Tiglath-Pileser finally conquered Damascus, as it had been lost since the time of Adad-Nirari III due to rebellions, and began the process of turning it into a province. A few years later, in 727, Tiglath-Pileser III died, but not before he crowned himself as the new king of Babylonia, calling himself King Pulu.

Tiglath-Pileser III was succeeded by Shalmaneser V, who ruled very briefly from 727 to722. During his short reign, he attacked Samaria (Israel) and took its capital city, also named Samaria, but only after three years of siege. King Hoshea of Israel was corresponding with the Egyptian pharaoh, Osorkon IV, who sent an army to help Israel fight Assyria. Egypt wanted a foothold in the land of Samaria, but Shalmaneser V could not allow the territories of his vassal kingdom to be taken. Shalmaneser V died during an expedition in Israel and was succeeded by his brother and commander of his armies, Sargon II, who ended the campaign in Israel quickly.

Sargon was already a middle-aged man when he took the throne. Some historians speculate that he was the one who disposed of his brother in order to ascend to the throne. Nevertheless, the beginning of his reign was marked with widespread rebellions. In Babylonia, Marduk-apla-iddina II proclaimed himself king and took the crown in 721, claiming Babylonia's independence from Assyrian rule. Sargon met Marduk-apla-iddina in battle near the city of Der in 720, where the Assyrian army was pushed back, allowing Babylonia to retrieve its territories in the south. Sargon did not give up on Babylonia, as he fought Marduk-apla-iddina many more times, and each time, Sargon was victorious. In 710, Marduk-apla-iddina abandoned his position as the king of Babylonia as he had to flee for his life. Babylonia surrendered and, once again, became a part of the Assyrian Empire in 709. Marduk-apla-iddina continued his rebellion against Assyria, though, and led military operations against them. This continued until the rule of Sargon's son, Sennacherib, who finally defeated Marduk-apla-iddina in 703.

In 718, Sargon led a campaign in Tabal, a Neo-Hittite kingdom in south-central Anatolia. He had to secure the entire territory of Tabal against the Phrygians in the northwestern territories, who often organized military incursions that endangered Assyrian borders. In order to achieve this, Sargon created one united kingdom of southern Anatolia named Bit-Burutash, with the Assyrian ruler Ambaris as its king.

Right after his campaign in Tabal, Sargon II received the news that the king of Carchemish, Pisiri, was secretly communicating with Mita, the king of the Mushki, which was an act of treason since it broke the treaty Carchemish had with Assyria. Sargon could not risk losing the strategically positioned city of Carchemish, as it would damage Assyrian authority in the western regions. Without even allowing Pisiri to explain his actions, Sargon attacked his kingdom, plundered it, and took its king and his whole family back to Assyria. In 717, Carchemish became an Assyrian province and ceased to exist as an independent kingdom.

In 714, Sargon decided to make a preemptive strike against the Urartian kingdom. A possible motivation for this was Urartu's weakness after numerous incursions by the Cimmerians, a nomadic tribe of the steppes. This was Sargon's eighth military campaign, and it was against King Rusa I, the ruler of Urartu. The campaign was well documented by Sargon himself in his letter to the god Ashur. He wrote about one of his armies that had to cut a forest and disassemble chariots and carry them in order to traverse the impassable terrain toward Urartu. He also mentioned his crushing victory over Rusa's army, making the king of Urartu flee for his life. Urartu was torn apart by the Assyrian military expedition, on top of the existing Cimmerian incursions, and as a result, King Rusa committed suicide after these events.

It is interesting that during the campaigns in 713, Sargon himself did not lead the armies. Instead, he stayed in his capital, and it is unknown why. It is speculated that he acted this way due to his advancing age. His army, however, was successful in taking Cilicia and Karalla, and they successfully completed a campaign in Tabal, while Persia and Mede offered tribute to avoid aggression.

In 711, Sargon had to deal with various unrests in his western provinces, mainly in the state of Gurgum, where King Tarhulara, who was loyal to Assyria, was assassinated by his son, the usurper Muwatalli III. Muwatalli proclaimed Gurgum's independence and probably had secret dealings with the Urartu kingdom, as well as with Phrygia. Sargon responded by aggressively removing Muwatalli from Gurgum's throne, annexing his kingdom and turning it into an Assyrian province, which would hold that status until the fall of the Neo-Assyrian Empire.

During Sargon's rule, the Assyrian Empire was at its highest. Even the Greek kings of Cyprus accepted his sovereignty. Phrygia and its king, Midas, submitted to Assyria in 708, and Kummuh became another Assyrian province as well. Sargon died in 705 while on an expedition to pacify Tabal, which had rebelled under the leadership of Gurdi the Kulummaean.

Sargon II was succeeded by his son Sennacherib, who ruled somewhere between 705 and 681 BCE. There are actually three proposed dates (705, 704, and 703) of his succession, which might imply that his coming to the throne wasn't without some turbulence. His name also indicates he was not Sargon's firstborn son. Sennacherib decided to move the Assyrian capital from Dur-Sharrukin to Nineveh. During the first years of his rule, Sennacherib encountered a problematic rebellion that required his full attention: Cilicia attempted to gain independence with the help of the Greeks. Sennacherib defeated Cilicia's rebels and their Greek allies.

In 701, Sennacherib had to turn toward Babylonia, where his first military campaign started. Marduk-apla-iddina II took the crown of Babylonia yet again, proclaiming himself as king, but his rebellion was short-lived. He was defeated, and once more, he had to run. This time he found sanctuary with his ally, Elam. Strangely enough, even though the city of Babylon was plundered, its population was not harmed. Evidently, Sennacherib either wasn't as bloodthirsty as his predecessors or he saw some possible gain in leaving the citizens alone. On the throne of Babylonia, he placed an Assyrian puppet king called Bel-ibni, and Babylonia remained at peace for some time.

However, Marduk-apla-iddina did not give up on his rebellion against Assyria. Soon after, he allied himself with Egypt. This alliance led to disaster for some of the Canaanite cities that were conquered, among them being Byblos, Ashdod, Ammon, and Edom. They all paid tribute to Sennacherib without further resistance. Egypt was defeated, and then the Assyrian king turned toward Jerusalem. He besieged the city but never captured it. Biblical sources mention an intervention from God's angels who smote 180,000 Assyrian soldiers; however, reality wasn't nearly as dramatic nor devastating. Sennacherib's scribe mentions a tribute being paid by the Kingdom of Judah, which satisfied Sennacherib, who decided to leave the city's gates.

Marduk-apla-iddina again tried to incite a rebellion against Assyrian rule, this time backed with his allies from Elam. In 694, Sennacherib destroyed the Elamite base in the Persian Gulf with the help of the Phoenician fleet, but while he was doing this, the Elamites managed to capture his eldest son, Ashur-nadin-shumi. They also placed Nergal-ushezib, the son of Marduk-apla-iddina II, on the Babylonian throne. Babylon fell under Assyrian rule in 689 but not after a few more attempts at rebellion. Unfortunately, it took a great amount of destruction and devastation for Sennacherib to finally put an end to the Babylonian problem.

Very little is known about his rule in the following years, and Sennacherib was assassinated in 681, most likely by one of his sons. He was succeeded by Esarhaddon, who describes the unrest that followed Sennacherib's death and how he took the throne while his brothers were fighting over it. He doesn't mention a possible murderer, but this may be because he tried to avoid further dynastic unrest. Other sources, like the Babylonian Chronicles, various biblical documents, and later Assyrian documents, imply that Sennacherib was murdered by one of his sons.

Esarhaddon ruled from 681 until 669 BCE and was the youngest son of Sennacherib. His first military excursions were against the Aramean tribes in southern Mesopotamia. During the first years of his rule, he had to reinforce the borders of his empire, as its provinces were under attack by the Cimmerians from the shores of the Black Sea, as well as by the Scythians who crossed the Taurus Mountains, coming from the southern steppes of today's Russia.

In 677, the king of Sidon, Abdi-Milkutti, rose against Assyria, but he was quickly defeated and beheaded. The capital city of Sidon was completely destroyed but was rebuilt as Kar-Ashur-aha-iddina. Esarhaddon continued the tradition of repopulating newly conquered areas with people from other parts of his empire in order to secure his dominance in the region.

The Scythians proved to be a nuisance to Assyrian rule. In 676, Esarhaddon conquered the cities of Sissu and Kundu in the Taurus Mountains before bringing King Ishpakia of the Scythians to heel. After the fall of Phrygia, Esarhaddon gave his own daughter to be wed to the Scythian prince, Partatua of Sakasene. This act was done in order to improve relations between the Assyrian Empire and the Scythian nomads, as well as to assure their loyalty.

The most important military campaign during Esarhaddon's rule was against Egypt and Pharaoh Taharqa of the Nubian dynasty. Esarhaddon left parts of his army to deal with a rebellion in Tyre, and with the remaining army, he took Egyptian lands. In the summer of 671, Esarhaddon reached Memphis, and with the help of some of the Egyptian princes, he captured it, forcing Taharqa to flee back into Nubia. Memphis was raided and sacked, its citizens were slaughtered, and their heads were gathered in piles in order to warn the Egyptians against rebellion. However, as soon as Esarhaddon left, Egypt rebelled. It was Esarhaddon's son, Ashurbanipal, who would continue to fight Egypt. It is believed that Esarhaddon died due to an illness. There are texts written by him that talk about his weak constitution during his final years. But there is also a possibility of him abdicating in favor of his son in 668 and that he died a year later.

Ashurbanipal succeeded his father and ruled between 668 and 627. He continued his father's efforts in Egypt but was also distracted from time to time by insurgents from the Medes in the east and the Cimmerians and Scythians in the northern territories of the Assyrian Empire. Ashurbanipal is considered the last strong ruler of the Neo-Assyrian Empire; after his death, the empire began its continuous decline. He was also a popular king amongst his subjects but was known to be very cruel and bloodthirsty toward his enemies.

Ashurbanipal didn't personally lead his first military campaign in Egypt. He chose to stay in his capital city Nineveh, but the army he sent managed to defeat Pharaoh Taharqa's army near Memphis. However, they failed to capture or kill Taharqa, and he fled to Upper Egypt. Soon after, in 664, he died, and his nephew, Tantamani, took his place and invaded the Assyrians in Egypt, killing all the nobility that remained loyal to the Assyrian Empire. As a result, Ashurbanipal sent an army to Egypt once again, and this time, he also employed a number of Carian mercenaries from western Anatolia. Ashurbanipal defeated Tantamani, invading Egypt all the way to Thebes, which he sacked. Eventually, Egypt gained its independence under Pharaoh Psamtik I, who remained on friendly terms with Assyria. It is not known how Psamtik managed to do this, but from that point onward, Egypt was free of Assyrian rule.

During the rule of Ashurbanipal, Assyria was one of the largest empires known to the civilized world. It stretched from the Caucasus in the north to North Africa in the south, and from

Cyprus in the west to central Iran in the east. Ashurbanipal's empire was vast, and he decided to start a dual monarchy by installing his own brother, Shamash-shum-ukin, as a vassal ruler in Mesopotamia. At first, Shamash-shum-ukin accepted vassalage under his brother, but soon after, he rebelled and became a Babylonian nationalist. He allied himself with other people who were known for their anti-Assyrian policy. Among them were the Suteans, Chaldeans, Arameans, Persians, Arabs, and the divided kingdom of Elam. Shamash-shum-ukin sent a letter to his brother, declaring he was the ruler and that Ashurbanipal was to become his subject and the governor of Nineveh. Ashurbanipal delayed his attack against his brother due to various bad omens, but when he finally launched an attack, he was victorious. The city of Babylon was besieged for two years until Shamash-shum-ukin committed suicide, as the defeat of the city was imminent. After this, the city surrendered to the Assyrian forces. Ashurbanipal decided not to destroy the city, but he did massacre all of the rebels and their allies. Babylon kept its semi-autonomous status and even formalized it.

Assyria was peaceful during the last years of Ashurbanipal's reign. But overexpansion took its toll on the empire, and it started to decline. Ashurbanipal managed to hold his grasp over the whole empire while he lived. It was after his death that Assyria was torn apart by its constant internal struggles.

Ashurbanipal was succeeded by his son Ashur-etil-ilani, whose reign was very brief, lasting from 631 until 627 BCE. Immediately after taking the throne, he faced civil wars and rebellions throughout the whole empire. These civil wars were just the start of the rapid decline of the empire. Brothers fought for the throne, dividing the Assyrian citizens in who they supported. Sinsharishkun, another son of Ashurbanipal, seized the throne for himself somewhere around 622. Little is known about the last kings of the Neo-Assyrian Empire, as this period lacks sources. Assyria's colonies, provinces, and vassal states took the opportunity brought by the internal upheaval and broke off, claiming their independence. Amongst them were Chaldeans, Babylonians, Medes, Scythians, Sagartians, and Cimmerians. The Assyrian king was in no position to send any armies in order to reclaim those territories because he had to fight a civil war that was tearing the empire apart.

Of all the states that claimed independence, Babylonia posed the most serious threat, and a long war in the heart of this kingdom started. The rebelling citizens of Babylonia gathered under the rule of Nabopolassar, a leader of the Chaldean tribe that resided in southeastern Mesopotamia. He was Babylonia's new king, and he played a key role in the fall of the Neo-Assyrian Empire. Nabopolassar took Babylon as his capital, proclaimed himself king, and ruled Babylonia from 626 to 605. He was the founder of the Neo-Babylonian Empire.

Sinsharishkun did not want to allow Babylonia to regain its freedom. Instead, he gathered his armies and initiated a new military campaign. However, in the heart of Assyria, another rebellion started, and he had to send some of his forces back home. These troops, instead of defeating the rebels, chose to join them, and a new usurper began to threaten Sinsharishkun's throne. There are no records detailing who the usurper was and how the rebellion started as all the sources were probably destroyed during the civil war in Assyria's capital of Nineveh. Sinsharishkun managed to fight off the rebel forces and take the throne again, but he lost the opportunity to solve the Babylonian problem.

Nabopolassar had the time he needed to take Babylonia under his rule and secure his power. In 619, he captured Nippur, thus becoming the ruler of Babylonia. Then he tried to invade the Assyrian territories, but he was defeated and forced back to Babylon. For the next four years, Nabopolassar had to defend his throne from the Assyrian army that was trying to unseat him.

In 616, Nabopolassar had to form an alliance with the Medes in order to fight Assyria, who had joined forces with Egypt.

Nabopolassar's alliance was joined by the Scythians and Cimmerians, as well as with the Iranians, Sagartians, and Persians, whose lands he freed from Assyrian rule during the civil war. Now he had an army powerful enough to confront the Assyrian forces. In the following years, the Assyrian cities of Assur, Kalhu, Arbela, and Gasur, among others, were taken. Nineveh itself was besieged for over three months before it fell. This is probably where Sinsharishkun died, but the information about him is missing as the Babylonian Chronicles describing the siege of Nineveh have been damaged. Even though Assyria lost so many cities, it still endured with Harran being its new capital.

Assyria's last king was Ashur-Uballit II (ruled 612 to 608). He was a general in the Assyrian army, and it is speculated that he was the brother of Sinsharishkun, as he was a member of the royal family. He somehow managed to escape the siege of Nineveh, and with the help of the Egyptian army, he defended Harran. He resisted Babylon and its allies for some time, but in 610, the Egyptian armies were depleted, and he had to retreat home. In 609, the Babylonians, Medes, and Scythians sacked Harran. Ashur-Uballit II escaped the city and asked Egypt for help once more. Pharaoh Necho II joined him, and Ashur-Uballit marched his forces toward Assyria. However, the way was blocked by Josiah of Judah and his forces, who had allied themselves with Babylonia. The Egyptian armies had no problem defeating Babylonia, but they arrived to assist Ashur-Uballit in a weakened state. Nevertheless, the joined forces of Assyria and Egypt besieged Harran in 609, but they failed since their armies had been defeated.

Pharaoh Necho II retreated to northern Syria, and it is not known what happened to Ashur-Uballit as this is the last year where his name is mentioned. He disappeared from history, losing the Assyrian Empire forever.

Chapter 5 – The Cimmerians

Distribution of "Thraco-Cimmerian" finds

The Cimmerians are a group of people shrouded in mystery. Their existence is known through various sources of Assyrian, Scythian, and Greek origin, but their homeland is never mentioned. Their ethnicity and geographical affiliations are unknown as well. There is no archeological evidence of any kind that would allow historians to say for sure it is of Cimmerian origin. This is why terms like the "Cimmerian problem," "Cimmerian enigma," or "Cimmerian mystery" are commonly used.

Herodotus, the famous Greek historian, mentions the Cimmerians and claims their origin was from north of the Black sea, in the area of Crimea. Furthermore, he wrote that the Cimmerians were driven out of their lands by hordes of Scythians during the 7th century BCE. The Cimmerians are generally accepted to be of Scythian culture, but they share no ethnic bonds with them. Historians usually relate them to the Iranians or Thracians that had to migrate due to pressure from the Scythian expansion during the 9th century. Herodotus' thoughts on the Cimmerians were accepted as true until the 19th century when new archeological discoveries were made, namely the Assyrian clay tablets dating from approximately 714 BCE. These tablets, from the time of King Sargon II, mention the Cimmerians and specifically their nation of Gamir. This means that by the 8th century, the Cimmerians were settled not far away from Urartu. This places their homeland to the south instead of the north, which was how it was previously believed. The Assyrian tablets may be more accurate in giving information about the Cimmerians; after all, they are several centuries older. But the teachings of Herodotus are not so easily dismissed. Instead, there is a widespread opinion that the newly discovered Assyrian tablets confirm the Cimmerian presence south of the Caucasus, where they wandered during their migration to Asia Minor.

Herodotus placed the Cimmerian migration due to the Scythian attacks during the 7th century, but the Assyrian texts proved it to be even earlier. The assumption is that the migration the Cimmerians undertook happened somewhere during the 8th century and possibly even the 9th century BCE. Because of what the Assyrian sources had to tell, some historians proposed the Cimmerian homeland not to be near the Bosporus in northwestern Turkey or the Pontic Steppe in today's Ukraine but somewhere to the east of Urartu. This is an area that they inhabited during Sargon II's rule and in the century that followed. There was never any archeological evidence found in the area of the Pontic steppe that would even remotely shed light on the Cimmerians' presence in those areas. Even archeological findings in the area of the Black Sea that were attributed to the Cimmerians might be from some other Late Bronze Age or Early Iron age cultures. Historians also never found more evidence for the Cimmerians actually being in the areas of the Bosporus besides their mention in Greek traditions. But this might also be because the Greeks met some other culture that was similar to that of the Cimmerians. The answer to the question where do the Cimmerians come from is based on shaky ground, as there is no evidence that will, for sure, give us a clue where to look.

The land of Gamir was first mentioned in a letter sent to King Sargon II of the Neo-Assyrian Empire. In this letter, the informants from the empire's border with Urartu sent a report to the king describing how Gamir suffered at the hand of Rusa I, the king of Urartu. This letter even contained the specific location of Gamir, saying that the land of Guriania separates Gamir from Urartu. But some linguistic problems are encountered in later studies. Historians often think of Gamir as a dialectic version of Kamir, which is in Cappadocia (modern-day central Turkey), and that would put this kingdom to the west of Urartu. This position would then identify today's Gurunt as the land of Guriania, which would have separated Urartu from Gamir. But later sources, from the time of King Esarhaddon, mention Gamir in the same context as the Mannaeans, Medes, and Umman-Manda, who operated in the northeast of Mesopotamia, which would place Gamir to the east of Urartu.

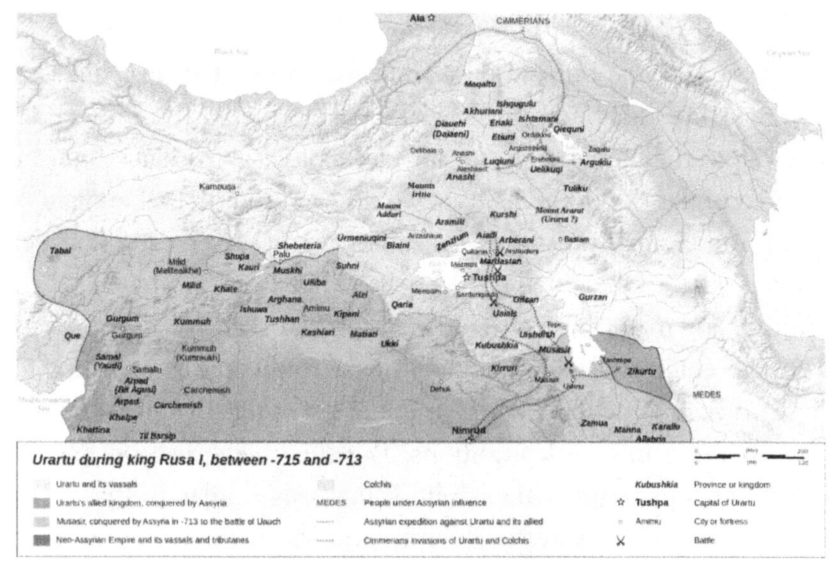

Map of Urartu between 715 and 713 BCE

© Sémhur / Wikimedia Commons https://commons.wikimedia.org/wiki/File:Urartu_715_713-en.svg

From the letter to Sargon II, historians were made aware of a battle taking place in Gamir. Apparently, Urartu was at war with the Cimmerians inhabiting these lands at that time. The reason for the war is still unknown, but the letter specifically describes King Rusa I of Urartu fleeing from Gamir in defeat. Because the letter was dated from being around 714 BCE, most scholars agree that the Battle of Gamir must have happened somewhere around that year, maybe even in 715.

Another Assyrian intelligence report dating from approximately the same time describes the Cimmerian invasion of Urartu, but this time from the territories of Mannea, a land south of Lake Urmia. Some scholars claim that this report also refers to the Battle of Gamir, but the context of the letter is completely different. Instead of Rusa attacking Gamir and losing the battle, the Cimmerians were the aggressors who invaded Urartu. The difference in context leads to the conclusion that this was a second confrontation the Cimmerians had with King Rusa I. Most likely, the Cimmerians joined Sargon II in the war against Urartu, and the combined forces were victorious, driving Rusa to commit suicide.

There are numerous mentions of the Cimmerians in Assyrian documents, but they only describe battles. The Assyrians were a military empire, prone to expansion; therefore, the majority of their surviving documents are battle reports. There are still no accounts that would explain the Cimmerian culture, ethnicity, politics, or economy.

From many Assyrian reports, it is known that Transcaucasia was a base from which the Cimmerians attacked and raided the Assyrian borders or the Assyrian vassal states. However, in 679, the Cimmerians were defeated by the Assyrian army led by King Esarhaddon. This is when the Cimmerian king is mentioned by name for the first time. According to Esarhaddon, the Cimmerian king was named Teushpa, but he also mentions him as the king of the Umman-Manda, which is Akkadian for "the horde from who knows where." This term was used to describe a poorly known tribe of the ancient Near East. The Umman-Manda have been attributed to different peoples the Assyrians fought in their history: Hurrians, Medes, Cimmerians, Elamites, and Scythians. It is thought they came from central Anatolia, but the Akkadian saying pretty much sums up how historians view this culture.

During the same year of 679, a Cimmerian detachment of soldiers was serving in the Assyrian army. At one point, the Cimmerians allied themselves with the Medes, attacking Shubria (a country bordering Lake Van), Parsua, and maybe even Ellipi. Again in 671/70, there are mentions of the Cimmerians serving in the Assyrian army.

Another Cimmerian king mentioned by name was Tugdamme, better known as Dugdammi in classical Greek teachings. He ruled during the mid-seventh century, presumably between 660 and 640. He is known for attacking the Greek cities in coastal Asia Minor. But in 653, he turned his attention toward the Assyrian Empire, which was ruled by King Ashurbanipal at that time. Assyrian reports on this confrontation mention Tugdamme as the king of Saka and

Qutium, a nomadic people of the northern, eastern, and western parts of the Eurasian Steppe. Ashurbanipal also called him "Sar Kissati," which roughly translates to "King of the World." This suggests Tugdamme ruled a vast kingdom. Tugdamme was defeated and killed around 641 or 640 BCE. Assyrian texts mention Marduk (a Mesopotamian deity) killing Tugdamme, which alludes to some other force being responsible for his death, not the Assyrians.

After Tugdamme, Ashurbanipal mentions Tugdamme's son, Sandakhshatra, as being the next king of the Cimmerians. There are some speculations that Sandakhshatra was, in fact, Cyaxares, the king of Media, and that he helped in bringing down the Neo-Assyrian Empire. There is no archeological or historical evidence to support these claims, however.

Ashurbanipal also speaks of a permanent Cimmerian settlement in Anatolia. In 665, the Cimmerians attacked Lydia but were defeated, as Ashurbanipal himself sent help to King Gyges of Lydia. The Cimmerians succeeded in defeating the Lydians, either in 654 or 652, and took over their capital city of Sardis. Gyges died during this battle with the Cimmerians. In 640, under the leadership of King Tugdamme, the Cimmerians attacked the Greek cities of Ionia and Aeolis. There are also mentions of their activity in the regions of Paphlagonia, Bithynia, and Troad. Around the same year, the Cimmerians tried to ally themselves with the Assyrian vassal state of Tabal in order to bring down Assyrian rule, but King Tugdamme fell ill, and it is believed he committed suicide.

The last mention of the Cimmerian people is from the end of the 7th century BCE when the Lydian king, Alyattes, defeated them in eastern Anatolia. From this point onward, sources no longer mention them; however, it is believed they settled in Cappadocia.

Chapter 6 – The Scythians

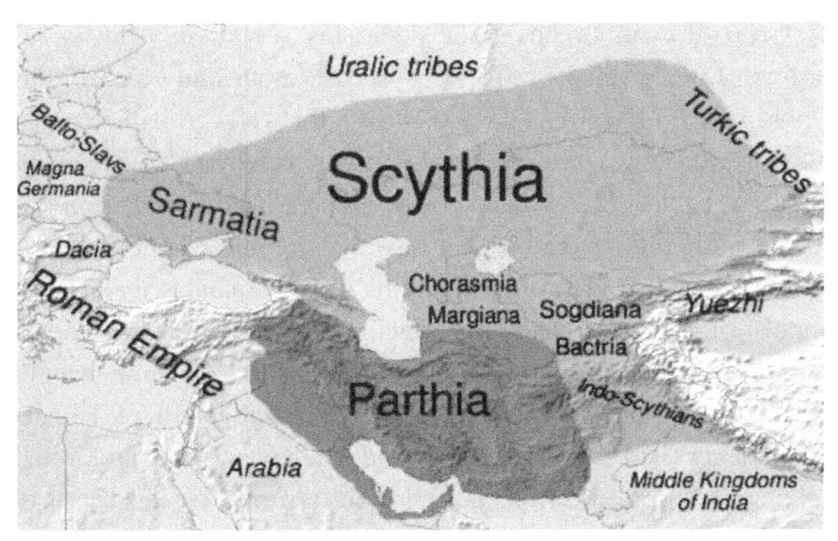

The extent of Eastern Iranian languages in the first century BCE

The word Scythians used to be used in a wider sense, mainly to describe the nomadic peoples of the Eurasian Steppe. What was common for all these people was the nomadic way of life and some similar aspects of culture. This is why today the term "people of Scythian culture" is used to describe various peoples who covered the same territory and shared a similar way of life. But ethnically, these people were different, and in time, historians started making a difference between them.

It is believed that the Scythians are of Iranian origin because their language is a branch of Iranian languages. But they also practiced a form of the Iranian religion. Herodotus noted that the Scythians came from the northern areas of the Black Sea as they pursued the Cimmerian tribes they had driven out of the Pontic Steppe. The Cimmerians crossed the Caucasus Mountains, but the Scythians followed them and entered Anatolia, where they would influence the region from the seventh to third century BCE.

There are two groups of sources that reveal the history of the Scythians. One is in Akkadian cuneiform texts, and the other one is of Greco-Roman origin. The Akkadians reveal only the earliest history of the Scythians, while the Greco-Roman sources cover their whole history. However, Greek sources that refer to early Scythian history, which was the seventh and sixth centuries BCE, are not always reliable. The Greeks often mixed history with common folktales; therefore, reading these sources requires critical analysis. The earliest document that mentions the Scythians is the Assyrian annals of King Esarhaddon, which speaks of a retreat of the Mannaeans after a battle. The Mannaeans at that time had the Scythians for allies, who were under the leadership of Ishpaka. Ishpaka also had the Cimmerians and Medes for allies, and in 678, he planned an invasion of the Assyrian territory. He died in battle against the Assyrian forces, which were led by Esarhaddon, around 675 and was succeeded by Bartatua (or Partatua). Bartatua couldn't keep the alliance whole, and he was defeated by the Assyrians. In order to keep the peace, he agreed to marry Esarhaddon's daughter in 674/6; this act made him an Assyrian vassal. He helped the Assyrians in their conquest of Media somewhere between 653 and 652, and the Assyrians gifted Media to the Scythians as a reward for their help. Bartatua died in 645 BCE. By 620, when the fall of the Neo-Assyrian Empire became inevitable, the Scythians gained more freedom. By taking advantage of the Assyrian situation, they started their own lengthy campaigns.

The Scythian king Madyes (Madius) inherited the throne after Bartatua, and he marched the army to the borders of Egypt. The Scythians plundered the region of Palestine, making the Cimmerians retreat from these territories. According to Herodotus, the next 28 years would be known as the years of Scythian rule over Asia, but Pompeius Trogus, a Roman historian, places the Scythian domination over Asia in a period of only eight years. This is where the influence of Scythian folklore on Herodotus is evident. The reality was that there was no Scythian rule but rather a large number of lengthy and successful raids.

Media finally liberated itself under the rule of King Cyaxares, who killed all the Scythian leaders during a feast at his palace, according to Herodotus. The Scythians stopped raiding the Middle East in the last decade of the seventh century BCE.

During the early sixth century, the Greeks started founding their colonies in the territory ruled by the Scythians on the shores and islands of the Black Sea. The relations between these two people were peaceful at that time, but there is new evidence that suggests the possible destruction of the Greek city Panticapaeum at the hands of the Scythians approximately during the middle of the sixth century.

Probably the most important event in the sixth century in Scythian history was the campaign for the lands of Darius I, a Persian king known for his victorious military expeditions. Before encountering the Scythians, Darius conquered parts of Eastern Europe until he reached the Danube. He invaded European Scythia between 520 and 507. Many historians put the year of this invasion in 513, but it is difficult to pinpoint the year of the invasion based on surviving sources. To cross the Bosporus, Darius I built a bridge out of ships. If Herodotus is to be believed, his army numbered 70,000 men. At the time of the Persian invasion, the Scythians were separated into three kingdoms with three different kings. However, King Idanthyrsus was considered the overlord, while the other two kings, Scopasis and Taxacis, were his subordinates. The Scythians did not receive support from their neighbors in the fight against the Persians, so they decided to implement scorched-earth tactics and moved the civilians with their livestock to the north. Darius chased the Scythians, but they retreated to the east, burning the countryside and blocking the springs and wells, as well as destroying the pastures. The Persian army chased the Scythians in hopes of openly fighting them but found themselves deep into the steppes, where there were no cities to plunder to resupply their army. Darius was frustrated by the Scythian tactics, and he openly challenged King Idanthyrsus to fight or else surrender. Idanthyrsus replied he would not fight Darius until they reached the tombs of the Scythian forefathers. He continued his tactics of retreat, as they had nothing to lose; there were no cities or villages, just open steppes. The Persian army chased the Scythians for a month, and Darius lost a number of his forces due to sickness, fatigue, and constant Scythian skirmishes. Finally, Darius stopped his chase at the banks of the River Volga and turned toward Thrace. However, Darius already conquered so much of the Scythian territory that most of the areas had to submit to Persian rule. Even so, Darius was still considered to have been defeated in this battle.

Even though the Scythians formally lost against the Persians, their endurance made their neighbors see them as invincible. This tradition of thinking of the Scythians as being invincible continued during the classical period, where it found its place mainly in literature.

The Scythians were a nomadic people, which means that they lived in tribes. However, these tribes would form a confederation when it came to the defense of their lands. The Scythian tribes also formed something close to a modern-day institution that would regulate pastures and agricultural lands of these equestrian herdsmen. Animal breeding exceeded the needs of the settled agricultural societies of the Scythians, and they started developing trade with other nearby nomadic peoples.

Herodotus mentions three Scythian tribes that were ruled by three brothers: Lipoxais, Arpoxais, and Colaxais. In folklore, these tribes received divine gifts: a plow, a yoke, an ax, and a bowl (or drinking cup). Traditionally, these three tribes are treated as if they occupied geographically distinct territories, but historians are proposing that the three divine gifts refer to social occupations. This would mean that the plow and yoke are symbols of farmers, the ax is a symbol of warriors, and the bowl or cup represent priests.

When it comes to warfare, almost the entire adult population of the Scythians, including women, joined the armies. The Scythians had a reputation of being invincible, as historical sources often said that the Scythians could not be defeated without outside help. They were known for their horse-riding skills and the use of bows from horseback. The Scythians were an aggressive people, and many became mercenaries. They often used barbed and poisoned arrows in their battles as well.

The Scythian religion was pre-Zoroastrian in nature and was related to the Proto-Indo-Iranian religion. It also may have influenced Slavic, Hungarian, and Turkic mythology. The Scythians worshiped seven gods and goddesses. However, eight of them are mentioned by Herodotus, who claimed these were gods worshiped by the royal family. First amongst them was Tabiti, the queen of gods and protector of homes. Later she was transformed into Atar or Agni, a fire deity of Zoroastrian origin. The Scythians offered animal sacrifices to their gods, with the most prestigious sacrificial animal being the horse. The Scythians also allowed a certain caste of priests, the Enarei, to play a significant role in the political life of the lands. It was believed that these priests received a divine gift directly from the gods and were able to foresee the future. The Enarei used strips made out of linden tree bark to read the future, and they were known to dress in female garments.

Scythian art was known for its small objects, such as jewelry made out of gold. During the early period of Scythian art, they were modeling animal figures, presenting them in combat poses. Art historians suggest that Scythian art was mainly influenced by the Near East during their military expeditions in these regions. It is commonly thought that Scythian art originated from the eastern part of the Eurasian Steppe, which was mainly under Chinese influence. During the sixth century, their artwork started depicting mythological creatures as a result of direct Greek influence. Early Scythian art often presents warriors with almond-shaped eyes using composite bows. Later, under the influence of Greek and Persian art, the warriors in Scythian art started having rounder eyes and longer beards and mustaches. During the Scythian golden age, the Greeks were the ones hired to produce their art. The Greeks crafted objects that represented Scythian legends or were used in religious rituals. By the end of the third century BCE, original Scythian art disappeared under the pressure of Hellenic culture. However, the Scythians continued to produce anthropomorphic gravestones.

Herodotus notes the royal lineage of Scythian King Idanthyrsus, stating that his father was Saulius, his grandfather Gnouros, great-grandfather Lykos, and his great-great-grandfather was Spargapeiths. Herodotus also speaks of Anacharsis, who came from the same royal family and was the brother to Saulius and the son of Gnouros. Anacharsis was a Scythian wiseman who traveled from the northern Black Sea all the way to Athens, where he became a renowned figure of "barbarian wisdom." He became popular in Greek literature, where he is numbered as one of "seven sages." Ephorus, another Greek historian, used the image of Anacharsis to describe his idealized image of the Scythians. There is no historical evidence of any existence of Anacharsis, who was a Hellenized Scythian prince, but the possibility is there. Even Herodotus admits that the

Scythians had no knowledge of Anacharsis' existence. Everything we know about this mysterious figure comes from Greek sources and literature, and there is no mention of this persona in Scythian history.

What we do know about Scythian history is that Darius' campaign into the Scythian lands led to a political consolidation amongst the Scythians and their neighbors. Scythian power grew considerably, and in the 490s, they launched an expedition into Thrace, reaching Chersonesos. In Thrace, the Odrysian Kingdom put up a resistance against the Scythian invasion, and new borders between the two dynasties were set. There are records of marriages between the Scythian and Odrysian royal families. For example, the Scythian king Oktamasades was the son of an Odrysian princess.

At that time, the Scythians chose to expand their lands north and northwest, where they destroyed several fortified cities and subjugated the citizens of the Odrysian Kingdom. They also tried for the first time to conquer the Greek colonies in the Pontic regions. Because of their previous friendly relations, the Greek settlements had no fortifications or walls to protect them. This resulted in the abandonment and total destruction of some cities but also in the quick fortification of others. Eventually, the Scythians were successful in having control over various Greek colonies. Herodotus confirms that King Scyles of the Scythians had a residence in Olbia. In Nikonion, for instance, coins that bore the name of Scyles were found.

At this point in history, during the 5th century, a change was happening in the Scythian Empire. With their increasing power, their wealth grew as well. The Greeks mentioned the existence of two Scythian kingdoms, Scythia Minor in today's Romania and Bulgaria, and Greater Scythia, which extended from the Danube to the lower Don Basin. Because of the vast lands that they controlled, the Scythians developed a division of responsibilities inside the empire. They had all the political and military power, but they left the urban citizens to deal with trade themselves, no matter what ethnic group they belonged to. The locals were also responsible for all the manual labor. The Scythians obtained much of their riches through slave trade, over which they had full control.

The Scythians were successful in conquering the Greek colonies to some extent, but the Greeks quickly united against them and formed an alliance under the leadership of the city of Panticapaeum. This alliance of Greek city-states later developed into the Bosporus Kingdom, also known as Cimmerian Bosporus. The Greek colonies that fell under Scythian rule started rebelling and gained their freedom. In the lower Don River territories, a Scythian settlement known as Elizavetovka was established. The Scythians wanted to continue their trade with the Greeks, so they allowed a Greek minority to inhabit this city, but the Scythians took trading, for the most part, of this city into their own hands. Even with a lack of evidence, some archeological sites allow us to assume that the Scythians were suffering some internal struggles. A related Iranian people, known as the Sarmatians, began invading from the east and conquered some Scythian territories. The Sarmatians intermingled with the Scythians, and although it seems they destabilized the political power of Scythia, the situation grew calmer over time.

During the fourth century BCE, Scythian culture blossomed. Most of the known monuments are dated to these times. Of the 2,300 discovered monuments in the steppes the Scythians lived, 2,000 belonged to the fourth century. The burial mounds archeologists found were also the richest during this period. Good relations with the new Bosporan Kingdom influenced the rapid Hellenization of the Scythians, especially the royal family and nobles.

The political life of the Scythians during the fourth century is mostly tied to King Ateas, who ruled sometime between 429 and 339 BCE. He united the Scythian tribes under his rule while invading Thrace at the same time. Ateas allied himself with the Macedonians and successfully conquered Triballoi and Istrianoi. His expansion toward the west caused a conflict with Philip II of Macedon, even though they were often allies. In 339, Philip launched a military campaign against the Scythians, and King Ateas died in battle. With his death, the Scythian Empire disintegrated, even though the Scythian people continued to exist. Alexander the Great continued his father's struggles against them after Philip's death.

A general of Alexander the Great, Zopyrion, led a campaign against the Scythians in 331/30. His army counted 30,000 men when it reached Olba and besieged it. However, they were unable to take the city, and they had to retreat. Zopyrion himself died during this battle.

One more Scythian king is mentioned in history from this period. His name was Agaros, and he was probably meddling in the civil war of the Bosporan Kingdom, where two brothers fought for the throne in 310/9 BCE. He allied himself with Satyros II, who was defeated during this war. Agaros gave refuge to the son of Satyros, Paerisades. Nothing else is known about his rule, but the fact that he intervened in the internal struggles of the Bosporan Kingdom may indicate he ruled over the Crimean steppes, which bordered the Bosporus.

At the beginning of the third century, Scythian culture suddenly disappears from the North Pontic region. The reason is unknown, but there are many speculations, from climate change to economic collapse. The third century was truly a dark age for the Scythians. They were expelled from the Balkans by the Celts, while in the east, the Sarmatians were expanding, slowly overwhelming them. In turn, the Scythians focused on the Greek cities of Crimea. By the middle of the third century, Chersonesos lost all of its settlements in northwestern Crimea.

The Scythians of the second century BCE only inhabited the territories of Crimea, the lower lands of the Dnieper River, and Dobruja. These territories were now known as Scythia Minor. The Scythians returned to their nomadic way of life, but they were also intermingling with the local populations. They established a new kingdom between the Dnieper River and Crimea during this period, and Scythian Neapolis became its capital.

This new Scythian kingdom was Hellenic in nature and even resembled the Greek monarchies instead of the fourth century Scythian kingdom of nomads. The kingdom had a habit of tying themselves to the Bosporan Kingdom through marriages. The most widely known Scythian king of the late period was Skilurus, and he reigned around 125 BCE. He ruled not only Crimea but also some of the territories of the northwestern Pontic region. He continued to be hostile toward Chersonesos and attacked it, but his army had to retreat when faced by King Mithridates VI of Pontus. A general of Mithridates' army, Diophantus, successfully campaigned against the last Scythian king, Palakos, the son of Skilurus. It took Diophantus three campaigns, which took place between 110 and 107, to completely wipe out the Scythians from their territory, and they even took their capital city. Now, only the Scythians of Dobruja existed, but they were of far less interest to anyone. Eventually, Scythia Minor fell under the rule of Mithridates VI.

The Scythians continued to exist after this, but they renounced their nomadic way of life entirely and began settling themselves. In the first century CE, the Scythians grew in strength enough to attack Chersonesos, which asked Rome for help. Rome easily defeated the Scythians, and they never allowed them to return to this region again. During this period, the Romans mention the Tauro-Scythians, who historians recognize as being a mixed population of the Crimean region. From these times, many Greek and Roman historians use the term Scythian to describe any nomadic people who were of Slavic or Turkish origin.

Chapter 7 – The Persians

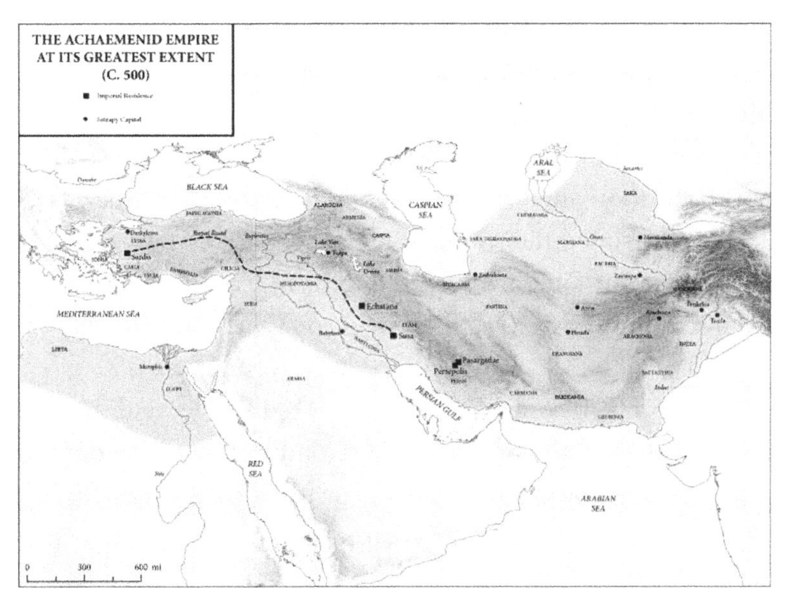

Map of the Achaemenid Empire at its greatest extent

Original creator: MossmapsCorrections according to Oxford Atlas of World History 2002, The Times Atlas of World History (1989), Philip's Atlas of World History (1999) by पाटलिपुत्र, CC BY-SA 4.0 <https://creativecommons.org/licenses/by-sa/4.0>, via Wikimedia Commons

https://commons.wikimedia.org/wiki/File:Achaemenid_Empire_at_its_greatest_extent_according_to_Oxford_Atlas_of_World_History_2002.jpg

The ancient Persians belonged to the group of Iranian peoples who inhabited the Persis region in southwestern Iran, today known as the Fars Province. There is little information about the first centuries of their history, which was between 1000 and 600 BCE. The first appearance of Persia in old documents is of Assyrian origin from the third millennium BCE. It is written in the old Assyrian form as Parahse, indicating the region that was inhabited by the Sumerians. The Iranian nomadic tribe from this region migrated west of Lake Urmia, taking the name of their homeland with them. Eventually, they were called Persians, and the land they occupied became known as Persis, what historians call Persia proper and the heartland of the later Persian Empire. At first, these nomadic Persians were influenced by the Assyrians, who had ruled them for over three centuries. However, a new power rose in the region.

Medes, another group of Iranian people, organized their own kingdom known as Media, uniting the region against Assyrian rule. Media became a political and cultural power in this region by 612 BCE. In 552, Persis, under the Achaemenid dynasty, was Media's vassal state. Soon after, though, in 550, they rebelled against Media and not only gained their independence but also conquered Media. The first Persian king, who is credited as being the founder of the Persian Empire, was Cyrus the Great, or Cyrus II, who ruled from 600 to 530. The Persian Empire was formed in 550 after the rebellion Cyrus II organized against Media. He had help from various nobles of the Median court and the commander of the Median armies, Harpagus, in overthrowing King Astyages.

Cyrus the Great commanded all of the vassal states that used to bow before Media. His uncle Arsames was the ruler of the city of Parsa, and he willingly gave up his throne to Cyrus. This is how Cyrus managed to unite two kingdoms ruled by the same Achaemenid dynasty. Parsa and Anshan became Persia.

The king of Lydia, Croesus, planned to take advantage of the unrests in the Median kingdom and seize some of its territories for himself, but he had to face a counterattack organized by Cyrus the Great. The exact year of these actions is unknown, but speculations place it in 547 due to information provided by the Nabonidus Chronicle. The Lydians attacked the city of Pteria in Cappadocia, which they besieged and captured. In response, the Persians invited the citizens of Lydia to revolt against Croesus, but they refused. Cyrus decided to lead an army and march against Lydians. His army gained numbers as he recruited more men from the nations he passed through on his way to Pteria. Neither side won in the battle, and both the Persians and the Lydians suffered great losses. King Croesus was forced to retreat back to his capital in Sardis.

Croesus called for his allies to help him, but Cyrus attacked again by the end of winter, so Croesus' allies had no time to send aid. The Persians besieged Sardis for fourteen days when Croesus finally decided to meet Cyrus in open battle, known as the Battle of Thymbra. The battle took place on the northern plains of Sardis, and the Lydian army outnumbered the Persians two to one. However, Harpagus, the renegade Median commander who still advised Cyrus, pushed to put camels in the front row in order to confuse the Lydian cavalry, whose horses were not used to the smell. This proved to be a tactic that decided the fate of the battle. The Persians won, and Sardis fell. Herodotus writes that Cyrus spared Croesus and made him his own advisor, but this information contradicts the Nabonidus Chronicle, which states that the Lydian king was killed. Nabonidus, who the chronicle was named after, was a Babylonian king who also suffered from a Persian invasion led by Cyrus. As it is from the same period, historians are inclined to trust his chronicle more than Herodotus' version of history.

The Persian commander Mazares, a former Median general, was entrusted with dealing with small uprisings in Lydia. After Lydia was subdued, Mazares continued into the Greek territories, where he took the cities of Magnesia and Priene. He continued his conquest in Ionia but soon after died of unknown causes. Harpagus was sent to finish the conquest of Asia Minor, and he captured Lycia, Cilicia, and Phoenicia. After ending his campaigns, he returned to Persia in

542.

In the winter of 540, Cyrus conquered Elam and took its capital, Susa. He continued to the city of Opis on the Tigris River, situated just north of Babylon, where he forced the Babylonian army to retreat. On October 10th, 539, he conquered the city of Sippar, where the Babylonian king Nabonidus resided. However, the king fled to the capital city, Babylon. Only two days later, the Persians entered Babylon; its citizens showed no resistance, and the Persians captured King Nabonidus. When Cyrus entered Babylon on October 29th, it proclaimed the end of the Neo-Babylonian Empire. With the fall of Babylonia, the Persians gained all of the territories this empire possessed, including Syria and Judah.

With the fall of Babylonia, Cyrus became the king of the largest empire the world had ever seen at the time. His empire occupied territories from Asia Minor in the west to the Indus River in the east. In the Cyrus Cylinder, a declaration made on a clay cylinder after the fall of Babylonia, Cyrus claims he improved the lives of his citizens. He repatriated the displaced peoples and worked on restoring the temples and sanctuaries. Some historians regard this cylinder as the first document describing human rights, but the majority sees it in the context of new policies of Mesopotamian kings who began their reign with announcing reforms to the kingdom.

There are many sources that describe the death of Cyrus the Great, but they all differ from each other. Some say he died during the invasion of Massagetae, a tribe that lived in the southern parts of modern Kazakhstan, and others say he died peacefully in his capital city. Furthermore, there are records of Cyrus being killed by his wife Tomyris, who was also the queen of Massagetae. And finally, the Greek historian Ctesias claims Cyrus died while quelling a rebellion that happened in the northeastern regions of the River Syr. The common belief is that the remains of Cyrus the Great were buried in the capital city of Pasargadae.

The second king of the Achaemenid Empire was Cyrus' son, Cambyses II, who ruled from 530 to 522. Even though his reign was brief, he is known for conquering territories in Africa, particularly Egypt. But before he became king of the vast Persian Empire, he was appointed as the governor of Babylonia. When his father, Cyrus the Great, decided to march against Massagetae, he became co-ruler and eventually the sole ruler after his father's death.

Cambyses didn't have trouble ascending to the throne, as the empire was stable, so all he had to do was preserve his authority over Persia's vast territories. The last prominent power in the Near East at the time was Egypt, and Cambyses took it upon himself to conquer it. Hearing of Persia's aspiration to take Egypt, some of the allies of Pharaoh Ahmose II (Amasis II) decided to abandon him and join forces with Cambyses. Egypt's former ally, Polycrates, the Greek king of Samos (better known as the tyrant of Samos), helped the Persians capture Cyprus, which was under Egyptian rule. This turned out to be a heavy blow to Ahmose II. Soon after, the pharaoh died and was succeeded by his son, Psamtik III, who only ruled for six months before facing the Persians and losing the Battle of Pelusium in 525. This battle took place at the eastern edge of the Nile Delta, and records say that the Egyptians had a strong defense, but the Persians were, nonetheless, victorious. Psamtik ran to Memphis, where he tried to resist the siege, but soon after, he was captured and carried in chains to Susa, where he committed suicide.

After the fall of Egypt, the Lydians and Greeks of Cyrene and Barca acknowledged Persian rule without resistance. Showing generosity, Cyrene allowed the widow of Pharaoh Ahmose II, who was Greek, to return to her home in Cyrene. To present his conquest of Egypt as legitimate, Cambyses used propaganda to claim he was of Egyptian origin, that he was the son of Princess Nitetis, daughter of Pharaoh Apries. Furthermore, he took titles belonging to the previous Egyptian pharaoh, naming himself the "King of Upper and Lower Egypt."

Cambyses had to leave Egypt in the spring of 522 to deal with a rebellion in Persia. While traversing Syria, he was wounded, and the wound turned gangrenous. Cambyses died three weeks later, and he left his empire without a direct successor. So, the throne was taken by his younger brother, Bardiya.

Bardiya was known to the Greeks as Smerdis, and allegedly, he ruled for only a few months. The story of Bardiya's rule has many variations according to different sources. Darius the Great claims that Bardiya was killed by his brother, King Cambyses II, who did it to ensure his position on the throne. Herodotus claims Bardiya was assassinated later during the invasion of Egypt and that an impostor took his place in court. They both agree that a certain mage-priest from Media impersonated Bardiya and took the throne. It seems that sources do not agree on the name of this mage as Darius calls him Gaumata, Herodotus Oropastes, and according to Ctesias, his name was Sphendadates. A group of seven Persian nobles discovered that the new king was an impostor and plotted to kill him. He was stabbed to death in September of 522. Not much is known about the rule of the imposter Bardiya, but some records mention his exemption of taxes for three years, which was probably why nobody rebelled against him.

Today, historians are inclined to believe that the usurper Gaumata, was actually the real throne successor, known to history as King Bardiya. Darius himself came up with the story of the mage who came from Media and became the pretend ruler to justify the assassination of the original king and make his coup legitimate. Several days after Gaumata was killed, Darius was crowned in Pasargadae.

Darius I, also known as Darius the Great, ruled as the fourth king of the Achaemenid Empire from 550 until 486 BCE. During his rule, the empire was at its peak. It included the territories of West and Central Asia, the Caucasus, the Balkans, the coast of the Black Sea, the Indus Valley, Egypt, and the northern parts of Africa, eastern Libya, and Sudan's coast.

Darius was a son of a noble who served in the Persian court. Herodotus mentions he was a *doryphoros,* a spearman of Cambyses II. Many historians interpret this as being the king's personal spear-carrier.

Herodotus provides an improbable story of Darius' ascension. To decide who would take the crown after the assassination of Gaumata, Darius and six other nobles agreed on taking a test. Each one of them would ride on his horse outside of the palace walls at sunrise. The noble whose horse would be the first to neigh, greeting the sunrise, would become the new monarch. The story goes that a slave called Oebares rubbed his hand over the genitals of a mare and approached Darius' horse, which became excited by the smell and neighed first. The clouds thundered at the same time, and the other six nobles dismounted, kneeling in front of their new king. Herodotus continues the story with Darius erecting a statue of himself, which presents Darius on a neighing horse with the inscription "Darius, son of Hystaspes, obtained the sovereignty of Persia by the sagacity of his horse and the ingenious contrivance of Oebares, his groom." Herodotus is known for often mixing folklore with history; therefore, this story is considered an unlikely one, albeit an interesting one.

After the coronation, Darius had to face a number of revolts across the country, as Bardiya had many supporters. Elam and Babylonia were the first to rebel, but Darius had no problem ending these revolts, as it took him only three months to end the Babylonian resistance. Soon after, there was a revolution in Bactria, Persis, Media, Parthia, Assyria, and Egypt. By 522, almost the whole empire was in revolt against Darius. However, with his loyal army, Darius had no problem suppressing the revolts and rebellions in just one year.

In 515, Darius launched a campaign to conquer the Indus Valley, continuing where his predecessor Cyrus had stopped in 535

BCE. The exact areas he conquered during this expedition are not known, as Darius himself writes it as the lands of Hindush. Modern scholars propose this area to be in the middle and lower Indus Valley, but there is no archeological evidence of Persians being there.

In 513, Darius had to turn his attention toward the Scythians, who threatened to close the trade routes between Central Asia and the shores of the Black Sea. Darius crossed the Black Sea with his army, using bridges made out of boats. But before entering Scythia, he conquered most of Eastern Europe. The Scythians undertook scorched-earth tactics as they retreated, but the Persian army followed the Scythians in their retreat, hoping to engage in open battle.

Toward the end of his campaign in the Scythian lands, Darius ordered eight forts to be built, with a distance from each other of eight miles. These forts were the frontier defense, marking the end of his progression in Scythia. However, he abandoned this project due to the winter that was coming. In order not to lose any more troops, Darius turned his army toward Thrace. He had failed to bring the Scythians into open combat, but the Scythians failed as well by losing a great deal of land to the Persians. Darius couldn't secure the territories he conquered in Scythia, and he never returned to them. This campaign turned out to be a very expensive stalemate.

The Greeks living in Asia Minor submitted to the Persians by 510, but there were also pro-Persian Greeks in Athens. In order to attract Greek traders, Darius opened his court to all those who wanted to come and serve Persia. The Greeks came and served as soldiers, statesmen, and artisans, but back home, the remaining Greek power was concerned about the strength of Darius' empire. This concern would culminate into a conflict between some Greek cities and the Achaemenid Empire.

The first to revolt was Miletus, under the leadership of its ruler Aristagoras. Soon after, Eretria and Athens joined and sent their troops and ships to help Miletus. They burned the city of Sardis, but the Persians responded fast and were able to reoccupy the Ionian and Greek islands. Thrace and Macedon declared independence, but that didn't last long. In 492, the Persians managed to quickly take control of them. Until then, Macedon was a Persian vassal state that had always kept its autonomy. It was only after the last conquest that it was brought entirely under the Achaemenid Empire. As a result of the Ionian revolts, anti-Persian parties gained popularity in Athens and Sparta, and they expelled their political opponents who were pro-Persian. Darius responded to this by sending an army across the Dardanelles. However, the Thracians blocked their way by harassing them until they chose to return to Persia. Darius, in his anger, gathered a larger army of 20,000 men under the joint command of Median admiral Datis and Persian general Artaphernes, who were successful and captured Eretria. In 490, the Persians met the Athenian army at the Battle of Marathon. The Persians were defeated, and this event marked the end of the first invasion of the Achaemenid Empire into Greece.

Darius had spent three years preparing a second invasion into the Greek territory; he even planned to lead the expedition himself instead of giving the command to others. But Egypt revolted, which affected Darius' health considerably. In October of 486, Darius the Great died. He was embalmed and buried at Naqsh-e Rostam, a necropolis he built about twelve kilometers (about a little over a mile) from his royal capital of Persepolis.

Darius I was succeeded by his son, Xerxes I, or Xerxes the Great. His name translates to "He who rules over heroes," and like his father, he ruled the Achaemenid Empire when it was at its peak, ruling from 486 to 465. In the Bible, he is mentioned under the name of Ahasuerus.

Xerxes was the child of Darius and Atossa, who was the daughter of the first king, Cyrus the Great. This fact helped Xerxes gain the throne as he was not the oldest child. His half-brother Artobazan wanted the crown for himself as he was the oldest of all the siblings. However, he came from a marriage Darius had with the daughter of his spear-carrier before he ascended to the throne. Xerxes received help from the Spartan king who was in exile in Persia, Demaratus, who argued that it is the first son born in a royal marriage that had the claim to the throne, which meant that it didn't necessarily mean the oldest son. Xerxes was crowned in October 486, and he was around 36 years old at the time. His ascension to the throne was smooth due to his mother's power, which not even Artobazan dared to challenge.

Soon after the crowning ceremony, Xerxes crushed a rebellion in Egypt by stationing his brother Achaemenes as the governor there. In 484, Xerxes confiscated a golden statue of Bel (Marduk) from Babylonia and melted it. This action outraged the Babylonians, who rebelled for the next two years.

During the rule of Darius I, the Athenians, Naxians, and Eretrians interfered in the Ionian Revolt, but due to his father's death, it was up to Xerxes to punish them. Xerxes started the preparation for the second invasion of Greece in 483 and ordered the digging of a canal through the isthmus of Mount Athos. At first, some Greek cities willingly joined Xerxes, such as Thessaly, Thebes, and Argos. Xerxes initiated the attacks on the Greek territories in 480, and the Persians were victorious in these battles, partly because Xerxes led the Persian army himself.

Herodotus exaggerates the numbers of his army to be over a million men, but modern scholars estimate it at being roughly 60,000. Herodotus also names the Persian elite infantry as the Immortals and claims Xerxes had 10,000 of them. The Immortals served as an elite imperial guard but also as a standing army, waiting to be called to battle if needed. They played an important role in the upcoming battle against the Greeks.

Xerxes is probably known the most for his role in the Battle of Thermopylae, which took place over the course of three days in August or September of 480 BCE. The allied forces of the Greek cities, under the leadership of the Spartan king Leonidas, clashed with the Persian armies of Xerxes I at the pass of Thermopylae. The initial idea of the Greek general Themistocles was to block the Persian advantage at the pass of Thermopylae and to simultaneously fight the Persian navy in the shallow waters of Artemisium, a cape in northern Euboea, Greece.

The Persian army marched toward Greece and was met by 7,000 Greek men who were blocking the pass. The Greek army was vastly outnumbered, as the Persian force numbered anywhere between 60,000 and 150,000, but they endured for seven days (only three days had actual fighting). After the second day of battle, a Greek soldier named Ephialtes betrayed his countrymen and revealed to the Persians a small path that would lead them right behind the Greek forces. Realizing his armies were outflanked, Leonidas chose to stand his position and fight to the death together with 300 Spartans and 700 Thespians, who guarded the retreat of the rest of Greece's army. There were reports of other members of the Greek allied forces standing their ground with the Spartans and Thespians, like the helots and Thebans, but they surrendered almost immediately.

At the same time, a naval battle took place at Artemisium, where the Greek army under Themistocles blocked the passage of the Persian armada. Upon hearing that the pass of Thermopylae was lost, Themistocles chose to retreat; in order for Greece's tactics to work, they would need both passes to be held. The Greek ships withdraw to the island of Salamis, and the Persians then overran the region of Boeotia and also captured Phocis, Attica, and Euboea. However, the Greek fleet attacked the Persians at the Battle of Salamis and won.

In order to avoid being trapped in Europe where he had no footholds, Xerxes had to return his forces to Asia. He lost most of his army due to starvation and disease. He left Mardonius, a military commander, with part of the Persian army to complete the invasion of Greece, but the very next year, the Greek army completely wiped out the Persians at the Battle of Plataea. This battle ended the Persian invasion.

The Battle of Thermopylae was an example of patriotism in modern and ancient literature. Even though greatly romanticized, this battle was a symbol of love for one's country and one's will to defend it. This battle is by far one of the most famous military clashes in ancient European history, as it is referenced in all spheres of culture, whether ancient or recent.

Xerxes was known for his rage, and upon retrieving the body of the Spartan king Leonidas, he ordered it to be decapitated and crucified. This was unusual for the Persians since usually they treated their brave and valiant enemies with respect. After the Persians abandoned the pass of Thermopylae, the Greeks returned to bury their fallen soldiers and to erect a statue of a lion dedicated to Leonidas. It took forty years for the Spartans to retrieve the bones of their king and give him a proper burial with full honors. In his memory, they started a tradition of funeral games being held each year.

On top of the burial mound of the Spartans at the site of the battle, a stone with an epitaph was raised to commemorate the event. It is written by Simonides, a Greek poet, and it reads, "Oh stranger, tell the Lacedaemonians that we lie here, obedient to their words." The Greeks often referred to the Spartans as Lacedaemonians because of the name of the region where Sparta was located, and by "obedient to their words," it means that they fought to their death, as they were ordered to by King Leonidas.

Xerxes was assassinated in August 465 by the commander of his royal bodyguards, Artabanus, who had the help of a eunuch serving in the harem. Artabanus planned to overthrow the Achaemenid dynasty, and after the assassination, he placed his own seven sons in key positions at court. Artabanus became the regent of Persia during 465 and 464. It is uncertain whether Artabanus also killed crown prince Darius, the son of Xerxes, or if he accused him of patricide while leaving his execution to the people. However, it is certain that both Xerxes and Darius lost their lives around the same time. The dynasty of Artabanus is uncertain, as some reports claim he named Artaxerxes I as king but acted as the reagent of the empire, while other sources say he claimed the throne for himself, wishing to end the royal dynasty, but due to the betrayal of general Megabyzus, he met his end by the sword of Artaxerxes.

Xerxes I was succeeded by his third son, Artaxerxes I, who ruled from 465 until 424. During his reign, Elamite stopped being the language of the government; instead, the Aramaic language was popularized. In addition, the solar calendar replaced the old national calendar while he was the king. The main religion of the state under Artaxerxes was Zoroastrianism.

Early during his rule, Artaxerxes had to deal with uprisings in Egypt, which lasted for six years (460 to 454 BCE). The revolt was led by Inaros II, the son of a Libyan prince. With allies from Athens, Inaros II defeated the Persian army and besieged Memphis. The Persian army under Megabyzus ended the siege of the city, defeating Inaros in 454, who was captured and delivered to Susa, where he was executed.

Artaxerxes continued his father's ambition to conquer the whole of Greece, and he employed new tactics against Athens. He funded Athens' enemies in hopes of weakening it enough that it would surrender. However, this strategy sparked a series of conflicts. The Greeks formed the Delian League in 478 during the second Persian invasion, which was an alliance of 150 to 300 Greek cities under the leadership of Athens. Wars fought between the League and the Achaemenid Empire were just a continuation of the Greco-Persian

Wars started by Darius I. In 451, the Delian League attacked Cyprus under the command of Cimon, an Athenian general. Their fleet numbered 200 ships of Athenians and their allies. They besieged the city-state of Kition in Cyprus, where Cimon died. Because of a lack of provisions, the League had to retreat toward Salamis. The Persians attacked the League's forces that were leaving Cimon by sea as well as by land. The League was ultimately victorious, and with the defeat of Artaxerxes' armies, the end of the Greco-Persian Wars was finally achieved in 449. A peace treaty was signed by both parties, and it included the autonomy of all Greek cities, as well as forbidding Persian armies from entering Greek lands or maritime territories. Furthermore, the Athenians were not to send troops into Persian territories.

Artaxerxes I died in 424 and was immediately succeeded by his only legitimate son, Xerxes II, who was assassinated after 45 days by his half-brother, Sogdianus, who ruled for a little over six months. Sogdianus met his end by the hand of his half-brother Ochus, who took the name Darius II upon his crowning.

Darius II ruled the Achaemenid Empire from 423 to 404. There are not many resources that describe the reign of Darius II. It is known there was a rebellion led by the people of Medes in 409, and a mention of Darius' name in harem intrigues. Some sources depict him as being dependent on his wife Parysatis, an illegitimate daughter of Artaxerxes I, with whom Darius had four sons. Her favorite son of all four was Cyrus, and she used her influence to give him command over western Anatolia while he was in his early teenage years.

Darius II commanded his satraps in Asia Minor, Tissaphernes and Pharnabazus, to attack Athens. The Persian satraps allied themselves with Sparta and started a war, which ended in Athens' defeat in 404. Under Darius, Persia managed to conquer a large part of Ionia. However, soon after, Darius II died in Babylon of illness. While he was on his deathbed, his wife Parysatis begged him to crown his second eldest son, her favorite Cyrus, but he refused.

Artaxerxes II instead inherited the throne, and he arrested his younger brother Cyrus, who was plotting to assassinate him. He was preparing to execute Cyrus when their mother intervened and begged for Artaxerxes to spare his brother's life. Cyrus was spared and given control over Lydia, where he prepared a rebellion. He employed Greek mercenaries known as the "Ten Thousand" to take his brother's throne for him.

The Ten Thousand fought at the Battle of Cunaxa against the Persians in 401. Xenophon, a Greek historian, reports that the Persians were scared of the mercenaries and that by the end of the battle, the Ten Thousand had only one wounded man. However, Cyrus died in that battle, and having no employer, the mercenaries decided to end the campaign and turn back to Greece. At first, they tried to find a new employer who would hire them to finish the job Cyrus started. They offered their services to Ariaeus, a general that was allied with them, but he refused, stating that he could not be the Persian king as he was not of royal blood. The Ten Thousand then approached Tissaphernes, the satrap of Lydia, but he refused them, too. In order to avoid conflict with the mercenaries, Tissaphernes funded their way home.

Artaxerxes involved himself in a new war against the Spartans, the Corinthian War, which lasted from 395 to 387. Agesilaus II, the Spartan king, began invading Asia Minor in 396. Artaxerxes then bribed the Greek states, particularly Athens, Thebes, and Corinth, in order to start a war with Sparta. These bribes were paid in darics, the main currency of the Achaemenid Empire, and they were the means of starting the Corinthian War. At the Battle of Cnidus in 394, the Persians, with the help of allied Athens, managed to defeat the Spartan fleet. The Persians increased pressure on Sparta by raiding the Peloponnesian coast. Athens felt strong enough to return some of the Greek cities of Asia Minor back under their fold. However, this worried Artaxerxes, as Athens' power suddenly grew.

In 386, Artaxerxes made a deal with Sparta and betrayed his allies. In the Treaty of Antalcidas, which ended the Corinthian War in 387, he forced his former allies to return the former Greek city-states of Ionia and Aeolis in Anatolia to the Achaemenid Empire. He also gave Sparta the power over the Greek mainland territories.

In 385, Artaxerxes undertook a campaign against the Cadusii, an ancient Iranian tribe. The sources do not offer reasons for this campaign, but it is believed it was to stop a revolt and make them pay tribute to Persia. Plutarch, a Greek biographer, describes this campaign, saying that the Persian army, numbering around 300,000 infantry and 10,000 cavalries, went deep into Cadusii land, but the mountainous region of these lands had no food to sustain such an army. Soon, they began to starve. At first, they ate their supplies, but later, they had to eat their own mounts. Tiribazus, a Persian general, came up with the idea to divide the Cadusii tribes, convincing their leaders that their opponents sent envoys to join the Persian army. They all submitted to Artaxerxes, which ended the Cadusian campaign.

During the reign of Artaxerxes II, Egypt managed to regain its independence. It all began with a revolt that was organized during the first years of his reign. In 373, Artaxerxes sent an expedition to regain Egypt, led by Pharnabazus, a satrap of Phrygia, and Iphicrates, an Athenian general who commanded a group of mercenaries. Due to the distrust between the two generals and the annual flooding of the Nile, the Persians lost what was supposed to be an easy victory. This event was the end of Pharnabazus' career. The second expedition to Egypt was led by Datames, a satrap of Cappadocia, but he, too, failed.

This defeat in Egypt was the spark that ignited unrest among the Achaemenid nobility. In 372, this unrest culminated with the Great Satraps' Revolt against Artaxerxes. Datames, the satrap who was sent for the second attempt to regain Egypt, suddenly felt exposed to too much risk at the royal court because of his opponent's machinations. He abandoned his loyalty to the Persian king and started a revolt by returning to Cappadocia with his troops. He managed to persuade the satraps from within Persia to revolt as well. Egypt was openly financing this rebellion against Artaxerxes, but the Persian king was successful in ending it by 362. Not long after these events, legend has it that Artaxerxes II died of a broken heart caused by the behavior of his sons.

When Artaxerxes II died in 358, he was succeeded by his son Artaxerxes III, who ruled until 338 BCE. He came to power after his older brother was executed and the other one had committed suicide. To secure his crown, Artaxerxes III murdered over eighty members of his family.

Upon taking the throne, Artaxerxes III had to deal with the rebellion of Artabazus II, the satrap of Phrygia, who gathered allies and fought for independence. Among the allies of Artabazus were Athens, Thebe, and Mysia, and with such a force, Artabazus managed to defeat the royal Persian army in 354. But the very next year, Artaxerxes' army came back and defeated Artabazus, who sought refuge with Philip II of Macedon.

In 351, Artaxerxes launched a new campaign to recover Egypt. After a year of fighting the Egyptian pharaoh, Nectanebo II, the Persians suffered defeat and were forced to retreat. At the same time, an uprising in Asia Minor broke out, and Artaxerxes had to abandon his plans of retaking Egypt, at least for the time being.

The rebellions in Cyprus and Sidon had a goal of making their states independent. They had some success in the early stages of their uprising when they defeated the Persian army led by Idieus, the satrap of Caria. But after this defeat, Artaxerxes gathered a large army of over 300,000 men, including a number of mercenaries he hired and the Greek armies who came to help. The Persian king was successful this time, and he managed to completely crush the rebellion. Sidon was burned to the ground, but the sources are not clear whether the Persian army burned the city or harmed its citizens. The estimations are that there were at least 40,000 civilian deaths, though. After the fall of Sidon, Artaxerxes sold its ruins to speculators who hoped to dig out various treasures from the ashes.

After ending the rebellion, Artaxerxes returned to his plans to retake Egypt. In 343, he gathered an army of 330,000 Persians, 14,000 Greeks, 4,000 mercenaries, 3,000 men sent by Argos, and 1,000 from Thebes. Pharaoh Nectanebo II managed to resist this army for some time with his 100,000 men. His tactical position gave him a good fighting chance, but the pharaoh did not have generals capable of leading his army, so he was defeated. Nectanebo fled to Memphis and then continued to Ethiopia. After conquering Egypt, Artaxerxes started looting its temples and terrorizing its citizens. He raised taxes on Egypt and persecuted its native religion in hopes of weakening it so they would never again revolt against the Achaemenid Empire. Egypt stayed under Persian control for the next ten years until Alexander the Great finally conquered it.

Artaxerxes spent the last years of his reign in peace, as there were no rebellions in his empire. However, the power Philip II of Macedon managed to gather called for a Persian response. Artaxerxes tried influencing the neighbors of Macedon in an effort to constrain Philip's power, but Philip had already started planning the invasion of Persia. He was just waiting for the Greeks to join him as allies.

Artaxerxes III died of natural causes in 338, although a Greek source by Diodorus of Sicily claims it was from poisoning by a eunuch named Bagoas and his own physician.

The next king of the Achaemenid Empire was Artaxerxes IV, also known as Arses (ruled 338 to 336). He was the youngest son of Artaxerxes III, but since all of his older brothers had died before he became king, Arses became the new king. It is believed that the eunuch Bagoas wanted to become a kingmaker, so he placed young Arses on the throne, believing he could control the inexperienced king. Being unsuccessful in controlling him, Bagoas decided to poison Arses as well and placed Darius III on the throne, Arses' cousin. During this time, Philip II of Macedon gained the alliance he sought from the Greeks in his plans to invade Persia.

Darius III ruled from 380 until July 330 BCE. Greek historians say he poisoned Bagoas and watched him die once he learned of his predecessor's fate. During Darius' rule, the empire was affected by constant rebellions, as the satraps were jealous of each other's power and indulged in scheming and plotting.

In 336, the Hellenic League, also known as the League of Corinth (a confederation of Hellenic states established by Philip II), authorized Philip II of Macedon to launch a military campaign against the Achaemenid Empire for destroying and burning the temples of Athens during the Persian wars that happened over a century before. But Philip's campaign was quickly suspended due to his death. He did manage, however, to recover some Greek cities in Asia Minor that were under Persian rule, but soon after that, he was assassinated.

Philip was succeeded by his son, Alexander the Great, who invaded Asia Minor in 334. He was victorious against the Persians in his very first battles. The Battle of Granicus in 334 BCE was fought near the site of Troy, and it marked the fall of Asia Minor under the rule of Alexander the Great. This was one of the three major battles that led to the fall of the Achaemenid Empire. Darius III did not participate in these first battles, leaving them in the hands of the Persian satraps in Asia Minor. A year later, in 333, Darius appeared at the Battle of Issus, where his forces finally met the Macedonian army of Alexander. Even though the Persians outnumbered their opponents two to one, they were outflanked and forced to retreat. However, the beginning of the battle didn't go so well for Alexander's army. Historians report that the Macedonians lost 128 officers in the first military confrontation. Alexander took control of the battle by mounting his horse and charging directly at Darius and his bodyguards, who were forced to flee. Seeing the

Persian king leave, the Greek mercenaries were the first to abandon the battle, followed by the rest of the Persian army. Alexander's cavalry continued to pursue the Persians as long as the day lasted.

Darius' wife, Stateira I, was captured after the battle, as well as her daughters and Darius' mother, who had followed him as he battled throughout the lands. It is said that Alexander treated the captured women with great respect; he even married Darius' daughter, Stateira II. Darius wrote letters to Alexander asking for his family back, but he refused to liberate them for as long as Darius denied acknowledging him as the new king of Persia.

The third and final battle that marked the end of the Persian Empire was fought in 331, and it took place near the city of Gaugamela. Darius' army was greatly outnumbered by the Macedonians, and the initial clashes were in his favor. He was already on the battlefield with his forces, waiting for the arrival of Alexander the Great. Again, Alexander himself led the final charge in the center of the Persian army, and he destroyed Darius' royal guard and forced Darius to run with whatever troops he could gather around him. When he was on the run, Darius gave a speech to encourage his fighters, promising another battle where they would have the opportunity to avenge their loss. He planned to raise another army to help him fight Alexander at Babylon, but his satraps refused to send him any help.

Darius was murdered during the retreat by one of his satraps, Bessus, later known as Artaxerxes V. Upon finding Darius' body, Alexander was disturbed to see his respected enemy killed in such a fashion, and he gave the Persian king a proper burial at Persepolis. The following year Alexander captured and killed Bessus, and the rest of the Persian satraps eventually pledged their loyalty to Alexander. Even though Bessus was a member of the royal family and proclaimed himself the king of kings, Darius is considered to be the last king of the Achaemenid Empire.

Chapter 8 – The Seleucid Empire and Romans in Anatolia

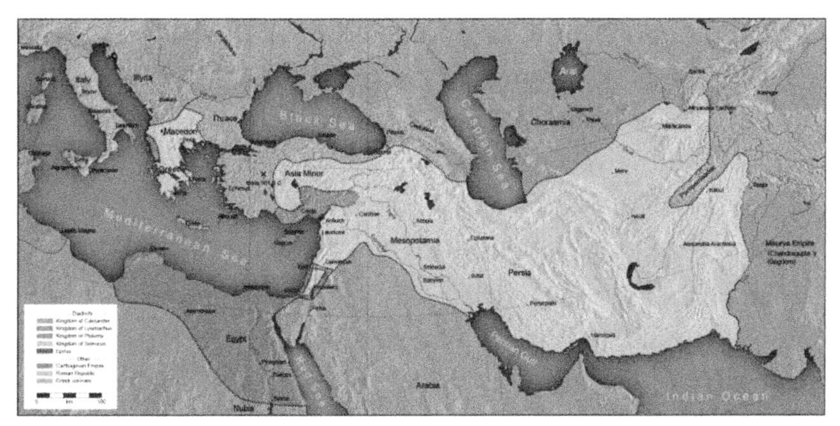

The Seleucid Empire under the reign of Seleucus I Nicator

Diadochi PT.svg: Luigi Chiesa (talk · contribs)derivative work: Morningstar1814, CC BY-SA 4.0 <https://creativecommons.org/licenses/by-sa/4.0>, via Wikimedia Commons https://commons.wikimedia.org/wiki/File:Diadochi_EN.png

Alexander the Great died in 323 BCE in the palace of Nebuchadnezzar II, the king of Babylonia. The circumstances of his death are unknown, but he left no successor, although his wife was pregnant at the moment of his death. Alexander's brother was alive at the time, but he wasn't capable of ruling due to his mental health issues. So, forty years of infighting in Macedon followed, as various "successors" fought against each other. The unity of Macedon seized to exist, and the kingdom was finally divided into four smaller ones: Ptolemaic Egypt, Seleucid Mesopotamia and Central Asia, Attalid Anatolia, and Antigonid Macedon.

The Seleucid Empire was founded in 312 by Seleucus I Nicator, whose dynasty ruled the lands until 63 BCE. The Seleucids took control of Babylonia after the division of Macedon, but they expanded into an empire. At its highest, the Seleucid Empire included central Anatolia, Persia, Levant, Mesopotamia, and parts of today's Kuwait, Afghanistan, Pakistan, and Turkmenistan.

In 301, Seleucus I expanded his territories to eastern Anatolia as well as northern Syria. He allied himself with three famous generals who served under Alexander the Great: Lysimachus, Ptolemy, and Cassander, and they went against Antigonus, another general. The wars between them are known as the Wars of the Diadochi, which would determine the boundaries of the new Hellenistic kingdoms. Later, in 281, Seleucus planned to take the territories of his former ally Lysimachus, expanding his kingdom to western Anatolia, but he was assassinated by Ptolemy Keraunos, the second king of Ptolemaic Egypt who also crowned himself king of Macedon.

Previously, Seleucus defeated Lysimachus in the Battle of Corupedium in 281 BCE. Lysimachus' kingdom fell apart, and the capital city of Pergamon was taken by Philetaerus, a nobleman and officer in the Macedonian army. He founded the Attalid dynasty of Pergamon in Anatolia. Even though Pergamon was officially under Seleucid rule, it continued enjoying autonomy under the rule of Philetaerus, as he was the one holding Lysimachus' treasury. He used all the wealth he acquired by taking the city to gain influence and extend his power beyond the city. He defended the city from the Gauls and built fortifications and temples, thus gaining prestige and trust amongst his subjects.

His successor Eumenes I was the one who gained complete independence from the Seleucid Empire in 263 through a series of organized rebellions. He extended the kingdom's borders south of the Caiscus River, all the way to the Gulf of Cyme. During the existence of the Pergamon Kingdom, there were constant wars over territories against the Seleucid Empire, and the kingdom's borders often changed. During the reign of Attalus I, who ruled from 241 to 197, the kingdom lost all of its territories and was reduced to the city of Pergamon. During the First Macedonian War in 214, the Kingdom of Pergamon allied itself with the Romans and supported Rome in all future wars. The last king of the Attalid dynasty, Attalus III, died in 133, leaving his kingdom to the people of the Roman Republic.

Antiochus I Soter, son of Seleucus I, inherited the throne, but he was unable to fulfill his father's plans of expansion. During the reign of Antiochus I Soter and his son Antiochus II Theos, Asia Minor was under constant war. The struggle for territory wasn't just with Ptolemy II of Egypt, as the Celtic invasions started increasing as well. Various provinces managed to gain independence during these times, including Cappadocia, Bactria, and Parthia. Hellenistic culture was blooming in the newly-freed regions, and Bactria even allied itself with the Greeks and formed the Greco-Bactrian Kingdom.

Seleucus II Callinicus, the next successor to the throne, lost even more of the Seleucid territory. Torn between the war against Ptolemy III and a civil war against his own brother, Seleucus II was unable to remain in control in Pergamum. The Attalid dynasty instead ruled in Pergamum once again during the 230s. Even more territories of Asia Minor were lost, and the Gauls settled in Galatia in the highlands of central Anatolia.

However, the son of Seleucus II, Antiochus III the Great, pushed to regain the former territories of the Seleucid Empire. He took the throne in 222, after his brother Seleucus III, and almost immediately began a new war, which he lost. Even though he was defeated on one front, he spent the next ten years being victorious and successful in returning old territories to his kingdom, such as Bactria and Parthia. After subduing these territories, he allied himself with Philip V of Macedon in order to conquer and divide the territories of Ptolemaic Egypt. During yet another war, which lasted from 202 to 195, Antiochus III defeated Ptolemy V and gained control over Coele-Syria.

This situation did not last for long. Antiochus' ally Philip V was defeated by the Romans in 197, who attacked Macedon, arguing that they were freeing the Greek city-states. Seeing the opportunity to take over some Macedonian territories, Antiochus sent a military force, but Rome created new innovative war tactics that the Seleucid army couldn't match. Antiochus was defeated in two major battles, Thermopylae in 191 and Magnesia in 190. He was forced to sign the Treaty of Apamea in 188 BC and made peace with Rome. The major clause of this treaty was for the Seleucids to completely retreat from Anatolia and never to enter the territories west of the Taurus Mountains again. The former lands of the Seleucid Empire in Anatolia were given to Rome's allies, mainly Rhodes and Pergamum.

This might look like Rome was generous by not taking the Anatolian territories for itself, but by dividing the lands between its allies, Rome made sure none of them would become powerful enough to pose a threat. This way, Rome also ensured it stayed involved in all Anatolian affairs.

The next few decades were quite peaceful in Anatolia, and Rome did not meddle in its affairs to much extent, but it was still a force that protected the freedom of its allies and the new kingdoms that came to be after the Seleucids abandoned these territories. The Galatians were the only remaining problem in Anatolia, as they often organized raids, until the war against Bithynia. At the time, the ruler of Bithynia was Prusias I, who, during the Roman war against Antiochus III, did not want to choose a side, and he actually managed to stay neutral. It is not known what started the war, but it was concluded by 183.

Rome had full control over the rulers in Anatolia, and even though they had no lands of their own, they enacted their influence on the events concerning Anatolia. The first province Rome officially adopted was in 133 when King Attalus III bequeathed Pergamon to the citizens of Rome.

In the year 91 BCE, Rome had to focus its attention on their homeland due to the Social War breaking out. The Kingdom of Pontus saw the opportunity to expand its territories, as the kingdoms in Anatolia lacked Rome's protection. Mithridates VI of Pontus' first strike was against the Kingdom of Bithynia, which he conquered. He had help from some of the Greek cities in Anatolia who were rebelling against Rome. A Greek philosopher, Metrodorus of Scepsis, who was known for his hatred of Romans, advised Mithridates that he should slaughter all the Roman civilians inhabiting the region, including women and children. This action, he assured the king, would destroy Rome's grasp on the lands permanently. The date of the massacre is not known exactly, but it is presumed it happened around May of 88 BCE. Some Roman historians claim 88,000 people were killed while other sources go even higher in numbers.

This massacre provoked Rome to such an extent that they immediately proclaimed war on Mithridates and his Greek allies. The relations between the Greeks and the Romans were never the same after these events, and the Greek cities lost their Roman protection. The Roman consul Lucius Cornelius Sulla besieged Athens, who had sided with Mithridates. Sulla's armies stormed the city and took its harbor Piraeus, completely destroying it.

Sulla and Mithridates clashed with their armies at two prominent battles: the Battle of Chaeronea (86) and the Battle of Orchomenus (85). In both battles, Rome was victorious, and Sulla forced Mithridates to sign a peace treaty. The Treaty of Dardanos, signed in 85, returned everything as it was before the war. This means that

Mithridates had to return the provinces of Bithynia, Cappadocia, and Paphlagonia to Rome and pay a war indemnity from his own wealth. The treaty was signed in haste since Sulla had to go back to Rome and deal with a rebellion.

Mithridates also had to deal with a rebellion in his own kingdom. He prepared a large army to deal with the uprising in Colchis, an area in today's Georgia. However, the Roman general Lucius Licinius Murena, who had stayed in Asia Minor with his garrison, saw the Pontic army's preparations as a threat to the Roman citizens of Cappadocia. He did not trust Mithridates and attacked his kingdom under the excuse of preventing another massacre of Romans, thus starting the Second Mithridatic War, which lasted from 83 to 81. Eventually, Murena invaded the territories of the Kingdom of Pontus, and Mithridates believed he was doing it under the command of Rome. Mithridates responded by attacking Roman villages and met Murena on the battlefield. The king of Pontus defeated Murena, who had to flee and seek refuge in Phrygia. Sulla did not approve of this attack on Mithridates since he did not want to break the treaty. The war ended with Mithridates making a deal with the king of Cappadocia, Ariobarzanes I. He returned some of the Cappadocian territories but kept most of what he had conquered. As a sign of peace, Mithridates engaged his own daughter, who was only four years old, to Ariobarzanes.

The Third Mithridatic war, which took place between 73 and63, was the last and longest war between the Kingdom of Pontus and the Roman Republic. Sulla died in 78, so the strongest promoter of peace between the two nations was gone. The Roman Senate decided not to ratify the Treaty of Dardanos, as the general opinion of Rome was that Sulla was too generous when drafting the treaty and that Mithridates did not deserve to keep all the territories of his kingdom. This angered Mithridates, and he decided not to wait for the Romans to come to his kingdom. He attacked Bithynia, which was just bequeathed to Rome upon the death of its last king,

Nicomedes IV. Rome sent two generals to oppose Mithridates, Lucius Licinius Lucullus and Marcus Aurelius Cotta. But Mithridates defeated Cotta at the naval Battle of Chalcedon in 74, trapping him within the city walls with no other choice but to wait for Lucullus to come to his rescue. Lucullus arrived and besieged Mithridates' army, which was occupying the city of Cyzicus at the time. Famine and plague forced Mithridates to retreat to his Kingdom of Pontus, but he was chased by Lucullus and his army, and a final battle took place in Pontus near the city of Cabira. The Roman army was victorious, and Mithridates had to run for his life to Armenia.

In Armenia, Mithridates convinced his father-in-law Tigranes II to not turn him over to Rome and to instead prepare for war. The Armenians lost all the battles against Rome, but there was some unrest in the Roman ranks. Pompey the Great had risen to power and wanted to replace Lucullus as the general of the Roman army during the Third Mithridatic War. Through scheming and inciting unrest in Lucullus' armies, Pompey was sent by the Senate to take over the command.

At the Battle of Lycus in 66, Pompey had his first victory over Mithridates, but the decisive battle was in 65 at the banks of the Abas River. Here is where Pompey defeated the main allies of Mithridates, making them unable to give further support to the king of Pontus. After this final blow, Mithridates VI fled to Crimea, where he gathered a small army in yet another attempt to regain his lost kingdom. Even his son, Pharnaces II, the king of Cimmerian Bosporus, refused to help him as Rome had just recognized his kingdom. Mithridates decided to kill his son and take the throne for himself. However, his younger son, enraged by his father's actions, raised the populace and led a rebellion. Mithridates could not bear the defeat and his own son's betrayal, so he decided to commit suicide. His death in 63 BCE marks the end of the war, and with it, the Kingdom of Pontus fell into Roman hands.

Conclusion

Even with the rising power of Rome, Anatolia managed to keep its diversity in culture and enter the new age as rich as ever. It enjoyed relative peace from the time of Rome to Constantine the Great.

Anatolia grew and developed its regions, especially after the taxes to Rome were lifted under the reign of Emperor Augustus. Agriculture boomed, as smart investments were made, and there was no lack of money. Rome also built roads throughout Anatolia, which helped the development of trade with other parts of the world. Trade enriched the already diverse culture of Anatolia by bringing merchants from exotic places such as China and various parts of Europe. It survived even the fall of the Roman Empire and set itself as a center of the civilized world through the achievements of Constantine I and the Byzantine Empire.

This is where history marks the end of the ancient times of Anatolia, a region with a rich culture that influenced the entire known world. From the Early Bronze Age to the heights of the Iron Age, Anatolia enjoyed a diversity of languages, religions, and ethnicities, even if it was constantly being torn apart by wars as countless armies marched across Anatolia. Populations moved, either migrating in the search for more fertile lands or by being relocated by ruthless kings, they all contributed to the living, breathing land that is Anatolia.

History is rich in this region, as is best shown by the constant archeological excavations that are taking place. Even today, there are many undiscovered places, whole cities that historians are still searching for. Some were probably destroyed by wars and may never be found, but there is an enormous cultural heritage in Anatolia, one is that too huge for just one book to cover.

Here's another book by Captivating History that you might like

Free Bonus from Captivating History (Available for a Limited time)

Hi History Lovers!

Now you have a chance to join our exclusive history list so you can get your first history ebook for free as well as discounts and a potential to get more history books for free! Simply visit the link below to join.

Captivatinghistory.com/ebook

Also, make sure to follow us on Facebook, Twitter and Youtube by searching for Captivating History.

References

Gregory D. Mumford, *The Oxford Handbook of the Archaeology of the Levant: c. 8000-332 BCE,* Edited by Ann E. Killebrew and Margreet Steiner

William W. Hallo & William Kelly Simpson, *The Ancient Near East: A History*, Holt Rinehart and Winston Publishers, 2nd edition, 1997. ISBN 0-15-503819-2.

Marc Van de Mieroop, *History of the Ancient Near East: Ca. 3000-323 B.C.*, Blackwell Publishers, 2nd edition, 2006 (first published 2003). ISBN 1-4051-4911-6.

Ergil, Doğu, PKK: The Kurdistan Workers' Party, in Marianne Heiberg, Brendan O'Leary, John Tirman, eds., *Terror, Insurgency, and the State: Ending Protracted Conflicts,* University of Pennsylvania Press, 2007.

Liverani, M., *International Relations in the Ancient Near East,* 2001. Palgrave Macmillan UK, ISBN. 978-0-230-28639-9.

Cultural Atlas of Mesopotamia and the Ancient Near East, An Andromeda book, An Equinox book, Armenian Research Center collection, Facts on File, 1990, ISBN 0816022186, 9780816022182

Jack M. Sasson, John Baines, Gary Beckman, Karen S. Rubinson, *Civilizations of the Ancient Near East,* Book 1, Scribner, 1995.

William H. Stiebing Jr., Susan N. Helft, *Ancient Near Eastern History and Culture,* Taylor & Francis, 2017, ISBN 1134880839, 9781134880836

Daniel C. Snell, *Life in the Ancient Near East, 3100-332 B.C.E. New Edition,* ISBN-13: 978-0300076660, ISBN-10: 0300076665

Louis Lawrence Orlin, *Life and Thought in the Ancient Near East,* University of Michigan Press, 2007, ISBN-10: 0472069926, ISBN-13: 978-0472069927

Donald B. Redford, *Egypt, Canaan, and Israel in Ancient Times,* Princeton University Press; New Ed edition, 1993, ISBN-10: 0691000867, ISBN-13: 978-0691000862

Mark Van De Mieroop, *The Eastern Mediterranean in the Age of Ramesses II,* ISBN:9781405160698, ISBN:9780470696644

Pierre-Louis Gatier, Robert-Louis Gatier, Eric Gubel, Philippe *The Levant: History and Archaeology in the Eastern Mediterranean,* Konemann, 2000, ISBN-10: 3829004958, ISBN-13: 978-3829004954.

Nicolas Grimal, Ian Shaw (translator): *A History of Ancient Egypt,* 1992, Oxford: Blackwell Publishing, ISBN 978-0-63-119396-8.

Michael Rice: *Egypt's Making: The Origins of Ancient Egypt, 5000-2000 BC.* Taylor & Francis, London/New York 1990, ISBN 0-415-05092-8.

Luckenbill, Daniel David (1927). *Ancient Records of Assyria and Babylonia.* Ancient records. 2: Historical records of Assyria: from Sargon to the end. Chicago: The University of Chicago Press. *Retrieved 3 February 2019.*

Arnold, Bill T. *(2005). Who Were the Babylonians?* Brill Publishers. ISBN 978-90-04-13071-5.

DeBlois, Lukas *(1997). An Introduction to the Ancient World. Routledge.* ISBN 978-0-415-12773-8.

Van De Mieroop, Marc *(2005). King Hammurabi of Babylon: A Biography.* Blackwell Publishing. ISBN 978-1-4051-2660-1.

Liverani, Mario. *Imagining Babylon: The Modern Story of an Ancient City.* Translated from Italian to English by Ailsa Campbell. Boston: De Gruyter, 2016. ISBN 978-1-61451-602-6.

Seymour, M. J. *(2006). The Idea of Babylon: Archaeology and Representation in Mesopotamia (Doctoral thesis).* University College London. OCLC 500097655

D. T. Potts, *The Archaeology of Elam: Formation and Transformation of an Ancient Iranian State.* Cambridge World Archaeology. Cambridge University Press, 2015 ISBN 1107094690

Bierbrier, M. L. *The Late New Kingdom in Egypt, C. 1300-664 B.C.: A Genealogical and Chronological Investigation.* Warminster, England: Aris & Phillips, 1975.

Thomas, Angela P. *Akhenaten's Egypt.* Shire Egyptology 10. Princes Risborough, UK: The Shire, 1988.

Morkot, Robert. *A Short History of New Kingdom Egypt.* London: Tauris, 2015.

Briant, P. (2006). From Cyrus to Alexander: a history of the Persian Empire. Winona Lake, IN: Eisenbrauns.

Bury, J. B., Cook, S. A., & Adcock, F. (1976). The Assyrian Empire. Cambridge: Cambridge University Press.

Kuhrt, A. (2010). The Persian Empire: London: Routledge.

Matthews, R. (1998). Ancient Anatolia. Ankara: The British Institute of Archaeology.

Petrie, W. M. F. (1940). Hutchinsons story of the nations: containing the Egyptians, the Chinese, India, the Babylonian nation, the Hittites, the Assyrians, the Phoenicians and the Carthaginians, the Phrygians, the Lydians, and other Nations of Asia Minor. London: Hutchinson & Co.

River, C. (2015). The Assyrians: the history of the most prominent empire of the ancient near east. San Bernardino, CA.

Savage, R. (2019). Mesopotamia: a captivating guide to ancient Mesopotamian history and civilizations, including the Sumerians and Sumerian mythology, Gilgamesh, Ur, Assyrians, Babylon, Hammurabi and the Persian Empire.

Steadman, S. R., & McMahon, G. (2016). The Oxford handbook of ancient Anatolia: 10,000-323 B.C.E. Oxford: Oxford University Press.

Made in the USA
Coppell, TX
12 June 2024